JOHN LANGDON-DAVIES was a journalist, war correspondent
and author of more than forty books.

He was born in Zululand in 1897 and raised in Kent. He won
a scholarship to Oxford to read history. A Quaker and pacifist,
when he was called up in 1917, he refused to fight. As a result,
he lost his scholarship and left Oxford without a degree. After
his first marriage and the birth of two sons, the family moved to
Catalonia in the 1920s. Langdon-Davies loved Catalonia and is
the author of *Dancing Catalans* (1929), one of the best pieces of
writing ever published about the Sardana, the emotionally and
politically charged national dance of Catalonia.

After the publication of *Behind the Spanish Barricades* (1936),
Langdon-Davies returned to Barcelona for the *News Chronicle*,
where he witnessed the bloody street battles between the
Republican factions that broke out in May 1937. His account
of these events form part of the book *La Setmana Tragica de
1937* published in Catalan in 1987. The same year, Spain's
predicament prompted him to name his third child by his second
wife, Jennifer Dolores.

In 1937 he founded Foster Parents Plan for children in Spain
with Eric Muggeridge to help the vast number of children who
had lost their parents in the conflict. Today that organisation is
called Plan and works with 11 million children in 60 countries.

Fascist air raids on Spain, which he witnessed first hand
convinced him Britain had to prepare for mass aerial
bombardment. He wrote the influential book *Air Raid* (1938) and
advised the British government on civil defence.

As a war correspondent, he covered the Russo-Finnish War for
the *Evening Standard*, a dangerous assignment that produced,
Finland: the First Total War (1940). His experiences on the
Finnish frontline influenced his *Home Guard Training Manual*,
in which he incorporated tactics he had learned from the Finnish

partisans, and which formed the basis of his work at the Home Guard Training School that he founded in Sussex, for which he was awarded the MBE.

In the late 1940s, he settled in Catalonia with his third wife. His compassion for the country he loved more than compensated for his dislike of living with a fascist regime. In Sant Feliu de Guixols, he concentrated on writing, raising four children and running the hotel Casa Rovira. He entertained the guests with late night discussions on literature, world politics and society, and was able to introduce them to the history of Catalonia and its culture.

A man of boundless curiosity he wrote prolifically. His other works include: *Militarism in Education*, *The New Age of Faith*, *A Short History of Women*, *The Future of Nakedness*, *Man and his Universe*, *Science and Common Sense*, *Fifth Column*, *Nerves versus Nazis*, *American Close-Up*, *Gatherings from Catalonia*, *Sex, Sin and Sanctity*, *The Cato Street Conspiracy* (as John Stanhope), *Carlos, the Bewitched* (as John Nada).

He created the ground-breaking *Jackdaw* series for *Jonathan Cape*, history folders which reproduced original documents and artefacts and were one of the first examples of educational multimedia.

His life was divided between England and Catalonia. He died in Shoreham, Kent in 1971.

PAUL PRESTON is the Príncipe de Asturias Professor of Contemporary Spanish Studies and Director of the Cañada Blanch Centre for Contemporary Spanish Studies at the London School of Economics. He is the author of *Spanish Civil War. Reaction, Revolution, Revenge* (2006); *Juan Carlos. A People's King* (2004); *Doves of War. Four Women of Spain* (2002); *¡Comrades! Portraits from the Spanish Civil War* (1999) and *Franco. A Biography* (1993). In 2006, at a ceremony presided over by the King of Spain, Paul Preston was inaugurated into the Academia Europea de Yuste, where he was given the Marcel Proust Chair.

NIGEL CHAPMAN is the Director General of the *BBC World Service* and the Chairman of Plan UK. He has worked for the *BBC* for more than 20 years, holding senior management and editorial posts in television, radio and online, many with a strong emphasis on news and current affairs. He is also Chair of *the BBC World Service Trust* - the *World Service's* charitable arm, which uses communications to aid development in some of the world's poorest countries.

John Langdon-Davies

Behind the Spanish Barricades

Reports from the Spanish Civil War

With Introductions by
Paul Preston and Nigel Chapman.

REPORTAGE PRESS

Reportage Press
26 Richmond Way, London W12 8LY, United Kingdom
Tel: 0044 7971 461 935
Fax: 0044 20 8749 2867
e-mail: info@reportagepress.com
www.reportagepress.com

Behind the Spanish Barricades was produced under
the editorial direction of Rosie Whitehouse
First published by Martin Secker and Warburg Ltd, 1936
Introduction © Paul Preston, 2007
Preface © Nigel Chapman, 2007
Footnotes © Rosie Whitehouse
Published by Reportage Press, 2007

British Library Cataloguing in Publication Data.
A catalogue record for this book is available from the British
Library.

ISBN-13: 978-0-9555729-4-4

Cover design and layout by Joshua Haymann

Printed and bound in Great Britain by Antony Rowe Ltd,
Chippenham, Wiltshire
www.antonyrowe.co.uk

Behind the Spanish Barricades

Reports from the Spanish Civil War

PREFACE

John Langdon-Davies's book about what he called 'the greatest atrocity of all - Civil War' is written both in sorrow and anger. He was special correspondent to Spain for the *News Chronicle* and had fallen in love with the country and knew it well before the war broke out. The book, written like a true journalist in five weeks, is a very vivid portrayal of the front line and is an authentic piece of war reporting. It is also the impassioned writing of the true campaigner and humanitarian.

In many ways he was faced with the dilemma that haunts many journalists; when do you stop reporting and get involved? When should you drop the pen or the camera and pick up the elderly refugee or the child? In 1937 John Langdon-Davies literally did pick up the child. A plea from the father of a small boy: "This is José. I am his father. When Santander falls I will be shot. Please, whoever finds my son take care of him for me," led to the foundation of a charity that rescued many children whose lives had been overwhelmed by the war.

He and his colleagues set up the first colony, a safe place for 200 children, in Puigcerdà on the French border in the summer of 1937. They raised funds in the UK, persuading hundreds of people to 'sponsor' a child. Today, seventy years on, that organisation is called Plan, originally Foster Parents Plan for Children in Spain, it works with 11 million children in over 60 countries. His campaigning journalism and writing certainly had an impact but his compassionate response to Spain's children has left an extraordinary legacy that few of us in his profession can match.

In his preface he writes "this book does not lay claim to permanence". It has stood the test of time and so also has his work with children, spanning decades, continents and reaching into the lives of millions of people. *Behind the Spanish Barricades* is a portrait of an extraordinary time by an extraordinary man.

Nigel Chapman
Chairman of Plan UK, Director General
of the BBC World Service
London, 2007

INTRODUCTION

One of the greatest journalists to cover the Spanish Civil War, Herbert L. Matthews, took enormous pride in his work and his personal ethic demanded that he never wrote a word that he did not fervently believe to be true. In Spain, he would endure the bitterness of seeing the side he supported lose. Over thirty years later, he concluded that: 'All of us who lived the Spanish Civil War felt deeply emotional about it. I always felt the falseness and hypocrisy of those who claimed to be unbiased and the foolish, if not rank stupidity of editors and readers who demand objectivity or impartiality of correspondents writing about the war… those of us who championed the cause of the Republican government against the Franco Nationalists were right. It was, on balance, the cause of justice, morality, decency. The war also taught me that the truth will prevail in the long run. Journalism may seem to fail in its daily task of providing the material for history, but history will never fail so long as the newspaperman writes the truth.' It is for that reason that John Langdon-Davies's *Behind the Spanish Barricades* remains such a valuable work seventy years after its first publication. It was in many respects an 'instant', essentially journalistic book, written very quickly after a rapid visit to Spain in the late summer of 1936, and published barely four months into the Spanish Civil War. However, as Matthews argued, good journalism is the first draft of history and Langdon-Davies's book is an important component of that first draft.

Writing the truth meant, to quote Martha Gellhorn, 'explaining that the Spanish Republic was neither a collection of blood-slathering Reds nor a cat's-paw of Russia.' She would have no truck with what she called 'all that objectivity shit', seeing as morally repugnant the adoption of a neutrality equidistant between two very different sides. Similarly, John Langdon-Davies would declare: 'I think one side right and the other criminally wrong, but beyond that I am obsessed with the disintegration of human nature that comes with the greatest atrocity of all, Civil War'. The idea that the Spanish Republic was a front for 'blood-slathering Reds' was habitually used by conservatives in Britain, France and the United States to justify their governments' policies of non-intervention, ostensibly adopted to confine the conflict to Spain and prevent general war, but with the effect of guaranteeing victory for the rebel forces. In the words of the poet, Sylvia Townsend Warner, the Republic was thus left 'drilling with broomsticks and fighting against the weight of Europe'. In the case of the British government, underlying the adoption of non-intervention, there was not just class prejudice but also an element of almost racist disdain for the ordinary Spaniard. In this context, the subject of Langdon-Davies's book, the events in the Republican zone in general and in Catalonia in particular, were of central importance. A particularly acute obstacle stood in the way of his efforts to show that the Spanish Republic was certainly not a front for 'blood-slathering Reds'. British policy, already founded on deep-rooted prejudices, was being decisively influenced by reports sent from Barcelona by the deeply conservative consul there, Norman King.

This is not to suggest that, initially, the Spanish Republic did not face serious problems. The military rising of 18 July 1936 was aimed to put an end to the various reforms of the Republic. A huge reforming agenda, in welfare, agriculture and education, aimed at improving the lot of the humbler members of society, had been attempted at the same time as efforts to curb the power of the Army and the Catholic Church. All of this, plus the granting of autonomy to Catalonia and plans to do the same for the Basque Country and Galicia, had infuriated the highly centralist officer corps. Their coup denuded the Republican government of a significant portion of its armed forces and also left the regime bereft of forces of law and order. In the short term, the Republic's lack of military units was spontaneously, albeit inadequately, made good by untrained militia units. The problem of the Civil Guard and the armed police known as the Assault Guards was less easily resolved. In the main, their loyalties lay with the insurgents and even where they did not, the old forces of order were the object of understandable mistrust. The revolutionary enthusiasm which took workers to the front did not serve to make them volunteer to become policemen. As a result, the first two months of the war saw a break-down of law and order in the Republican zone. The Republican authorities made every effort to control the 'uncontrolled' elements but for several months their efforts were in vain. In the words of Julián Zugazagoitia, the editor of the daily *El Socialista*, 'the power of state lay shattered in the street'. The consequence was that, as George Orwell gleefully noted, the working class was 'in the saddle'. Barcelona was the centre of an anarcho-syndicalist revolution.

There was widespread terrorism in the Republican zone for a period of about four months, mainly directed against the supporters of right-wing parties and the clergy. This situation was facilitated by the effective disappearance of the police force and the judiciary together with the fact that revolutionary crowds had opened the jails and released the common prisoners. Accordingly, behind a rhetoric of revolutionary justice, acts of violence of all kinds were perpetrated. Some violence was certainly an expression of popular outrage at the very fact of the military coup and its attempt to destroy the advances made by the Republic. Acts of revenge were directed at the sections of society on whose behalf the military was acting. Thus, hatred of an oppressive social system found expression in the murder or humiliation of parish priests who justified it, Civil Guards and policemen who defended it, the wealthy who enjoyed it and the employers and landlords' agents who implemented it. In some cases, the acts had a revolutionary dimension – the burning of property records and land registries. But there were also criminal acts, murder, rape, theft, and the settling of personal scores. Courts were replaced by revolutionary tribunals set up by political parties and trade unions.

About 55,000 civilians were killed in the Republican zone in the course of the war. It is difficult to find a simple explanation. Some, like the imprisoned army officers killed at Paracuellos del Jarama and Torrejón de Ardoz during the siege of Madrid, were victims of decisions based on an assessment of their potential danger to the Republican cause. Some were executed as known fifth columnists. Others died in explosions of mass rage which occurred as news arrived of the savage purges being carried out in the Nationalist zone and especially of atrocities committed by Franco's Moors. Air raids on Republican cities were another obvious trigger of popular fury. Whatever the reasons behind the violence, it seriously damaged the reputation of the Republic abroad and undermined its efforts to secure international support. Bizarrely, the atrocities in the Nationalist zone did nothing to diminish its standing even in British and French government circles, let alone in Berlin or Rome.

Norman King's consular despatches from Barcelona built a lurid picture in which 'anarchists, and the escaped criminals with other armed hooligans for a time spread terror throughout the town'. Even when things had calmed down, he speculated almost gleefully that economic collapse 'will produce widespread distress, and possibly lead to a massacre' and predicted that 'a time is not far distant when a wave of xenophobia might set in'. In contrast to King's alarmism about 'raw undisciplined youth armed to the teeth and mostly out of control', *The Times* correspondent commented that 'our escorts and the Republican crowds in the towns, all armed to the teeth, were the most amiable and solicitous revolutionaries one might wish to meet' and that: 'The danger to foreigners in Barcelona seems small. Even the Communists and Anarchists have shown respect for foreigners.' In mid-August, King was reporting that the left was committed to 'the deliberate wiping out of the better classes' and that 'the common people talk openly and ignorantly of their schemes for overthrowing the well-to-do'.

It is clear from his own memoirs that Anthony Eden, the British Foreign Secretary, was much influenced by the despatches from King reporting that 'pillaging and murder are still taking place'. In one such, a gruesome description of a visit to the morgue, King alleged that 'most of the victims have been murdered in cold blood either by the Government militia or agents of the anarcho-syndicalists with whom the Government is now working hand-in-glove'. It was described by an appalled Eden as rivalling 'the most harrowing of Goya's drawings'. The profound impact of these reports is reflected in Eden's comment that 'wholesale executions over a long period far exceeded anything warranted by the abortive revolt'. *The Times* praised the efforts being made by President Lluís Companys and the government of the Generalitat to put an end to terrorism and to save the lives of hundreds of rightists and religious personnel. In contrast, King blamed the Generalitat for the violence of extremist 'ruffians' which 'would disgrace the most backward race of savages known to humanity'. He dismissed the efforts to restore order as tantamount to the imposition of Bolshevism.

An important effort to present a more realistic view to a British audience was made by John Langdon-Davies. Since first visiting Catalonia in 1920, and living there during the years 1921-1922 and 1927-1929, Langdon-Davies had been an enthusiastic student and advocate of Catalan culture. His book, *Dancing Catalans*, published in 1929, reflected his admiration for the humanity and egalitarianism that he believed were the essence of social relations in rural Catalonia. The persecution of the Catalan language and popular culture under the dictatorship of General Miguel Primo de Rivera (1923-1930) intensified Langdon-Davies's sympathies for Catalan nationalism. Unsurprisingly, the establishment of the democratic Second Republic on 14 April 1931 seemed to him to promise a freedom for the region that he loved.

On 6 August 1936, barely three weeks after the military coup, he arrived at Puigcerdà on the Spanish border on a second-hand motorcycle with his fifteen-year-old son, Robin. They had been obliged to bring it through France by train. After leaving Robin with Catalan friends in Ripoll, he went on to Barcelona as a special correspondent of the now defunct liberal London daily, the *News Chronicle*. There, he was fortunate that an old friend, Ventura Gassol, was Minister of Culture in the Catalan Government, the Generalitat. While most correspondents had serious difficulties in getting their despatches to London or New York, Langdon-Davies was allowed to telephone his from the Minister's office. Between 11 August and 7 September, on an almost daily basis, he wrote articles in which he tried to put the disorder and church-burnings into their historical context. Thereafter, he went to Valencia, Madrid and Toledo before returning to England on 19 September. He used the material gathered as the basis for lectures on behalf of the relief organization, Spanish Medical Aid, and for *Behind the Spanish Barricades* which he wrote in barely five weeks in the intervals between his lectures, a precipitation belied by the clarity, colour and vigour of its prose.

During his brief time in Spain, Langdon-Davies was quickly convinced that the British policy of non-intervention was disastrous for both the Spanish Republic and for Britain. This brought him into direct conflict with the views being propounded by Norman King. In September 1936, he visited the Foreign Office in London in an attempt to counter-act the apocalyptic view of Companys and of the Catalan situation that was emanating from right-wing sources. He mistakenly underestimated the scale of the killing in Barcelona, and this led to officials checking his figures with Norman King. The Consul gloated and he seized the opportunity to brand Langdon-Davies as a Communist, which he certainly was not: 'when one finds people like Langdon-Davies deliberately misrepresenting conditions one cannot help wondering as to his motive. The only conclusion one can draw is that he and other communistic minded people wish to introduce into England the same earthly paradise they find in Spain'.

He was more successful in setting down his own opinions on both in *Behind the Spanish Barricades*. He had come to regard Companys as 'the greatest man in Catalunya today' despite an initially very unfavourable impression: 'I had never liked the look of him. He is too much like those caricatures of the German Crown Prince that helped us to win the war to save democracy. A weak man, I thought, and a sentimentalist. I was completely wrong. I went to see him at his private reception room at the Generalitat. [...] Companys leaned back in his chair and smiled. A foreigner who could speak to him in Catalan! He relaxed. The conversation that followed seems to me to contain a statement of certain political truths of the first importance to any student of politics in this changing world.' Essentially, after his early poor impression, Langdon-Davies subsequent admiration derived from Companys's realistic support for the Spanish Republic.

In the course of their lengthy conversation, Companys spoke of his relationship with the anarcho-syndicalists. Langdon-Davies commented: 'Ever since the rebellion Companys has insisted in having the CNT take part in the responsibilities of government. Of course, short-sighted people have thought that this meant that the Generalitat had become a mere shadow in the hands of the CNT. But the wisdom of Companys has borne fruit. He has tied down the anti-political philosophers to the job of having to organise and to govern. If he had not vigorously supported a policy of making the anarcho-syndicalists responsible for what happened, they would have blamed the bourgeoisie for anything that went wrong; as it is they are themselves forced to justify their existence by learning how to keep public order; they have to control their own extremists.' Langdon-Davies was equally impressed by the fact that Companys seemed to have mobilised the petit bourgeoisie for the anti-fascist struggle. He concluded: 'For every thousand that has heard of Hitler and Mussolini probably only one has heard of Companys; but that does not alter the fact that he is one of the key-men in Europe today.'

Despite his sympathy with the Republic, Langdon-Davies did not try to pretend that revolutionary violence did not exist but he made an effort to understand what lay behind it. In the case of the shooting of thirteen fascist sympathizers in Ripoll, the town where he left his son, he faced a grave moral dilemma: 'as I thought of those superb, simple-hearted working men and peasants in overalls, organizing as best they could to keep the Moorish invasion from saving Christianity by killing Spanish Christians; as I thought of their gentleness, their zeal, their courtesy, and how in spite of it all they had been moved to get up and kill thirteen fairly harmless men, my heart hardened against those who had brought to Spain the most horrible atrocity of all, civil war.' The blame, he concluded, lay with 'those who let loose the supreme horror of civil war'. The book was published by Secker & Warburg in November 1936 with considerable critical success, hailed perhaps most significantly in the *New Statesman* by Gerald Brenan, perhaps the only man in England who knew Spain as well as Langdon-Davies.

Throughout the rest of the Civil War, Langdon-Davies returned to Catalonia with frequency. He was deeply shocked on a visit to Barcelona in February 1937 by the plight of the thousands of refugees who inundated the city. In the spring of 1937, he helped set up the National Joint Committee for Spanish Relief. Langdon-Davies was a Quaker and with the help of the Friends, the Committee put a huge effort into setting up homes for refugee children. With his friend, Eric Muggeridge, Langdon-Davies devised a 'Foster Parents Scheme' whereby families in Britain and the USA would 'foster' a named, individual child. It's equivalent in the USA was called 'Foster Parents Plan'. The idea was enthusiastically welcomed by the Catalan government and soon there was a home for refugee children established at Puigcerdà, a small market-town on the French border in the north-west of the province of Girona. There were soon several homes and the idea would be the basis for Langdon-Davies's later and much wider scheme, Plan International.

The humanity that underlay the creation of Plan resonates

throughout this book. Early in the preface are words that resonate today as pro-Franco propagandists, the equivalent of holocaust deniers, continue to peddle wild fantasies about Communist conspiracies and Muscovite skulduggery: 'To the many readers who quite sincerely believe in the insincerities of our philo-fascist press I say, "I beg of you to believe it possible that you have been misled. Read and imagine things in terms of human men and women; of simple folk, insulted and injured, whose hope of an end to the Dark Ages has been destroyed by rebellion subsidised from abroad. If you saw your family doomed to the conditions of the Spanish peasantry and workers, would you need Moscow gold to make you cling to the little you had and fight for a little more? Remember all that you have heard of the age-long tyrannies of Spain; do you realise that a victory for the Rebels means their re-imposition on the remnant left alive?"'.

Paul Preston,
Director of the Cañada Blanch Centre for Contemporary Spanish Studies at the London School of Economics
London, 2007

EDITOR'S NOTE

This edition is based on the book published by Martin Secker and
Warburg Ltd in 1936, which contained fifty-five photographs and
illustrations. Some of these are now lost and due to the constraints
of modern publishing we have not been able to reproduce them
all. For that reason we have had to make limited alterations to the
text. The book was also published in the United States in 1937.
This edition reproduces the original cover. Reportage Press has
made all possible efforts to track down the original designer to
credit the 1936 jacket design, but to no avail.

CHRONOLOGY

1914-18 Spain is neutral during the First World War.

1917 A general strike is crushed by the army. Anarchist and socialist movements grow. Political violence escalates.

1923-30 General Miguel Primo de Rivera is appointed Prime Minister by the king and rules as a dictator.

1931 Second Republic declared. It is led by a coalition of the left and centre. A number of controversial reforms are passed in the face of strong opposition from the former elite. The Agrarian Law of 1932 distributes land among poor peasants; the miltary is reformed and cut back and anticlericalist legislation is passed. King Alfonso XIII goes into exile.

1933 The Spanish Confederation of the Autonomous Right, *Confederación Española de Derechas Autónomas* (CEDA), wins the largest number of seats in the Spanish parliament, but not enough to form a majority. The President refuses to ask its leader, José María Gil-Robles, to form a government, and instead invites Alejandro Lerroux of the centrist Radical Republican Party to do so. CEDA supports the Lerroux government;

1934   *October* CEDA demands and is given three ministerial posts. The Lerroux/CEDA government then tries to annul the social legislation that had been passed by the previous government. The move provokes a general strike in Valencia and Zaragoza, street fighting in Madrid and Barcelona, an armed uprising of miners in Asturias and an autonomist rebellion in Catalonia. The rebellions are suppressed brutally. Mass political arrests and trials follow. The country polarizes politically.

1936   *February* The Popular Front coalition of parties on the left wins a majority of the seats in parliament with 34.3% of the vote.

1936   *March-May* Street riots, strikes and general anarchy in some parts of Spain. Political tensions rise. There are numerous assassinations and politically related acts of violence.

1936   *April* The liberal Manuel Azaña becomes President. He is the object of intense hate for the Spanish right as he was responsible for pushing the reform agenda through parliament between 1931-33. The Spanish generals particularly dislike Azaña as, while Minister of War, he cut the army's budget and closed the military academy.

1936   *July* Military uprisings in Spanish Morocco and some parts of the Spanish mainland. The government dissolves the regular army. General Franco flies to Spanish Morocco where the Nationalists are almost unopposed

in assuming control.Hitler agrees to help the Nationalists. Stalin offers assistance to the Republican government. German and Italian planes airlift Franco's army
to the Spanish mainland. Tens of thousands of people
caught on the 'wrong' side of the lines are assassinated
or summarily executed. Numbers are probably compa-
rable on both sides.

1936   *August* First International Brigade volunteers arrives in
Spain.

1936   *September* Nationalist forces win a significant victory
when they relieve the Alcázar in Toledo where a Nationalist garrison has held out since the beginning of the
rebellion, resisting for months thousands of Republican
troops.
A military junta names Franco as head of state and chief
of the armed forces of Spain.

1936   *October* The Nationalists launch a major offensive toward Madrid. The first aid supplies from Russia arrive
for the Republican side.

1936   *November* Nationalists launch a major assault on Madrid.
The government flees to Valencia. There is fierce fighting and the Nationalist assault is repulsed.
Germany and Italy officially recognize Franco as head of
the Spanish government.

1936   *December* Italy sends its own 'volunteers' to fight for the
Nationalists.

1937   *January-February* Nationalist assault on Madrid again
fails.

1937   *March* Guernica bombed.

1937   *May* Running street battles in Barcelona between different factions of anti-fascist Republican troops.

1937   *June* Bilbao falls.

1937   *July* Republican counter offensive around Madrid.

1937   *November* Nationalists close in on Valencia. Government moves to Barcelona.

1938   *April* Nationalists take part of the Mediterranean coast and Spain is effectively cut in half.

1938   *June-October* Battle of Ebro. Government launches a major campaign to reconnect their territory but fail. Moral is undermined by the Munich Agreement.

1938   *October* International Brigade leaves Spain.

1939   *January-February* The Nationalists conquer Catalonia.

1939   *February* The Franco regime is recognized by the British and French governments.

1939   *March* Madrid falls to the Nationalists.

1939   *April* The last Republican forces surrender and Franco declares victory.

1939-1975 The Franco dictatorship. An estimated 100,000 Republicans are killed or die in prison as Nationalist repression follows the civil war. Many others are put into labor camps to build railways and monuments, drain swamps and dig canals. Hundreds of thousands flee abroad. Thousands of those who fled to France are captured by the Nazis during World war Two and die in concentration camps in Germany.

1975 *November* Franco dies. Succeeded as head of state by King Juan Carlos. With Juan Carlos on the throne, Spain makes the transition from dictatorship to democracy.

1977 *June* Spain holds its first democratic elections in four decades.

Spain,
1st August 1936

FRANCE

ANDORRA

Puerto de la Selva
Ripoll
Ribes
Vich
Puigcerdá
Gerona
Barcelona

Lérida

Palma

MEDITERRANEAN

Pamplona
Huesca
Zaragoza
Teruel

Valencia

Murcia

S. Sebastián

Oviedo
Burgos
Ávila
Madrid
Toledo
Cáceres
Badajoz

Granada
Málaga
Córdoba
Sevilla
Cádiz
Ceuta
Tánger
Melilla

La Coruña
Santiago
de Compostela

PORTUGAL

ATLANTIC
OCEAN

Lisbon

Santa Cruz
de Tenerife
Las Palmas
de Gran Canaria

Republican area

Nationalist area

DEDICATION

To the man whom I have called 'Paco', for his cheerfulness through everything; the 'Marquis', in memory of a day near Caceres; 'Borrull', for an evening in the Fifth District of Barcelona; 'the Captain', in the hope that he was not burned to death in Toledo; 'Puig' and 'Joan'. Also to my old friends Maria M—, Catholic poet, and Josep S—, Catholic capitalist, for their steadfastness. And to Ventura Gassol, President Companys, Alvarez Del Vayo, in proud thanks for their friendship. And to Ventura Sureda and Josep Gelabert in New York.

AUTHOR'S PREFACE

This book does not lay claim to permanence or to be considered as a work of art. It has been written in five weeks in the intervals of addressing meetings from one end of England to the other to collect funds for Spanish medical aid.

I have tried to draw a picture of the Spain I love as well as the Spain which is suffering. I cannot see the Spanish tragedy as a political affair on which one can take a vote. I think one side right and the other criminally wrong, but beyond that I am obsessed with the disintegration of human nature that comes with the greatest atrocity of all, Civil War.

I do not pretend that there were not many cheerful and light-hearted moments in my visits to Spain this summer, and I hope that something of their flavour has come through. Moreover, I have paid tribute to the virtues called out in simple folk by the terror that has come to them. But the abiding feelings must be sorrow and anger. And it is not so much anger against those who have brought all this to Spain, as anger against those in our own country who wish them well.

To the many readers who quite sincerely believe in the insincerities of our philo-fascist press I say, "I beg of you to believe it possible that you have been misled. Read and imagine things in terms of human men and women; of simple folk, insulted and injured, whose hope of an end to the Dark Ages has been destroyed by rebellion subsidised from abroad. If you saw your family doomed to the conditions of the Spanish peasantry and workers, would you need Moscow gold to make you cling to the little you had and fight for a little more? Remember all that you have heard of the age long tyrannies of Spain; do you realise that a victory for the Rebels means their reimposition on the remnant left alive?"

I have to thank first the Editors of the *News Chronicle* for sending me as their Special Correspondent to Spain. They never censored a word of what I had to say. Second, the publishers of the *Left Review* for permission to reprint a paragraph by Ralph Bates.[1] Third, Sir Peter Chalmers Mitchell for permission to publish his letter to *The Times*. And, last, innumerable Spanish friends, many of whose names I never knew, who by their acts of courtesy made my progress through a civil war so easy and left with me a new experience of what comradeship can mean.

1.Ralph Bates, (1899-2000) was an English novelist best known for his writings on pre-Civil War Spain. A communist sympathiser, Bates enlisted with the government forces and helped to organise the International Brigade.

CONTENTS

CHAPTER 1
ONE LAST PARADE

Madrid. May 1st, 1936.

A city given over to the proletariat. Those members of the bourgeoisie, who have not driven away the night before to some country retreat, are staying in bed or peeping with distaste from behind closed shutters.

I had never seen a continental May Day celebration in a large city. To me the festival of Labour meant little but a rainy day in Hyde Park effectively damping the ardour of a small crowd singing "England Arise the Long, Long Night is Over." Here was something different. For one thing there were no police; at least there were none in the Paseo del Prado. If you walked up a side street in any direction you came across platoons of them waiting behind corners; mounted police; armoured cars; rifles and machine guns everywhere. But in the Paseo del Prado all was given over without reserve to the marching proletariat; the forces of law and order had the courtesy to stay away.

All footsteps on that day pointed towards the glorious Paseo where in sunlight the statue of Velasquez, palette in hand, leaning forward, estimated the textures and surfaces of scarlet and royal-blue shirts formed up in marching order beneath the dappled plane-trees. The waiting procession stretched for miles, its tail twisted round behind the hideous Ministerio de Fomento, its brilliant head beneath the museum itself. Everybody laughs, cheers, sings.

"Oo, archie, pay; oo, archie, pay; oo, archie, pay." The united communist and socialist youth are marching by, and more beautiful young men and maidens you could not desire to see. Alternatively, socialist blue shirts and scarlet ties, and communist scarlet shirts, men and girls alike, but the latter very careful of their appearance. Got by Moscow out of Hollywood, you might say; while the men are clean-shaven, upstanding fellows whose appearance would have pleased not only Walt Whitman but Colonel Blimp.

"Oo, archie, pay; oo, archie, pay; oo, archie, pay." The letters U.H.P. stand for United Brothers of the Proletariat, and they are the rallying cry of the Spanish Popular Front.[1] Later, in Merida, beneath the shadow of a Roman monument to the Peace of Augustus, I was to see in the pottery market dishes, unaltered in design since Spain was part of the Roman Empire, except that U.H.P. was painted in the centre instead of the traditional leaf like pattern.

Also I saw scrawled up in a public lavatory, "Long live the Spanish Phalanx, death to the United Sons of Bitches"—for U.H.P. stands for that also.[2]

The banners are innumerable, and for those willing to under-

---

1. The Spanish Popular Front was an electoral coalition pact signed in January 1936 between various left-wing political organisations to contest an election in February of that year. The creation of popular fronts was in keeping with the Comintern policy at the time which advocated a broad alliance of the left as the best way to combat the rise of fascism. It won by a narrow margin but governed as if it had a majority, instigating a series of radical polices (among them the restoration of Catalan autonomy, an amnesty for political prisoners, the exiling of senior army officers like General Franco and General Mola from mainland Spain and agrarian reform,) which alienated the right and led to the military insurrection.

2. The Spanish Falange, *Falange Española*, was a fascist organisation that hoped to establish a fascist state similar to Mussolini's Italy in Spain. In the February elections, the Falange received only 0.7% of the vote but after the victory of the Popular Front it grew rapidly and by July of that year it had a membership of 40, 000. In the run up to the July insurrection it did more than any other group to cause disruption and on July 18th, it supported the military rebellion and became the dominant force in Nationalist politics.

stand they are warnings of the storm which will break ere long. As each banner passes, the crowd salutes, clenched fist, bent left or right arm, the salute of the Popular Front or, less frequently, but too frequently for the pleasure of those who may be peeping from behind the closed shutters, a straight arm with fist stretched skywards. The trees themselves, pollarded into gaunt skeletons, are raising their boughs in the communist salute.

A scarlet banner with white letters cries: *"Ni Tierras sin Cultivar: Ni Campesinos Con Hambre."* "Neither land uncultivated, nor peasants hungry." I was to see with my own eyes in Extremadura, in the province of Toledo, in Andalusia, why that banner spoke direct to the crowd's heart.

"Milicias antifascistas: obreras y campesinas" in red on a white banner. "Anti-fascist militia: working women and peasant women." I watched the beautiful girl who carried the banner on her shoulder. Here, I thought, was surely a chance for a movie director in search for talent. In less than three months she and her like were to be in workers' overalls, with rifles not banners on their shoulders, taking the place deserted by a rebel army, part of the new army, the Army in Overalls.

And here, closer together, walking not marching, come a group of women, old and young, and children. Above them flaps a banner: "Widows, mothers, and orphans of the Asturias miners." The crowd cheers with a slightly different tone. It is thinking of the men who were shot down by Foreign Legionaries in October, 1934, and thrown into a common grave.[3] Here are some of their families walking in Madrid lest anyone should forget what patriotism has done. If the rest of Spain had followed those miners in their desperation, how many tears would have been spared!

The procession moves on, stops, moves on again. Down very

---

3. In October 1934, a national revolt and general strike broke out, when CEDA, the Spanish Confederation of the Autonomous Right, *Confederación Española de Derechas Autónomas*, who were the largest party in the Cortes demanded three ministerial posts. CEDA was a rightist Catholic coalition regarded by some as the legal face of fascism. There was widespread anger as the administration tried to annul the social reform programmes introduced by the previous government. Notably it cancelled the land reform programme. (Millions of Spaniards lived in more or less absolute poverty under the

4 Behind The Spanish Barricades

near to the ground you can see the Anti-fascist Pioneers. The youngest is three, the oldest seven or eight. Too young to do more than one thing at once, they are having a difficult time. For they must march, and keep a fist in the air, and chant their marching song. It comes wavering towards us from stumbling little figures in blue and scarlet. "Oo, archie, pay; oo, archie, pay; queremos escuelas laicos; we want secular schools!" Nothing in the world seems less likely. A little girl of four lets her outstretched arm lie languidly on her head and doggedly follows the heels of the infant in front, every now and then she remembers to tell the crowd that she wants secular schools, she wants secular schools.

A new and curious sound comes from a section in white trousers, white caps, white collars and blue shirts, probably an Asturian or a Santander contingent. A rondalla of mandolins. Mandolins playing the Internationale. There is a block in the procession's progress, and the rondalla squat near the ground on their haunches and continue to play the Internationale on their mandolins. The Anti-fascist Pioneers stop wanting secular schools, and rest. I take their photographs. They all try to be in the front row, and in consequence all fall down. They fall towards me like the crest of a breaking wave, a foam of little white fists in the air.

The street vendors sell scarlet buttons, gilt sickles and hammers, stars. The beggars forget about the love of God, and beg their comrades for a halfpenny in the name of international solidarity. Girls coax coins from me in aid of the victims of fascism in Abyssinia; I hope they kept the pennies for the coming victims of fascism nearer home. I buy a copy of a new magazine, *Mujeres*, or *Women*. The voice of the anti- fascist women. Bread for our sons;

---

firm control of aristocratic landlords in an almost feudal system.) There was widespread street fighting and martial law was declared. The armed uprising staged by miners in Asturias, in northern Spain, was brutally suppressed by troops led by General Franco. The Spanish Foreign Legionaries, many of whom were criminals and fugitives, together with the locally recruited Moroccan troops went on an orgy of rape and pillage in the occupied villages. The revolt was followed by a mass of political arrests. Moderates on the left saw that the uprising was a disaster but it gave the extreme left a taste for armed insurrection and those on the right were left with the impression that the army was the only bulwark against revolutionary change.

happiness for our hearths. We do not want war, nor fascism. We want bread, work, peace, and liberty. The mothers of Abyssinia call us. The mother of Prestes begs us to save her son. Bread and justice for the widows and orphans of Asturias. For their rights, for their sons, for liberty and work, the women go out into the street on the First of May.

I buy another object that's a very interesting sign of the times, a strip cartoon. For centuries you have been able to buy in Spain picture histories like this, usually lives of Saints or accounts of some religious event. Here is the new version, eminently fitted for a people who still understand pictures better than words; all the hopes and desires of this huge procession on one sheet of paper, and in their expression strange survivals of traditional ways of thought. (See plates)

No. 1 shows the calendar open at the great saint's day, the day of Saint Proletariat, Martyr; in 2 and 4 we see abandoned tools and idle shops; in 5 we see the workmen going off to his outing; we see in 6 the disapproval of the leaders of the reactionary parties, and in 7 the union of the various workers' parties, "united they must triumph, then plenty of strife"; in 9 the great leader of Spanish socialism, Pablo Iglesias, whose name has taken the place of those of many saints and aristocrats on street signs; 10 shows that priests are fascists, and 12 that the proletarian fish knows better than to swallow their bait; 14 shows the aristocrat escaping with his money, and 15 shows Lerroux in his coffin;[1] 18 is homage to Quevedo, the "first antifascist"; 19 is the programme of the Popular Front "shortly to be carried out"; 20 the prisons from which 32,000 workers have been released, 21 the abolition of the death penalty; 22 new terms for workers; 23 capital taken from hiding in stockings and forced into use; 24 the symbol of the United Front on the pulpit of fascist priests; 25 "these signs of force must disappear"; 26

---

1. Alejandro Lerroux (1864-1949) was a centrist radical, leader of the Radical Republican Party. He served as prime minister in the Second Republic following the abdication of King Alfonso XIII and he was responsible for suppressing the revolt of 1934 which earned him the hatred of the left. In 1936, he fled Spain for Portugal, returning in 1947.

capitalism is on its deathbed as monarchism was; 27 these doctors in council exchange their fears; 28 they advise a dose of fascism; 29 but Dr. Proletariat has a word to say; and 30 Don Capital "requiescat in pace." This is the 'picturized' creed of a united people.

The last parade moves on again. Here are the veterans and the leaders. Besteiro, Indalecio Prieto, and above all Largo Caballero. The crowd shouts out their names. Caballero, Caballero, Caballero. He is sixty-seven years old; he has been condemned to death; he has been imprisoned six times. In less than three months he will be in blue overalls fighting on the Sierras against this thing called fascism...[1] A few days later I had coffee at the house of a courteous and distinguished old gentleman. I had come to see his Goya, and a very lovely Goya it was. "You know," he said, "things are very serious. We shall have to fight this attack on civilization which the Jews and Moscow are preparing." In less than three months he was in prison, or dead; I have not been able to find out which.

Merienda by the Side of the Manzanares.

They have furled their banners and put them away. They have stocked the shopping baskets with provisions, taken down the family clothes-line, filled their seven-litre jars with wine, and crossed the Manzanares. The street-vendors, having got rid of as many sickles and hammers, stars, scarlet buttons as possible, are trying their luck with nuts, ice-cream, small buns, and sherbet.

---

1. Although the three men marched together in the parade, they were long time political rivals with radically different ideas as to how reform should be carried out. These divisions were reflected in the left in general and weakened their cause. The main problem with the Popular Front was that it put centrist liberals and Marxist-Leninists in the same coalition.

Francisco Largo Caballero (1869-1946) was a trade unionist and the most radical leader of the Socialist Party (PSOE). He advocated a Bolshevik style dictatorship of the proletariat. His views were attacked by Indalecio Prieto (1883-1962), the leader of the right-wing of the PSOE, who drew most of his support from middle class and intellectual party supporters and was an advocate of the centre left alliance with the liberal republicans. Prieto was against street violence and the burning of the churches. Caballero did not allow the PSOE to take part in the Popular Front administration initially, largely in order to block Prieto from taking office as prime minister but also

An unending crowd of people, all with symbols of revolt about their persons, climbs through the pines of the Casa del Campo. Each family, or each pair of lovers, looks around for a place where they can stake out a claim. They select a knot of trees and encircle it with the family clothes-line, dump the wine-jar and the baskets in the middle, and relax. Those who have been there longer are already eating, and those who have been there longer still are skipping or playing blind man's buff. Everywhere little isles of possession bounded by clothes-lines, and in the distance the vast ex-royal palace.

A notice on the trees says "Those who attach swings to the tree-trunks should realise that they are injuring the trees which belong to the people." I close my eyes and see Goya's picture, *The Swing*, and his other picture, *The Picnic on the Banks of the Manzanares*, and again his picture, *Blind Man's Buff*. He lived in the valley just below, and though the first of May, and blue and scarlet shirts, and sickles and hammers and stars, had not been invented in his day, he must have wandered amid these trees watching the picnickers a hundred times. On the other side of the river is the church which Goya decorated with human, all too human, angels. It is now his tomb, and someone has scrawled up on its walls in red paint the words of an English bishop, "Religion is the opium of the people."

Goya did not know of the first of May, but of the famous second he left his unforgettable pictures. On that day in 1808 the people of Madrid rose against the Napoleonic dictatorship. The French rode

---

because he believed that the administration would play the same role as the Kerensky government had done in Russia. Caballero was dubbed by the communist press as the "Spanish Lenin". He believed that direct action and widespread strikes would bring about a revolution. Although the Popular Front manifesto was mild, it was Caballero's earlier speeches that alarmed the right and caused it to react so violently against their victory. Julián Besteiro (1870-1940) had resigned as President of the *Union General de Trabajadores* (UGT) an anarcho-syndicalist trade union now led by Caballero, as he disliked the radical path it had begun to follow. He had opposed the armed uprising of October 1934 to which Caballero had been deeply committed. In 1936, he won the highest number of votes for any candidate in Madrid. He argued strongly against direct action and the formation of militias. The three men attacked each other continually in the leftist press.

them down with their Mamelouk mercenaries and shot them in dozens next day. But the rising of the Spanish peasants and working men was the first step toward saving Europe from Napoleon.

If Goya were alive to-day, what would he see? I have no doubt that many of those people I saw surrounding themselves with clothes-lines in the Casa del Campo on the first of May are now dead. I know that they rose against the threat of a worse domination than that of Napoleon, and that by doing so they gave Europe one more chance. But I do not know if Europe will be willing to take it.

Over all those groups taking merienda by the side of the Manzanares was brooding the figure of death. Behind the shuttered windows, in the country houses, in the silent barracks, men were even then plotting to bring over the Mamelouks once more, to have firing squads over open graves, to put an end to picnics. Against them, rather to their surprise, has appeared an Army in Overalls. And Madrid when I saw it again in August was seemingly as empty of bourgeois as on May 1st. But the streets were barricaded, and behind the closed shutters was fear, not mere distaste. The smile of good humour has faded off the face of the crowds. The small children are no longer content to demand secular schools; they go about the streets dressed up as militiamen and hospital nurses, and nobody bothers to collect money for Abyssinians. The Paseo del Prado as I saw it in August was an odd sight, full of deserted booths and merry-go-rounds, shooting-galleries and peepshows. For the fascist rebellion swooped down on the midst of the annual fair, and no one has had the heart yet to cart away its neglected remains. But how I saw all this from the depths of an ancient hansom-cab, and why I did not have to pay for the cab, and who accompanied me— these shall be told later.

Blood in Barcelona.

I had come to Madrid from Barcelona. In the great Catalan city, which is everything that Paris is supposed to be, I had eaten lunch with M. and T. We ate from one until half-past-four, ate and discussed Catalanism.

M. is a sensitive poet, a strong catholic, and as aloof from mere politics as any Catalan can be. T. is an anti-catholic, a motor engineer, and a near-socialist— as near, that is, as a bourgeois, whose father started as a peasant and ended as a factory owner, is likely to be. When I first saw him in 1921 his factory was surrounded with barbed wire, and he was waiting to shoot any workman who seemed likely to attack it. Those were the days of the great strikes when post-war Spanish industry, a mushroom war-baby at best, was beginning to draw in and leave men stranded. Later he was defrauded of his share in the factory by an international scoundrel, and began to change his political views.

I have many of T.'s letters; here is an extract from one. "All seems very old in our Europe," he writes. "We are suffering a great crisis of arteriosclerosis. The poisons of our past life of orgies are desperately mixed with our blood in every cellule of every limb and organ. I am not a pessimist, because I know that all ends well, but I see my life, and even the life of the biggest men in the world, such a little thing to counteract the almost fatality of events. I cannot so much avoid feeling ironical at the efforts made by so many intellectual, artistical, and all sorts of highly-trained people that rather becoming another Don Quixote to look at, I prefer to be Sancho Panza…

"We are coming to an Individual Humanity encircling all the racial, political, national, and other differentiations, but this is impossible with the prejudices and narrowings of both mind and heart of the actual man… The nose against the window-panes, feeling in myself the vain centurial hope of millions of souls, let me dream of a certain dawn."

I think you can get past the barrier of imperfect English to T.'s type of mind. It is a type that is not at all likely to approve of the way things were going in May, 1936.

M. and T., different as they were in most things, were both firm Catalanists. To them 'Spain' was not merely a foreign country but an inferior one. The Catalans had that Greek quality of balanced wisdom called σωφροσύνη or in Catalan 'seny.' The Spanish, on the other hand, did not know how to behave. There had been more than one hundred churches burned in Spain since the February elections, and not one in Catalunya. People were being assassinated quite regularly in the inferior regions where Castilian is spoken; but the Catalans, thanks to their Mediterranean balanced wisdom, went about things in quite a different way. I, also, was once a Catalanist, but, since October, 1934, when the Catalans let the Asturian miners down, I have been less so. It is a very delicate question to bring up, but with that hatred of a perfect thing which is characteristic of the normal man I pointed out the mole on the face of Catalunya.

"Why did the Catalans fail to defend themselves and their government in the revolution of 1934?"

"Ah, that was a pity," said T. "But it was the fault of Dencàs and Badia. They would not arm the workers."

"Why not?"

"Well, you see, we are afraid of the F.A.I. and the C.N.T. To arm them is to put the power into the hands of criminal pistoleros. Dencàs and Badia were afraid to do that; so of course the Catalans could not resist."[1]

It was the first time I had heard of Badia, who was the chief of police in Barcelona in 1934, a young man who had come into prominence at the age of eighteen by trying to bomb King Alfonso in the interests of a free Catalunya.

I went out into the street reassured about Catalunya; its Greek 'seny' would see it through. I took a tram—owned almost entirely by retired minor rentiers in the home counties of England—and went towards the centre of the city. At the corner of the Calle de Montaner was a large crowd. In its centre a pool of blood almost covered with red carnations dropped there by sympathetic girls. The porter at the next block of flats was pointing out the bullet

---

1. **FAI**, *Federación Anarquista Iberica*, was a federation of anarchist groups that emerged out of the CNT, *Confederación Nacional de Trabajo*, an anarcho-syndicalist trade union allied to the Popular Front. Both had a strong following in Catalonia. FAI took part in several uprisings, including that in Asturias in 1934 and carried out numerous political assassinations. When the civil war broke out FAI helped to establish the anti-fascist miltias in Barcelona. The leadership of the Popular Front was unable to control its allies on the extreme left and to get them to respect the law.

marks in the window-sill.

"What has happened?"

"The brothers Badia have just been assassinated."

"By whom?"

"Oh, the F.A.I., I suppose, or the fascists."

The Catalan 'seny' had been caught napping for once. I went to see my friend Q.

Portrait of a Catalan Bourgeois Mystic.

Q. knew all about the assassination of Badia. It had been done by Murcians. Catalans never committed any act of violence whatever, and the only reason why Barcelona was notoriously the world centre of nihilism and criminal syndicalism was that there were so many people from Spain, and especially the disreputable parts of Spain like Murcia.

Now there is no doctrine in the world so absurd as not to have some kind of basis, and it is perfectly true that Barcelona as a great industrial centre has attracted large numbers of unskilled and un-educated workers from more backward parts. It is the same problem as faces the American social system. America is full of Italians and Greeks, and the one-hundred-per-cent nordic American will tell you that it is the presence of these degenerates that causes the police so much trouble. He forgets that when America opened its arms wide to the Italians and the Greeks, it was not asking for a Dante and a Pericles, but for cheap labour. And so it got Chicago.

In the same way Q., who believes in race-culture as firmly as Hitler, does not see that the demand for cheap illiterate labour has given Barcelona many of its problems. Like most nationalists he has never given a thought to economics. If everybody was a Catalan there would be no economic problems.

I remember Q. in the old bad days of Primo de Rivera.[2] He was

---

2. Primo de Rivera (1870-1930) was an aristocrat and an army officer who after he seized power in a coup d'état was appointed as Prime Minister by the King. He then ruled as a dictator from 1923-1930. His dictatorship was mild but he suppressed separat-ist movements in the Basque country and Catalonia where it was made illegal to speak

curator of a Catalan museum of prehistoric antiquity. The dictatorship, stupid as usual, was determined to stamp out the Catalan language. The specimens must be labelled in Castilian. The neolithic flake of flint must not be called 'neolític' but 'neolítico.' Q. said that only over his dead body should 'neolític' be turned into the Castilian 'neolítico.' So all the labels disappeared and we poor visitors were left in danger of mortal sin; we might easily think that the stones were paleolithic and not neolithic at all.

When I grumbled at this particular triumph of Catalanism, T. took me up. "You may laugh at Q.," he said. "But let me tell you, during the October Revolution it was Q. who did things. I met him one day, and he said to me, 'To-morrow at two o'clock you are to be in the Plaza de Catalunya, and a man will come up to you with a box which will contain bombs, and you must take them to so-and-so.' "

"What happened?" I asked.

"Well," said T., "I went to the Plaza de Catalunya, but the man with the bombs never turned up."

Not that Q. was altogether inefficient. He had organized the boy scouts of Catalunya and was busily arranging for them to fight for complete Catalan independence when they grew up. After October he was imprisoned on the *Uruguay*, the floating prison which to-day is crammed with fascists. When Q. and his colleagues went on deck, the guard saluted.

"Why do you salute us prisoners?" they asked.

"Well, who knows whether next time you will not win, and then we shall expect you to remember that we treated you with courtesy." 'Next time' has come, and there is nothing but sharp death given out on either side.

Q. took me to see the lying-in-state of the dead men. It was a moving affair. Apart from the fact that I had never seen a dead man before, I was chiefly impressed by Q.'s efficiency in boring his way through a milling crowd of about three thousand.

"This is Q.," he said; "Q. and a foreign journalist, make way

---

Catalan in public and to dance the sardana, the national dance. His fall led to the eventual abdication of King Alfonso XIII and the collapse of the Second Republic.

please," and before I knew what had happened we were at the dead men's side. Both had met death unshaven, and a strip of sticking plaster held together one lacerated cheek. Amid the candles stood a guard of honour, men and women in Catalan separatist uniform. Q. made a curious little dart at each face, peering down within an inch of the sightless eyes, and moved on weeping. The Murcians had reduced the Catalan race by two.

Next morning Q., knowing that I had come to learn as much about Spanish realities as possible in a short time, took me to see a man whom, he thought, I ought to know. This man was at the head of a movement which aimed at uniting the Provençal-speaking groups of southern France as far north as Toulouse and east as Marseilles to Catalunya. He assured me that already these Frenchmen looked to Barcelona rather than to Paris for their capital. He thought it very important for the British Empire. After all, Barcelona, Marseilles, and the Balearic Isles between them would be very helpful in keeping the way to India open. He showed me nicely-printed translations of Catalan books into Provençal and Provençal books into Catalan.

When I told Q. that my London paper would have very little space for such things, he was hurt. When I told him that I did not care in the least whether they spelt it econòmic or económico, but I did want to know what the Catalan government, free and sober, was going to do about economic problems, I saw him hunting for Murcian traits in the shape of my cranium. Then I left for Extremadura.

The Many Spains.

On the way to Extremadura I thought how strange it was that people should try and invent a unity called Spain. So far Q. was right. Catalunya was not Castile. But nor were Extremadura or Andalusia, Aragon or Navarre, Galicia or Asturias, the Basques or the Valencians. They were all regions with superb egoisms and separate problems.

Catalunya is the richest part of Spain, both agriculturally and industrially, and its riches it owes to two factors, the mountains and the sea. From the mountains comes water, carefully coaxed along innumerable channels to fertilize fields and gardens, shot down artificial falls to generate power. And the sea is the Mediterranean, an older civilizing force than the Atlantic. Barcelona, the most important town on the Mediterranean, gave Europe its first democratic parliament, its first code of seafaring law; while the water from the hills created a wealthy class of peasant proprietors, and later turned the wheels of industry until, with the coming of electricity, it made the great city of a million men a hive of industry, with all the problems and injustices that go with capitalism anywhere in the world.

You can see the history of successful capitalism on the face of Barcelona to-day. Its architecture reflects the rise of a purse-proud generation of *nouveaux riches*, without real traditions, clamorous to show in their stones and bricks how much money they had to spend.

In the Paseo de Gràcia there are gingerbread horrors of architecture which cannot be equalled elsewhere in the world. One house by the notorious architect Gaudí is built like granite sea-waves, without a right-angle inside or out, a sort of Mappin terrace for asses, not goats, to live in. They say that many of the room-walls are built of plate-glass, and that they are all curved and twisted. They say that the owner could not find a wall against which to put a grand piano, and telephoned Gaudí for advice.

"Do you play the piano?" he asked.

"No, but one must have a musical instrument in the drawing-room."

"Then I advise you to hang up a violin."

They say that the garage is at the top of the house, with an inclined plane to get you there, and that the young man of the house has his bed arranged so that he can tumble out of the car into it. They say -

Q. explained how the superb Catalan gothic, neither French nor Spanish, was typical of the Catalan spirit. He was right; the hard-headed merchants of the medieval city-state knew how to build without fuss, with strength, with 'functional' simplicity; their cathedral evidently came from the same practical spirit which gave the world the first code of mercantile law. But Gaudí and the monstrous mansions of the Paseo de Gràcia, and the fireproof cathedral of the Sacred Family—these are the Catalan spirit too. Even Q. admits it: "We Catalans are such individualists that our philosophy runs to anarchism. We will never submit to communism." So say the F.A.I. and the C.N.T., though Q. would rather that they did not.

Why is Catalunya Catalunya and Extremadura Extremadura? Even Q. admits that there is no such thing as a Catalan race. The true-born Catalan is a mixture of Greek, Celto-Iberian, Roman, Goth, Visigoth, Vandal, Norman, Suevi, and the rest. The explanation of the perfection of the Catalan spirit is the same as that of the perfect cocktail; fate hurled in all the ingredients haphazard, and (thank God) the Catalan was the result.

The Catalan has 'seny'; he does not burn churches; he settles up his quarrels by agreeing with his enemy in the way; he is democratic. In short, he is very like Victorian Manchester except that he believes in tariffs to protect his industries. His sole weakness is that he is at the mercy of Murcians. The uncatalan F.A.I., according to Q., are a bunch of criminal pistoleros in the pay of the fascists, dominating the C.N.T. or syndicalist unions and, of course, being Murcians, they are the snake in the paradise which is Barcelona.

They do not care, these F.A.I. and C.N.T., for the things that really matter. They would read a label with the word 'neolítico' without turning a hair. They are not interested in joining up with the south of France. Instead of the Catalan flag of four red bars on a golden background, they wave their own black and red flag. Instead of saying in good Catalan 'adeusiau,' godbewi'ye, they say Salud. They are perfectly willing to regard other Spaniards as their equals so long as they are anarcho-syndicalists.

While good Catalans devote their energy to dedicating fountains to dead poets and changing the Castilian notices in the streets into Catalan, the anarcho-syndicalists are otherwise busy. They have a code. "You must learn to kill without hate" is one sentence in their code.

Extremadura.

But as I looked at the illimitable horizons of Extremadura I thought of other reasons for the difference between one part of Spain and another, beside Q.'s theory of the admirable Catalan cocktail.

I sat in the huge Roman amphitheatre at Merida; I took a seat in the upper circle. Below me was the arena with all its excellent sluices and channels through which came the water when a shipwreck scene was to be shown. Down there they had actually manned the toy ship with a crew of wild beasts and Christians, and on those tiers had sat the crowds, the Sunday afternoon crowds, thrilled by the drowning livestock. On exactly such a spot as this had sat the little boy crying bitterly because one poor lion had got no Christian. This was the grandeur that was Rome, Rome that declined and fell. The Roman Q.s put it down to the Murcians from the distant empire. Wiser men said that latifundia destroyed Rome, just as latifundia have destroyed all this part of Spain. Just as latifundia, huge agricultural and pastoral estates owned by absentee landlords, must destroy any part of the world in the end.

Now the difference between Catalunya and Extremadura is this: in Catalunya, thanks to the sea and the mountains, there is more rain than evaporation; in Extremadura there is more evaporation than rain. Go there in May and you find a flower garden, but by the end of June there is nothing but an unending brown hell beneath a copper sky.

For centuries the Extremaduran feudal lords added acre to acre and village to village; in the towns Merida, Caceres, Trujillo, Badajoz, Medellin, they built their palaces and spent their money, the money which was squeezed from soil which was never replenished. Cultivation gave way to pasture; the peasant found that instead of having land to till he was jostled off the face of the earth by grazing herds. The wilder spirits became the conquistadores and slaked their burning thirst with the blood of the New World. Later, when adventure ceased, the big landlords toddled off to Madrid and lived in forgetful obesity. The land died and the peasants died with it.

So, in May, 1936, as the train laboured along through miles of despoblados and dehesas, miles of unused land all belonging to one man, and he a virtually unknown absentee living in a modern apartment in Madrid, with no other grounds for self-respect than his ancestral tree—as the train cut the endless wastes, every now and then I would see a peasant on a ridiculously small donkey riding to find work, and as the train passed I would see him greet it with a clenched fist raised to the sky.

Every few miles we would pass a little station or a group of farm buildings, and on the walls I could read, Death to Gil Robles;[1] Viva Rusia; and the letters U.H.P. Little children, clean and almost naked, turned to us laughing and gave the communist salute. Hour by hour in this land of Cortés and Pizarro, the strange isolated figures looking more than life-size in the slanting afternoon light raised that fist skywards, and sometimes one could hear a cheerful "Down with Fascism" through the rattle of the wheels.

The Marquis.

Of course there are those who believe that the reason why those fists are shot skywards is that Moscow has telegraphed a rouble to their owners to do so. People who cannot think, feel, or do anything unless it is suggested to them are great believers in world-wide conspiracies. It never occurs to them that a man may revolt against intolerable conditions because he has a will of his own. No Moscow Jew had trudged those Extremaduran wastes with a pail of red paint to put up on every broken wall the sickle and hammer of angry hope. The writing on the wall has come from men and women grown tired of waiting for the redress of centuries-old

---

1. Gil Robles (1898-1980) was the leader of the rightist coalition CEDA, *Confederación Española de Derechas Autónomas*, a controversial figure, regarded by some as the legal face of fascism. It was the appointment of three CEDA ministers to the cabinet that triggered the revolution of October 1934. After the revolt, he was made Minister of War and appointed General Franco as Chief of Staff. CEDA, which was supported by a broad sweep of voters from moderate Catholic republicans to the extreme right, was the largest party in the right wing National Front coalition in the elections of February 1936 which it narrowly lost. Its youth movement joined the Falange en masse in the spring of 1936. Robles, however, was to live in exile during the Franco regime.

wrongs.

I went to Caceres. Caceres is in two parts, one a busy provincial modern town, the other a silent amber city of medieval palaces, through whose halls scarcely a voice resounds, while in the streets there are none but school-children. The Republic has turned many deserted mansions into schools and the church squares are made dangerous by footballs.

I walked up the street. Two little boys dashed round the corner and, at the sight of me, "Jesus" they shouted.

"What is it?" came the cheerful voice of Jesus from behind the corner.

"Quick, come here, a foreigner." But Jesus missed his cue, and came skipping cheerily into sight. When he saw me his manner changed. He discarded radiance, energy, health in one gesture, and became the perfect beggar-boy. "Alms, for the love of God, sir. Help a poor ailing child."

"Certainly not," I said, "you're being ridiculous." Giving up at once, Jesus went rollicking down the hill after his companions. An example of how even brilliant acting can be unconvincing if the cue is missed.

It was just after my brush with Jesus that I met the Marquis. He was a sensitive, rather worn-looking, man, taking a photograph of a deserted Renaissance palace.

"You are German?" he said.

"No, English."

"O.K., we can talk to one another in English then."

"You are American?" I asked, not unnaturally.

"No, I am Spanish; but I have lived many years in America."

I told him that I was wandering round studying conditions and that I was particularly interested to see how the peasant lived. He said that he was the man to help me best, since he was taking a film of peasant life to show the absentee landlords what their conduct meant in terms of human misery.

We drove out into the country. Little cavalcades of men and women on mule back passed us. These scattered workers live miles and miles from the scenes of their labour. So deeply in their

blood lies the memory of days when all this country was frontier between Moors and Christians that even now they huddled
together in the town rather than risk the isolation of the endless
fields. Five and ten miles out of Caceres they must go every day
and back again at night, because five hundred years ago isolation
from the herd meant death at the hands of a marauder.

At last we came to a low, long building which housed six
families of human beings. These were the typical peasants of Extremadura. What we were to see could be seen a thousand times
over almost without variation. At one end lived some brazeros,
men who did not own an animal and depended on being able to
hire their own bodies out at harvest-time or seed-time to farmers
needing manual labour. When in work they received one shilling a day. They had never tasted meat in their whole lives. They
greeted us with the courtesy of any Spaniard. They talked and
laughed with precisely the same brand of wit as Sancho Panza
had. We went into a bedroom ten feet by ten, with a hole in the
wall one foot square for window. In this room, on sacking, slept
night by night three married couples.

This was no dumping ground for down-and-outs; these were
no worthless tramps, but typical representatives of the peasantry
of Spain showing us their home. They had nothing to hope for;
nothing else to remember when life ended. The universe of their
personal experience would be square miles of parched untilled
soil, and lost in the midst of the plain a room ten by ten shared
between six grown men and women.

At the other end of the building lived some families of yunteros,
owners of some sort of animal, a horse, a mule, a donkey, which
could be hired out, as well as their own bodies. Spotless rooms,
with whitewash on the walls. "We were able to do that," said the
father, "thanks to my post of correspondent for the Institute of
Agrarian Reform," a post which brought him half a crown a week.
Beds round all the walls; in the centre a few sticks burning to heat
the meal, the smoke disappearing through a hole in the roof, a few
pots and pans, a rams-horn of olive oil, sacking for blankets.

Here lived all their lives three families of handsome men and women. The horizon was the same as that of the brazeros further along, except for a little whitewash on the walls, and slightly more air to breathe at night.

We took our photographs and said good-bye. A dozen fists were raised to the sky in farewell. The Marquis shook his head. "That is something altogether new," he said. "If the landowners do not learn in time to give, give, give, it will be taken from them with a knife."

We passed on towards Madrid. At Navalmoral, we ate at a little inn. The daughter of the house served us. "That dish of meat has an excellent complexion," said the Marquis.

"Yes," said the girl, "but it is painted."

"With what?"

"With tomato."

To the right of us, hidden away, was Toledo. "Every year for many years," said the Marquis, "I have gone to Toledo for one reason only, to see Juan de Mena's wooden carving of San Francis. There you have truth and beauty. It is all that I feel most deeply."

We stopped at the village of Lagartera, so picturesque, so typical of all that has made Spain a tourist's paradise; the clothes, the embroidery, the dance that La Argentina took all round the world. In the village square they had written up, "Women fight fascism which kills your sons. Death to Gil Robles. Long live Russia."

"You should go to the monastery of Silos for a week's retreat," said the Marquis. "Once I nearly ceased to be a catholic; I read Fabre's entomological books; I was shaken in faith; I went to Silos, and I found they knew all about Fabre; they gave me back my faith."

We reached Madrid. We drank sherry at the Café Molineros, along with the Marquesa and her plump little daughter. In less than three months, Navalmoral was to be in ruins, Toledo a battlefront. I know not where the monks of Silos have gone, but the Café Molineros was full of anti-fascist militiamen in overalls, the Marquesa was in Portugal, and the Marquis —where was he?

Back for a while in Madrid I buried myself in crowds of people enjoying themselves. I do not believe that anyone can understand what has been happening in Spain unless he has lost his identity time and again in Spanish proletarian crowds. I went to Stamboul, which is never recommended to tourists. It is rather like a co-operative hall in an English suburb, and is run by proletarians for proletarians. I mentioned it to the Marquis and he shuddered. Of course he had never been there, but he had heard of it, and that was enough.

At Stamboul there was a concert of cante flamenco. There were two prices, a shilling, and nine pence. I bought an expensive ticket and so did about ten others; the rest of the audience, a few hundred, were content with nine penny seats; content, that is, until the first singer appeared, and then they came forward like a high tide and occupied the empty rows where we sat. It was much cosier that way.

But the first singer was very long in coming, and as I waited in Stamboul my mind went back and forth over audiences I had seen in Spain and their curiously revealing behaviours. There was the concert in the open court-yard of Charles V's palace at Granada, where I had seen bourgeois Spain in the presence of music. I had learned a great deal about the limitations of the Spanish bourgeoisie at that concert. There is nothing like observing economic classes when they are off their guard. The concert was supposed to start at ten p.m. By eleven the vast circle of the court-yard was half-full, and as each group arrived it took the chairs from the long cold rows and spread them about with much noise into irregular little intimate clusters. This in itself was all to the good, for informality conduces to a fuller enjoyment of art. Shortly after eleven the orchestra began to play and for half an hour a steady stream of people filed in at the two entrances and proceeded with much conversation to drag the chairs into fresh family groupings. Those who had already composed themselves to listen greeted each new noise with an explosive hiss, which drowned the original offending interruption and, as well, any music that might have floated through.

Meanwhile the excellent orchestra continued to unwind a symphony by a young Madrilenian composer. When the few who were in a position to know had told the rest of us that the work was at an end, a general scamper began for the promenade, where for the next half-hour beauty and pandemonium held equal sway. It was only too clear that this was the music all had come to hear. But after half an hour the conductor unfeelingly interrupted the serious business of the evening by raising his baton. *Scheherazade* struggled with the returning crowds who, having met with new friends in the promenade had to re-group their chairs amid a further babel of expostulatory hisses. Meanwhile the 'jealousy motive' thundered unheard in the distance.

Now the economic interpretation of the Granada concert is this: In Spain the bourgeoisie has not settled down to any mannered tradition; it is too *nouveau riche* to understand that audiences are to be seen and not heard; it has come too rapidly from the peasantry and the proletariat.

The bourgeois musical audience is to be seen at its very best at a London Promenade Concert, or faced by a phalanx of performers that are welded into one by a Stokowski or a Toscanini. Chamber-music and the little orchestra of Bach's days belong to the aristocracy who can enjoy themselves in the seclusion of their private houses, reserving opera for moments when they wish to show themselves to the vulgar world. Symphony orchestras are the musical media most suitable for democracy once it has achieved the supreme democratic virtue of sitting still and taking no part whatever in what is going on around. As this democratic virtue of passivity is the product of generations, your Spaniard has not got it. Moreover, he has not had long enough at it to make a successful snob— 'muy snob' in Madrid means 'trés chic'—and so he refuses to pretend to enjoy what bores him. But for our snobs we could not fill the Queen's Hall or Carnegie Hall, and as for Covent Garden and the Metropolitan Opera House, in a world without bourgeois snobbery they would be deserts through which the woodwinds howled unheard.

Compare the concert in Granada with another in Malaga. This was a musical and dramatic entertainment in which alleged scenes of Andalusian life, song and dance, were tied together with an

interminable recitation in rhymed couplets. The theatre was full.
We listened politely to the first rhymed harangue, and went wild
with enthusiasm at the second scene, where Angelillo and another
popular favourite quarrelled most heartrendingly in cante flamenco. We sighed audibly when the actor returned for the next
harangue, and at the third we threw programmes and hats at him
until he stopped.

Then Angelillo came forward to say that as the programme
was very long it had been decided to cut the couplets except when
they were absolutely necessary to the understanding of the plot. So
would we listen politely so as not to miss anything? We listened
politely. But when Angelillo excelled himself in the twenty-fourth
and last scene, just about as the clock struck three a.m., we went
wild. By this time Angelillo had discovered several dear friends
in the audience, and chattered to them between the verses of his
songs. We had become a happy family of fifteen hundred people.

It is that solidarity of emotion that distinguishes the proletarian
audience. It is an audience that never gives up its individuality to
become a listening cypher; it is self-conscious; it is alive. And now
in Stamboul, I remembered also how I had never made friends
with anyone by reason of going to the bourgeois concert in the
court of the palace of Charles V in the Alhambra. I would never
expect, for that matter, to come back enriched with new personal
friendships from the Queen's Hall, unless I went to the cheapest
seats, and even then it would not be likely. But after the Malaga
concert every other person in the streets seemed to know us; and
when we went, B. and I, to see the gardens in some suburb we
realised how lasting friendships can be made from little things.

At the concert of cante flamenco we had arrived at the sched-
uled time for beginning. It was the second house that we were
attending, and the first was not yet out. Nor was it out an hour
later, by which time a large crowd was waiting with us.

It was a 'rough' looking crowd, distinctly 'east side,' and I, who
had not then altogether got rid of my school-tie prejudices, did not
want to leave B. alone in it, while I myself visited the 'caballeros'. I
suggested that she should visit the 'señoras' next door, count sixty,

and return.

We went to our respective doors, and behold the 'señoras' door was locked. The crowd descended on us; the poor foreign lady wished to go to the senoras and the door was locked; Paco, Juan, Tomás, and Juanito ran to find the janitor; the rest waited and tried to console the foreign lady; "patience, it will be all right, you will not be kept long, etc."; at last a sigh of genuine relief as the janitor rushed up and opened the door; the crowd, which had been really distressed at the incident, bowed the lady into the señoras, where she counted sixty and then returned.

Next day as we drove to the gardens, turning a corner in the road, we came on a dozen young men. They put up their hands to stop us, and in case there was a good reason, like a hole in the road, which is quite likely in Spain, we stopped. They crowded round and greeted us like old friends.

"So you like cante flamenco?" said one.

"Yes," I answered, "so you were at the concert last night?"

"We all were," he said, "and it was I who got the key for the señora!"

You could not imagine any part of that incident coming out of a bourgeois musical audience. It could only happen in Spain where every proletarian is also a gentleman and an aristocrat. It was because I had not realised this that B. had been put to the bother of counting sixty behind closed doors. The crowd would have been friendly; the people who pinch ladies' behinds in the Paseos are not proletarians but the señoritos who are now helping Moors bring civilization back to Spain.[1]

At Stamboul, I thought of other Spanish proletarian crowds enjoying themselves. There were the fishermen and cork-factory workers listening to Wanda Landowska's harpsichord at Sant Feliu de Guixols.

I had heard her a few months before in New York. She played the same music, wore the same plum-coloured velvet dress. There

---

1. The term Moors refers to the large number of Moroccan regular troops in the Spanish Foreign Legion. The military uprising began in Morocco, where forty per cent of the Spanish army were based.

she played to the bourgeois who had honoured her with evening dress. Here in Sant Feliu most of the audience had on blue shirts without collar or tie, and caps. They stared at her with a burning concentration from the balconies, a solid mass of workers and fishermen who had never seen a harpsichord before. Not one sat down; they leaned over the parapet, or over the shoulders of the men in front; you could have heard a pin fall. Then they applauded like children.

It was these same men who used to come to my Wednesday evening gramophone concerts. They would ask for "La Quinta" of Beethoven, and sit in rows in the street listening through the open windows and always coming to express their pleasure afterwards. Anarcho-syndicalists to a man, they are now trying out libertarian communism in Sant Feliu.

These and other crowds flitted in and out of my mind as I sat waiting at Stamboul; but at last the concert began; two wicker chairs were placed for the guitarist and the singer; the ninepennies jumped the twelve empty rows in the shilling section, and we were soon one company. Communist, socialist, U.H.P., Popular Front symbols everywhere; these were the men who two months later became the Army in Overalls. I like to think of them all over Spain as I have seen them from time to time listening to music, not as we bourgeois do, but as if they were part of the living experience. What has happened to the key-keeper at Malaga? Angelillo I was to see at a huge United Front rally; for whereas the opera singers like Fleta went fascist, the greatest artists like Casals and all these singers of flamenco, remained with their audiences singing and fighting.

Zaragoza; C.N.T.

I went from Madrid to the capital of Aragon: Zaragoza, the ugliest town but one in Spain. The Ebro has carved out a canyon in mud, and out of mud human beings have built a dust-coloured dusty city.

Nothing can be more deplorable than the Arabic brick architecture of the Aragonese desert towns; Zaragoza, Teruel, Calatayud, Huesca. Calatayud is saved by the fact that a section of the inhabitants are so poor that they have to live in caves carved out of the mud cliffs. That is very picturesque, at least for tourists, who will be sorry when the ending of social injustice leaves them no more troglodytes to stare at. Huesca has one or two interesting bits, but Zaragoza and Teruel are blights.

The pride of Zaragoza is the Virgen del Pilar. In the Napoleonic wars when the common people of Aragon with a few incompetent generals defied the French for month after month, you could hear them singing jotas of which the words were:

> La Virgen del Pilar dice
> Que no quiere ser francesa
> Que quiere ser capitana
> De la tropa Aragonesa.

The Virgin of Pilar says that she does not want to be French; she want's to be the captain general of the Army of Aragon.

On the hot summer nights of July and August, 1936, you could hear the same jota being sung in the barricades of the loyal militiamen to these words:

> La Virgen del Pilar dice
> Que no quiere ser fascista
> Que quiere ser capitana
> De la tropa anarquista.

The Virgin of Pilar says that she does not want to be fascist; she wants to be the captain general of the anarchist party.

The Spanish people have always liked to appoint images of the Virgin to the highest military commands; and they have probably been right often enough in relying on them rather than on more earthly generals. Sometimes a saint was made a field-marshal, as when, in 1810, the Cortes of Cadiz gave the supreme command to Santa Theresa.

Zaragoza is first of all a pilgrim city. According to 90 foreign and 400 Spanish authors, several Popes and innumerable bishops, the Virgin came on January 2nd, A.D. 40, astride a jasper pillar, a broomstick-de-luxe, in order to wake up Santiago from a very long sleep and to command him to build a chapel on the very spot where the concerted ugliness of the Cathedral now stands.

I had only one reason for visiting it on this occasion, and that was to be able to say that I had seen the tenth-rate murals which Goya painted on the domes, long before he became the greatest of social philosophers-in-paint. It was an almost impossible task; the whole cathedral was full of scaffolding holding it together, and cracks a foot wide were visible in every cupola. The captain-general of the Aragonese forces was still there, well-lit with a thousand candles, but an air of the end of things hung about the atrocious and crumbling interior.

The life that once quickened the ancient temple was to be found now elsewhere, gathered into a dynamo of energy in the great bull-ring. Nor was it a bullfight that was occupying the minds of the crowds there. It was the annual conference of the C.N.T., the great syndicalist organisation of Spain. As I look back on my judgments of that C.N.T. conference from a distance of five fateful months, I realise how badly I misunderstood what was going on. Yet I had some excuse. When you think of the problems and resolutions discussed by the C.N.T. delegates in the Zaragoza bull-ring in May, 1936, how can you blame me for not knowing that, when the blow fell, it would be this C.N.T. that proved itself ready and organised to resist the evil!

They discussed everything on the face of the earth — nudism, vegetarianism, esperanto, marriage, and sex generally; the need for libertarian soviets, the possibilities of co-operating with social-ists and communists, programmes of strikes, sabotage and expro-priation.

They passed a resolution that if, in any village or town, the majority decided to abolish clothes, they would have the right to divest the minority. The argument that carried the day was that it would be psychologically intolerable to have one half free of clothes and the other half soberly dressed, and so all must be compelled to accept the medical good sense of the majority. Your syndicalist is a great casuist; he insists on arguing, and he insists on sticking formally to certain dogmatic assertions. He is against compulsion, he prefers compulsory persuasion; he fulminates against discipline, and demands in its place the better organization of indiscipline. You would have said surely that the theologians in the bull-ring at Zaragoza might be trusted to make a mess of a civil war.

But how brave in argument they were during those days! They took even sex by the horns in the Zaragoza bull-ring. They passed a resolution that if anyone, male or female, chanced to rouse the sexual feelings of another, it amounted to a gross and palpable interference with the freedom and happiness of that other, unless the guilty person was prepared to relieve the feelings he or she had produced. They therefore carried with acclamation the proposition that such a person, if they refused to alleviate the suffering they had imposed on another by rousing sexual feeling, must be exiled from the town or village where they resided for a period long enough for all fires to be quenched. "I say unto you that whosoever looketh on a woman to lust after her hath already committed adultery with her in his own heart," was thus completed with a suitable corollary.

All these things newspapers reported with their customary glee; but we none of us realised at all that the Zaragoza conference was to prove democracy's best and final council for defence. I travelled all day in the train with returning delegates. They were in most ways indistinguishable from delegates returning from a British labour conference; they were all exalted by the excited atmosphere of crowded deliberations. But when I talked to them, I realised that their way of thinking was such that no English socialist or communist could possibly understand them. They came from a totally different world.

What nobody knew in May, while syndicalists disputed in the bull-ring, was that in Zaragoza, very quietly and very determinedly, the officers in the barracks were laying their plans.

An Historic Note.

My constant companion in Spain is an early unexpurgated edition of the great Richard Ford's guide. Here in Zaragoza, where the present is so drab and the past so glorious, I have often turned to its pages and asked their help to shed a little afterglow on the mud-brown crumbling walls. When, last May, I had finished my account of the anarcho-syndicalist conference and sent it home to England, I sat up in my hotel bed and read what Ford had written about Zaragoza.

"The modern martyrs," wrote Ford, just under a hundred years ago, "are those brave peasants who fought and died like men; si monumentum quaeris, circumspice; look around at the terrific ravages of the invader, which testify his relentless warfare, and the stubborn defence during the two sieges which have rendered Zaragoza a ruin indeed, but immortal in glory. One word of record. This city, like others in Spain, rose after the executions of Murat on the dos de Mayo, 1808;[1] on the 25th Guillelmi, the governor, was deposed, and the lower classes were organised by Tio Jorge Ibort, Gaffer George, one of themselves; a nominal leader of rank being wanted, one Jose Palafox, an Aragonese noble, was selected because he was handsome, for in Spain, as in the East, personal appearance is always influential. 'There is none *like* him, long live the King.'

"Palafox had served in the Spanish royal body guard, and therefore, necessarily knew nothing whatever of the military profession; but Tio Jorge commanded, and with two peasants, Mariano Cerezo and Tio Maria, for his right and left hand, did the fighting;

---

1. On 2 May 1808, in Spanish the *'Dos de Mayo'*, the people of Madrid rebelled against the occupation of the city by French troops, an event that triggered the Peninsular War. The rebellion was provoked when Napoleon's brother-in-law, General Joachim Murat commanded that the daughter of Charles IV and Prince Francisco de Paula should be sent to the French city of Bayonne. A large crowd gathered in front of the Royal Palace in an attempt to prevent their removal. Murat sent the Imperial Guard to quash the demonstration. When they opened fire on the crowd, rebellion spread around the city. Hundreds died in street fighting before Murat regained control of the city. Hundred of prisoners were executed the following day, a scene captured in Goya's famous painting *The Third of May 1808*. The uprising sparked rebellions across Spain.

all the means of defence were 220 men, 100 dollars, 16 cannon and a few old muskets. Lefebure arrived June 15, 1808, but paused and thus enabled Tio Jorge to prevent a coup-de-main. To the French summons of surrender, the bold Tio replied, 'War to the knife.' Lefebure returned August 15, boasting, and with truth, that he had left the city 'un amas de decombres.'

"Palafox now went madder with vanity than any Gascon or Andaluz; reposing under his laurels, he neglected every preparation for future defence; meanwhile Buonaparte silently made ready for his great revenge, and in three short months, while Juntas were talking about invading France, crushed all the ill-equipped armies of Spain at one blow. Zaragoza was soon invested, and attacked by Buonaparte's sagacious suggestion on both sides, and especially from the Jesuit convent on the other bank of the Ebro, which the Spaniards had neglected to secure. After sixty-two days of dreadful attack and resistance, plague and famine subdued Zaragoza.

"The city capitulated Feb. 20, 1809, the rest of Spain having looked on with apathy, while Infantado, with an idle army, did not even move one step to afford relief—*socorros de España tarde o nunca*. Lannes had pledged his honour that Palafox should depart free, and that no one should be molested; but he pillaged the temples, shed innocent blood, put Boggiera and others to death under prolonged torture; insulted Palafox and robbed him 'even of his shirt' and sent him to the dungeons of Vincennes.

"These two sieges cost the lives of nearly 60,000 brave men, which were lost for nothing, as the defence of the town was altogether a military mistake, and entirely the result of popular impulse and accident, the moving power of things in Spain.

"And now Tio Jorge is scarcely mentioned by name, for it would offend the pride of Spain's misleaders to admit the merit of a peasant, whose valour and intelligence shamed the cowardice and incapacity of the Alaches and Imazes. The Tio was a true son of the people of Spain, and his treatment from his so-called betters is purely Oriental and national."

After copying this, I turned to Richard Ford on the famous Dos de Mayo, 1808, the day when the exasperated Spanish people rose against the legions of the French military dictator, and cried 'They shall not pass.' "This Dos de Mayo," says Ford, "is an exponent of Spanish nationality. Their philosophy was *españolismo*, i.e. impatience under foreign dictation; the conduct was accident, impulse of the moment, personal bravery, and contempt of discipline. Here three individuals, with only three cannon and ten cartridges, disobeyed orders, and dared to pit their weakness and want of preparations against the strength of a most military and powerfully organised foe; they had nothing fixed, but their own personal courage, and greater hatred of the invader, and they represented their countrymen at large. And although routed, because exposed to unequal chances by their inexperienced chiefs and left wanting of everything at the critical moment by their miserable juntas, yet thousands of gallant Spaniards rose to replace them in this *holy war*.

"The honest people neither required 'fanatic monks nor English gold' to rouse them, as the Buonapartistes falsely stated then and still state. They resented the *desprecio* of the foreigner, who assumed to be the regenerator of Castile; they spurned his gifts, scouted all prudential motives, and listened to nothing but the clink of his chains; it was national instinct; honour therefore eternal is due to the brave and noble *people* of Spain."

That was an English conservative speaking a hundred years ago. As I re-read his words in October, 1936, thinking of the Zaragoza scene amidst which I read them last, I wonder what Richard Ford would think of English conservatives to-day, who have crucified his heroes instead of sending them aid.

On the second of May, 1936, in Madrid I went to the spot in the Paseo del Prado where they commemorate the heroes of the people who died one hundred and twenty-eight years ago. As we stood there, some trouble-seeking students cried out 'Viva la Falange Española' and at once a thousand people were on their tracks. We chased them round the commemorative column and past the Post Office and across the Paseo until we reached the Cortes building, and there the police both rescued and arrested them.

They were searched for arms, and those that had them were

taken off to the police station while the crowd clapped hands. It seemed a rather childish thing to me at the time. Why not allow scatterbrains to shout whatever they please? Now, in October, I have changed my mind. Indeed I am glad that, as our democratic government is unable to preserve the democratic decencies, the people themselves stopped Mosley marching down Aldgate shouting 'We'll rid London of the Yid.' Those who have grown-up minds have suddenly found that the world is at the mercy of badly- educated children playing at soldiers.

However that may be, I was constantly to recall during the coming months Ford's words about the Spanish people and about those sieges of Zaragoza. They helped to save Europe and the nineteenth century from military dictatorship. In those days Europe was willing to be saved.

Strikes and Dead Poets.

Back in Barcelona I was to meet B. just come from England. I went to the hotel to book a room. "We can let you have a room, but we cannot feed you or give you baths to-morrow."

"But why not?"

"Because at midnight there begins the strike of the FOSIG."

It was the hotel proprietor explaining, and the FOSIG was the Federation of Syndicated Workers of the Gastronomic Industry, in other words the hotel and restaurant workers' trade union.[1] When a strike is announced in Barcelona the employers do not attempt to argue. They take every care to prevent a would-be black-leg from functioning. Their sole object is to avoid unpleasantness, and there is only one way of doing that.

By next morning, not a hotel, restaurant, café-bar, or kiosk was open. Opposite us the proud dimensions of the Ritz had become meaningless; in the Ramblas not a cup of coffee was to be seen. Our proprietor sat at a table gazing into vacancy. He was quite certain he was ruined. The new bases demanded by the workers were fantastic, and there was no doubt at all that they would have

---

1. Anarchist unions, like FOSIG believed that direct action would bring about a socialist revolution.

to be accepted.

The jeunesse dorée at the Ritz had motored away from trouble, and we were able to help ourselves; but sundry tourists, British and American, helpless and fanatically bent on getting all for which they had paid, showed signs of discouragement. But the normal inhabitants of the Ramblas, the strolling crowds, were the most visibly hit. All their lives these crowds had lived in a perpetual routine of drinking coffee and having their shoes cleaned, and now they could do neither; for though the shoe-shiners were not on strike there were no café tables at which to sit while the lights were lit on leather toecaps. Moreover, the heavens took it upon themselves to weep bitterly for the follies of mankind, and Barcelona with too much water and no coffee almost ceased to be Barcelona.

Meanwhile the moderate socialist party was due to hold its annual conference and its inevitable banquet. What could they do for cooks and waiters? They must beg the FOSIG to let them be served. The FOSIG said that sufficient waiters and cooks would be released in order to look after them, but on condition that they all wore blue shirts with scarlet ties, or scarlet shirts. Otherwise not a human being was waited on in Barcelona for three whole days. While this was going on preparations were being made for a really important function by the Ministry of Culture of the Barcelona Government; there was to be a fountain dedicated to a dead poet in a wood on a beautiful mountain-side. We were distinguished guests; we drove through the streets of Barcelona between cheering crowds with outriders on motor cycles and with Catalan flags on our bonnets. The Minister of Culture, Ventura Gassol, dedicated the fountain with a long speech, while the villagers and imported Barcelona literateurs stood waving branches of yellow broom.

The reason we were honoured guests was that my Catalan friends had the mistaken notion that I was a distinguished English poet, sympathetic with oppressed peoples and preferring to live abroad, in fact le Byron de nos jours. I blushed scarlet when the Minister of Culture pointed to the presence of ' the magnificent English poet' as a proof of the international reputation of the dead writer then in the act of being honoured with a fountain. I buried my face in the perfectly printed programme, and as I did so there came to my mind the words económico and econòmic, the Castilian and the Catalan, and I found myself saying for the fiftieth time, "whether they use Catalan or Castilian in discussing economic problems, have these people any answers to them?"

I was rash enough to ask T. that. I said, I don't care if you balance your budget in Catalan or Castilian, but are you going to balance it? I don't care if you liquidate the difficulties of capitalism in Catalan or Castilian, but are you conscious that those difficulties exist? T. reacted as you might have expected. He sent me a Catalan economic journal with an article on the use of certain differential-calculus equations in statistical research 'to show that we are capable of solving economic problems.' Well, the C.N.T. had a different method. Like the Murcians that they were, they were preparing to solve economic difficulties by learning "to kill without hate." But what with the resolutions on nudism in the Zaragoza bull-ring and the fountains in honour of the dead, there was evidently plenty of time for everything in the Iberian Peninsula. The only people who seemed anxious to hurry, though none of us knew it then, were certain generals and army officers who were hoping to complete their plans by June 15th. June 15th was an important date, since it marked the ending of one term of training for conscripts and the beginning of another. The new recruits had all been under the influence of the 'reds' and could not therefore be so completely relied on to be disloyal to democracy.

Another busy little group was too modest to make a display of its energy. These were the ant-like Germans, preparing huge dossiers of all sorts of things, prying into the lives of private individuals and card-indexing their nazi and anti-nazi doings. Here was a gentleman who had spoken ill of Germany in a Valencian newspaper. He had been so rude as to say that Germany was a war-loving country. Would Herr X find out all about him and how he could be influenced? Here was another man who had written favourably about Germany. Would the German Club at

B. invite him to a dinner? How was it possible to smuggle nazi propaganda into Spain at Z without exciting the interest of the customs officials? Yes, a most surprisingly ant-like industry, this building-up of a hidden structure, this eating the soil away from under people's feet. Later on accident was to bring it all to light.

Balletomaniac.

Then there was Kim's party for members of the Russian ballet. Kim is my dearest friend in Spain, a young but very successful lawyer, sentimental, almost eaten alive by his conscience, humorous, cynical, disillusioned. His great aunt has been highly recommended for sainthood. Kim gave me a small pamphlet setting forth her miracles, which were of a nice practical type. Thus:

"10 kilograms— the sixteenth of January of this year 1928, I received a letter from a young friend of mine in Cervera in which he said: 'My bodily health has much improved. If you were to see me you would scarcely recognise me. I have increased my weight by ten kilos. For this purpose I had made two Novenas to Doña Dorotea which have been very profitable, since from then on I have improved more noticeably.'"

A prayer to the old lady produced a postal order for two hundred pesetas by return post; and an organist, unable to pedal through a pain in his foot, praying to her found himself relieved bit by bit.

Of course one has heard of this sort of thing again and again, but Kim is the only man I know actually related to a miracle-maker, and I have sometimes thought that it was a pity that he did not appreciate the connection at what surely must be its true worth.

Not that Kim is not religious. When he was about twenty he came and stayed with me in England, and when I asked him if he wanted to go to the nearest Catholic church, five miles away, he said "No," but, as he confessed ten years after, he lay awake all night after in a cold sweat of shame.

Kim is another of those constant lovers who are constantly in love, and of recent years it has been members of the Russian ballet. I suppose if you begin at one end of the line of *Les Sylphides* there is nothing much to stop you until you reach the other end.

He is very serious on each separate occasion, and parts only with catastrophic force.

Kim looks as if, when he is old enough, he will be another El Greco portrait. It is not only that his face, as it is, has all the necessary characteristics, but, more important, that he is bound to have precisely those emotional experiences and to react to them in precisely the way that will, in the next twenty years, model his face as El Greco would have modelled it. Although he is a Catalan, I think of him whenever I want a type of españolismo. The weight of all the ages is in his smile; the burden of tradition on his brow; the conflict between free modern intelligence and medieval chains colours the workings of his mind.

"I am a fascist," said Kim suddenly as we sat eating lobsters. "You ought to shoot me." It was safe last May to say jokingly in Barcelona that one was a fascist.

"No, I am not one of them," he went on, pretending to joke. "They are too horrible … all those horrible people … they are altogether horrible." He said the word more expressively than an Englishman could. "Just think, John, things are so dreadfully bad here that I think I may have to join those awful, those horrible, people." The conversation drifted to all sorts of things. I reminded him how years ago when he was a very young lawyer he had wanted to start a crusade against the disgraceful legal position of women in Spain, and how he had supplied me with legal details for an article I had written on the position of women in Spanish social life. I told him of the letter I had had from someone in Madrid when the article appeared:

"Dear Sir:

"I have read your article on Spanish Women; a Romantic Myth Exploded. Your article certainly explodes romantic myth that Englishman never hits below the belt. But I may be mistaken, for although I have met several kinds of English blackguard, I have never met before one who is also the particular kind of bastard you are.

"Yrs. faithfully,
"JESUS DE FONTE, Madrid."

We laughed. I reminded him of the general who had a querida, and how he, Kim, had fought for her rights against him, and had nearly wrecked his career. But every now and then he would say: "Yes, they are all horrible people, these fascists, but I think I may join them." He would stop in the middle of changing a phonograph record and say, "John, you do not know I am altogether disgusting, horrible," and laugh. Then he went to a drawer and got out the largest Albacete navaja I have ever seen. It had a blade twelve inches long and a black sheath out of which the blade whipped with a crackle like a machine gun. "I will give you this knife," said Kim. "You will be able to use it to kill some of those horrible people perhaps."

"But what possible use can a knife that size be?"

"Well, in Albacete the muleteers use them. If the mule is on a precipice and is going to fall over, the muleteer very quickly whips out his knife and cuts the cords of the baggage so that only the mule goes over the edge, and the baggage falls on the path. Then they carry it home on their own shoulders." We improvised a ballet; the professional Russians who had come turned out to be without exception from places like Cleveland, Ohio, and San Diego Calif. There was also a middle-aged man who followed the ballet around.

The Minister of Culture, Ventura Gassol, had given the company a subsidy, and they were dancing, of course, in the famous Liceu, where years before an enthusiastic nihilist had exploded a bomb. It is a vast building, and like any other opera-house at once the glory and the shame of bourgeois dramatic art. But you can get into the top gallery for about one shilling and two pence. The ballet-girls thought the Barcelona audience just the cutest of all European audiences, and taught Kim the Lindy hop.

Late at night we went down the Paseo de Gràcia to the Oro de Rhin, the Rhinegold restaurant, haunt of the gilded youth. We drank liqueurs, and Kim shook his head and smiled. "This terrible place," he said, "for the horrible, too rich people. I hate these people. But they are my friends, too. Perhaps I will go to Australia. Perhaps I will join the Russian ballet."

Next time I saw the Oro de Rhin it had a huge barricade of sandbags at its entrance, and it had been requisitioned by the Left Republican Party for a red- cross hospital.[1] The man who paid for our liqueurs had been killed.

Practical Communism.

We left Barcelona and travelled towards the Pyrenees along the Costa Brava. It is here that the Greeks landed and established a trading colony, and to this day there is something classical about the way men look and feel. Or rather the influence of seafaring which helped mould the Greek character is still pervasive here.

It is a strange thing, the effect of the sea on human thought. All along this coast is a range of hills a few miles back from the shore, and many of the villages are double. There is, for example, Premia de Dalt and Premia de Baix, Upper and Lower Premia.

Upper Premia is full of ratas d'iglesia, it is priest-controlled and medieval; but the fishermen of Lower Premia are free-thinkers."[2] And the important thing," Kim said to me once, "is that in the villages on the hill the morals are bad; they do horrible things to the women; but among the free-thinking people below, the relationships are much better." Often enough the fishermen do not trouble to marry, but they live with their "comrade" far more faithfully than the legitimate husbands further inland.

The fishermen are the first to rise against oppression, and the most ruthless in their determination to break chains. In the fishing town in which I lived for two years there was still to be seen the burned-out ruins of the parish church which had gone up in flames during the Setmana Tràgica of 1909. At that time Sant Feliu declared itself a Libertarian Republic all on its own. I had not understood, when I lived there, how or why this had been, but now it is perfectly clear.

---

1. **Left Republican Party,** *Izquierda Republicana* **drew its support from skilled workers, small businessmen and civil servants and made up the bulk of the first government formed by the Popular Front after the February elections.**

2. *Ratas d'iglesia* **is a term used to describe women, usually elderly who are always in church.**

In my day the churches were not being burned in Sant Feliu. It was the cork-factories that were blazing. And it was not the workers who set them on fire, but the owners. Thanks to a huge gold reserve, Spanish currency was regarded as very sound in those days, and the peseta became dearer and dearer in terms of dollars and pounds. This meant ruin to the exporters of cork. One did not have to read quotations of foreign exchanges in the news-papers; if a cork factory or two had been burned down by accident the night before, one could be sure that the value of the peseta had gone up.

We went to Port de la Selva, one of those surprises for people who persist in imagining that social experiments are only to be found in Russia and America.

Port de la Selva is a little fishing village in a fold of the Pyrenees. The beauty of its white buildings reflected in a bay of ultramarine may be taken for granted. What is more important is that behind all the beauty, the picturesqueness, the tourist-value, there shelters less than the normal amount of social injustice. Port de la Selva is a fishing village practically owned by the Fisherman's Co-operative. The fishermen own the tools of their trade, not only their nets and their boats, but the curing factory, the stores and storehouse, the refrigeration plant, the shops where daily necessities are bought, the olive oil refinery, the olive groves, the transport lorries to take the fish to Barcelona, the café, the hotel, the theatre and assembly room, everything that they need and use. They have insurance against death, accident, loss of boats, and the other dangers of their trade.

Instead of having to work in boats belonging to middlemen, of having to sell their catch on the quay to middlemen, of having to buy their goods from the "open" market, they have organized an industry which at best can never bring a fortune, which normally gives its workers the barest of subsistences, into something rea-sonably secure.

The rules of the Cultural and Recreative Section of the Society "Posito Pescador" of Port de la Selva contain several interesting things. Thus Article 5 gives a list of people who do not have to pay a subscription to the section, the first being—"Women who have a common life in the same dwelling as a man who is a subscriber"; the second—"Women who are over sixty or who live in a dwelling where there is no man over fifteen."

According to Article 6, "The *diversion* of members will consist in dances," and according to Article 8, "The *expansion* of members will consist in theatre and movie shows, literary and scientific evenings, lectures on fishing, farming and pisciculture, concerts both instrumental and choral, and the installing of a casino for the selling of drinks."

Any member who does not dance on the Festa Major will have to pay a peseta for the privilege of not dancing. Anyone indulging in fisticuffs, screams, whistlings, wranglings, insults, or whatever is opposed to morality, decency or decorum will be fined twenty-five centimos.

It is a misdemeanour for any member of the Society to criticise or speak ill of its governing body in any public place or street, but any member with a grievance has a right to bring it up before the meeting of all members. Every member must pay a percentage of the value of his catch into the funds of the Society and any member may borrow from its funds in case of necessity. So that such borrowings shall only be spent in the co-operative shop, Port de la Selva has coined its own token money which passes more frequently than coin of the realm. In short, we have in this village beneath the Pyrenees a perfect example of a co-operative commonwealth in action. Here we see a virtually classless society, for the only economic division is between those who own a boat and those who work in someone else's boat, and there is no obstacle for any industrious person to pass from one to the other. By setting up a curing factory the co-operative protects itself from slumps. If the fish market is glutted, the catch can be withdrawn and cured. By providing each of its members with an olive-grove or a vineyard or a vegetable allotment, they are insured against the disaster of continued bad weather. When they cannot fish, they labour in the vineyard.

To sit in the café at Port de la Selva is to sit in an atmosphere of free men, and no one can understand Spain if he excludes from his idea of Spain this reality. For there is something very Spanish about Port de la Selva and its co-operation, the spontaneous local experimenting in the art of living together. It is something that must remain utterly incomprehensible to those who are condemned to live in a dormitory on the outskirts of London or New York, who are content therefore in Spain's hour of agony to think of it as a country full of reds in the pay of Moscow. Many a time in these last few months, when I have read atrocity stories and foul distortions in our gutter press, have I thought of the fishermen in Port de la Selva whose agony we have increased by the hypocrisy of non-intervention.

Ansó and Paredes.

I have thought, too, of certain peasants in Aragon. Off the road between Jaca and Pamplona, now the main artery of the fascists in the north, is a narrow road leading towards the mountains. It passes up a valley to a limestone gorge so narrow that it is sometimes built out over the stream and sometimes tunnelled through the rock. Beyond this narrow gateway the valley widens into an unexpected fairyland in the centre of which is Ansó. The women of Ansó wear Elizabethan ruffs and long pleated dresses of green, the men cover their heads with a black handkerchief, the knot of which hangs down like a pigtail, and over this they wear a black hat. Round their waists is wound a purple sash twenty inches wide; their knee breeches are slashed open at the knee showing a purple lining; their stockings are white, and their canvas sandals Roman. They dwell in houses that defy description save that they are like the illustrations to some German fairy tale.

At the butcher's shop you buy from a lady who might be Queen Elizabeth. The sheep, the kid, the calf, and the pig hang from the ceiling, and she cuts you whatever comes next, and whatever it happens to be comes out at the same price. There are no best ends here.

Like all communities where the occupations are seasonal, Ansó at certain times of the year seems to be a community at leisure.

The women work in the houses, of course, but the men, since the herds can look after themselves for the moment, sit all day long in the village square smoking. Among them sits the priest—or sat, for this was in 1932—smoking his cigar. He is a good man, and no one minds joining him in a smoke, but that is about his only function. For here, too, religion, even so long ago as 1932, had lost its hold.

You would think that Ansó was a happy medieval survival, nice and picturesque, hardly as advanced in social organization as one of our own villages, but from the point of view of tourists all the better for being a bit backward. But wait a minute.

The leading mind in Ansó is, as so often, the doctor. Often enough the Montague and Capulet of a modern Spanish village are the doctor and the priest. If you have a bad reactionary doctor then the village will be entirely in the hands of a vicious cacique. If the doctor is strong enough to stand out against the vested interests there is hope for the village. Here in Ansó the wealthiest family happens to be very progressive; it appoints a good doctor and, equally important, a good schoolmaster housed in a good school.

The doctor and the schoolmaster showed us the village library. "But where are the books?" I said, looking at almost empty shelves.

"They are all out being read."

I had found the perfect library at last, the library without any dead or sleeping volumes.

"We have only two people who cannot read here, and they are over eighty, so you cannot blame them." This is a country where in some parts there are 60 per cent of the population illiterate.

I wanted a household remedy. "You can get it at the pharmacy." We went to a nicely kept chemist shop with a businesslike man in white overalls dispensing. "How much?" I asked.

"Well that is a little difficult. You see, this is a municipal shop, and all taxpayers get their medicines free. I suppose we had better charge you cost price."

"Are the doctor's services free also?" I asked him.

"Yes, in this village I am paid by the municipality. It is much better, because in that way they can get a well-qualified man and I can get security. When I was a young man beginning, I answered an advertisement for a position as village doctor, and I found that one of my duties would be to shave the villagers. Here we have a separate barber!"

"Is shaving free too?"

"Oh yes, every taxpayer is entitled to a weekly shave. Of course there is another barber's shop run by private enterprise to which courting youths go for special treatment. But most of us are satisfied with a Saturday operation."

"You seem to have a great many public services."

"Oh yes, every taxpayer is entitled to the advice of the municipal veterinary surgeon if his animals are ill. After all, it is to the advantage of the whole community to avoid disease, isn't it? The only trouble here is that everybody is so lazy. They have their flocks, and they send the boys out to look after them, and their wives keep house, so what is there to do but just sit and talk?"

"What do they talk about? Politics?"

"No, we leave politics to the people in the capitals. If there were no politics life would be a great deal more easy."

There it is again, this constantly recurring Spanish theme of philosophical anarchism, this practical experience that if nobody interfered all went well. Ansó had long ago reached a state of social-economic equilibrium; its shepherd councillors had nothing to fear except what might come from Zaragoza or Madrid, and just like the co-operative fishermen of Port de la Selva the less the outside world interfered the better it was for everyone. I thought of Ansó and Port de la Selva as I read Indalecio Prieto's great Cuenca speech about the village of Paredes. Here is another Spanish village lost like a dying waif in the deserts of central Castile, the other side of the picture to Ansó and Port de la Selva, and like them a product of a tendency to anarchism and weak central control.

"As I was coming here," said Prieto, "a village appeared on the left of the road in the midst of the fields. I asked its name. 'Paredes' they told me. And then they told me how all the land in the village belonged to one man, down to the sacred soil of the cemetery, every cottage, the fields, the trees, bushes, blades of grass, the very dust of the tombs, all. And before this vision of medievalism my heart stood still. All that is one man's! And does he live in the village? Does he cooperate in the work of his neighbour? Does his sweat mix with that of those labourers whom I see scattered over his fields, pausing to greet us as we pass with a fist raised to the sky? No ! The Señor does not live in the village. Does he visit it? Ah, it would be better if he did not visit it. He comes now and again with a vicious bodyguard, with women who, to defend themselves from poverty, have to sell him their bodies. The honest inhabitants of Paredes, at his coming, lock their doors and draw the blinds, because these unhappy women, giving way to their degenerate caprices, run about the streets drunken and disgusting. And the man who creates these scandals calls himself a Catholic and even more scandalously a Christian. What was the use of our romantic Cortes at the end of the nineteenth century abolishing black slavery, if we still permit this white slavery in our own Spain? Why not abolish this slavery which I see on our own Castilian meseta? Paredes, Paredes, Paredes."

That was in the beginning of May, 1936. Let us turn to the faithful gazetteer of 1849. "Paredes" says Madoz, "property of the Marquis of Ariza, in the centre of a beautiful and fertile vega. Its climate is somewhat cold, well ventilated, little subject to illness. There are eighteen middling houses; a lovely chapel served by a priest in the pay of the Marquis of Paredes. The inhabitants pay one part in nine of all that they cultivate to the said Marquis."

In August, 1936, the economic descendant of the said Marquis, helped by the priest whom he wisely pays, have joined together to perpetuate precisely this state of affairs. Multiply Paredes by a thousand and you have what feudalism has done to Spain. If you have a momentary theory that it is all because the Spaniard is "degenerate," think of what co-operation has done in Port de la Selva or Ansó. And then remember that every barricade that falls in Spain before the advancing Moors perpetuates Paredes.

CHAPTER 2
THE STORM BREAKS

As May turned into June the atmosphere became more and more charged. Only people like Q. remained calmly in the middle of their dreams. He had been to Madrid over some secret mission or other and I met him on his return to Barcelona. "I am back from abroad," he said, "and very glad to be in my native land."

"How did you find Madrid?" I asked.

"Horrible. Just the same as usual, only worse. Strikes everywhere. All the hotels closed because of them. Castilian extremism, you know."

"But, hang it all, there has been a Catalan strike in Barcelona of waiters and so on. All the hotels have been closed."

"Ah, but only for two days; there you see the Catalan spirit of compromise. In Madrid they have been striking for three weeks and the Castilians will not compromise at all."

Now I had been in Madrid a week before, and there had been no strike then, and as for Catalan compromise, that is a very nice word to use when the strike ends with full acceptance of the strikers' terms—if you except a few demands thrown in without anyone expecting or desiring their acceptance. But it is no use arguing with dreamers. "Have you heard anything about a military plot in Madrid?"

"Not much," said Q. mysteriously. "There may be one, of course, in Castile."

"What about the military here in Barcelona?"

"They may try to rise, but we shall defeat them." There was no doubt about that "We." It meant Q. and men like him, together with his boy-scouts. They would defeat the military strictly in the Catalan language. They would not need any Murcians.

Incidentally the fact that the U.G.T.-C.N.T. waiters' strike had been settled so quickly thanks to the Catalan spirit of compromise might in cross-examination be used to show Q. that all the C.N.T. could not possibly be Murcians.[1] But what's the use!

T. was still troubled, chiefly about definitions. "What we need is a new definition of progress," he kept saying. It is a matter of historic importance that in May and June, 1936, while the military were consulting the fascist international in Rome and Berlin and Lisbon, men like T. were searching for a prolegomenon to a definition of the word 'progress'; and men like Q. were saying that, unless the discussion was carried on in Catalan, they would take no part in it.

Meanwhile the papers were full of discoveries of secret supplies of ammunition and money found in fascist private houses. Not a day passed without a successful government raid. More than this, evidence began to accumulate that the army officers were preparing something. For the most part the government seems to have decided to keep as much of all this as possible out of the papers, for it knew itself to be between two forces far greater than itself. It was a government which had to rely on the strength of others to be able to rule at all. On its ability to rule depended social peace.

Let us see how Spain had evolved up to 1936. The Monarchy came to an end in 1931, and two of the factors contributory to its end are worth recalling. First, in the secret "Pact of San Sebastian," the republican parties of the rest of Spain and the separatist parties

---

1. UGT, *Unión General de Trabajadores*, the General Union of Workers was a trade union affiliated to the socialist party and led by Largo Caballero.

of Catalunya struck a bargain. In exchange for Catalan support in getting rid of Alfonso, the Spanish republicans promised a big measure of self-government for Catalunya. Second, the immediate ending of the monarchy was due to something which was not 'national' at all, but local. The towns of Spain held municipal elections and elected republican mayors and councils. When this was known Alfonso immediately left the country "to avoid unnecessary bloodshed."

On April 14, the Republic was established, and one of its first acts was to dissolve some of the Religious Orders. The first government lasted just two and a half years, until, in September, 1933, a Lerroux-Gil Robles government of the most reactionary type took its place, and held disgracefully corrupt elections. This government established a reign of terror, complete with all modern devices such as concentration camps, and it set to work to destroy the mild liberal reforms of the past two years.[1] It struck blows at all workers' trade union organizations; it drew back from the original promises to the Catalans; it wrecked the first efforts at agrarian reform; it gave fascists carte blanche to misbehave; and it proved itself more corrupt than ever the Primo de Rivera dictatorship. In October, 1934, to save all the Republic had stood for in the minds of its original designers, armed insurrection broke out in two parts of Spain.

The October revolution is vital to the understanding of what is happening now. In Asturias it was a workers' revolution led by the miners whose lives had been made intolerable. They set up local soviets and fought until they had been butchered to death by the armed forces of the state. What was in their minds can best be seen from a document printed at the little mining town of Grado, in Asturias, during October, 1934.

"To The Workers And Peasants Of The County Of Grado.

---

1. Although mass arrests followed the revolt of October 1934, it is important to note that only two executions were ever carried out.

"Comrades! We are creating a new society. And, as in the biological world, childbirth is brought about amid physical lacerations and moral pains. It is the natural law that none can escape. The noblest man that Humanity has produced was born of a dying mother. This is fate. Death produces life. The agony of a dying being, its last sigh, go to sustain the lungs of a new-born babe, go to give life. It is not strange then, workers, that the World we are creating costs blood, sorrow, and tears. The whole earth is fertile.

"Well. This gigantic work needs the help of all. The young men are fighting in the streets with an enthusiasm and courage worthy of the cause they defend. They are the true heroes of this day's work which is going to free the workers. But there are other labours just as necessary.

"Supplies for the neighbourhood are complete. Lack of railway transport is a difficulty. It will be some days before we can get life going normally.

"Yes, yes. We are anxious to get things going again; we are longing to allow our young men to give themselves to creation instead of destruction; it is a caricature that anyone born to give life should use instruments of death. It will be a matter of hours only before we convince the holders of ancient privileges that they have lost them forever, just as feudal privileges are lost forever.

"Meanwhile we must all eat as little as possible. We must sacrifice our stomachs. Long Live the Social Republic."

The 'few hours' have lengthened out. The Asturian miners were shot and thrown into open trenches. When the February elections brought the people back to power their remains were rescued for reburial by men in gas-masks. Their widows and orphans marched in the May-day procession in Madrid. Their surviving comrades came to the rescue of democracy when fascism rebelled against it.

Asturias in October, 1934, produced one especial warning of the sort of thing that fascist patriots had up their sleeves—the miners and their wives were shot down by foreign legionaries and

Moors.[1]

In Catalunya quite another story was being told. In spite of everything that had happened, the separatists refused to realise that when the bourgeois go fascist, liberals can only survive by putting their trust in the workers. Throughout Barcelona and the countryside the workers flocked out into the streets and begged to be armed, the bourgeois government, trying to be revolutionary in a nationalist sense, dreaming no doubt of Garibaldi and Mazzini, failed to put up any resistance. President Companys gave himself up "to prevent useless bloodshed," just as Alfonso had done, and soon all was quiet.[2] The workers, seeing that it was all useless, went back home. The bourgeois leader hid in a sewer. Everyone else was bundled on to the prison-ship *Uruguay*. Gil Robles and Lerroux continued what had now become in very fact a reign of terror. I asked T. what he had done in October, and he told me that his daughter had sewn the separatist star on the usual Catalan flag, "a very dangerous act." It lasted until February, 1936, and then, in spite of the fact that the reactionaries held the electoral machinery and spent money like water, the centre and the left won the majority. It was the Popular Front that performed the miracle; without it democracy would have perished for a generation. Because the power behind the government was the Popular Front all the ancient privileges realised that the last fight had begun. From the moment that the February elections gave the legal power to the forces of progress, all the forces of privilege set to work to prepare to capture their lost positions by illegal means.

It is important to realise this. Between February and July there

1. General Franco used regular Moroccan troops and those of the Spanish Foreign Legion, which like the French Foreign Legion attracted criminals and fugitives. After the miners had been defeated there was widespread looting, rape and summary executions as the troops over-ran the towns and villages of Asturias.

2. Lluís Companys, (1882-1940) was the leader of the Catalan Republican Left, *Esquerra Republicana*, an essentially middle class movement. In 1934, he led a Catalan nationalist uprising and was subsequently imprisoned. In February 1936, he became President of the Catalan Generalitat. He supported the Republicans but on July 18th refused to arm anarchist militias. He fled to France in 1939 but was arrested by the Nazis and handed over to the Spanish government who condemned him to death.

was no pause at all in the preparations. Once the reaction found they could no longer buy votes, they began to buy arms. Once they found they could not use the common folk of their own country, they began to arrange for help from the fascist international in other countries.

Their policy was to prepare secretly, and meanwhile to prevent the new government from governing. Every sort of method of undermining public order was tried. Yet throughout it all the bourgeois parties, the government itself, seemed to have been unaware of the growing danger. Certain measures were taken; the Guardia de Asalto was strengthened and "purged of fascist elements"; cells of anti-fascists were established in the barracks to listen in on the plottings known to be going on there; but the government's chief obsession seemed to be to show how well it could keep order, how calm everyone should be. The long, long night was over, peasants were beginning to get land, nearly every strike was successful.

But the workers had more sense of impending trouble. They had no belief in democratic compromise; they had experienced the ruthlessness of the oppressors too recently to be complaisant. The slightest thing caused a panic. Early in May, I saw a crowd milling around the Government Building in the Puerta del Sol, a crowd of women. The rumour had been broadcast everywhere that someone had been giving children poisoned sweets, that the Madrid hospitals were full of dying victims. All the working-class districts of Madrid were in turmoil; crowds had to be hosed to disperse them. The papers on May 4th had to devote the whole of their front pages to denials of the rumours. Great banner headlines across the whole page said: "Señor Casares Quiroga will prosecute rumour-mongers. The minister of government affirms that it is absolutely false that there are poisoned children in Madrid—the socialist councillor Sr Redondo has visited every one of the institutions where it has been said that there are children hospitalized and has seen none." Who started the rumours? Nobody knows. According to the Marquis it was communists anxious to stir up feeling against nuns. According to most people it was a fascist attempt to produce a discrediting riot. If it had been in Barcelona some people would have seen a Murcian attempt to discredit Catalanism. Later events have shown that whereas socialists, communists, and syndicalists never at any time showed any desire to stir up trouble, the fascists were working ceaselessly.

At any rate, when I was in Caceres a few days later, I went to a churreria early in the morning and bought churros. I stood eating them at a street corner and there was one too many. I offered it to a little boy. At once there was a rush of women from the market, shouting to him as they came that he mustn't touch it, it might be poisoned.

I remonstrated. "Who has suggested this idea to you?" I said.

"We have all heard how there have been poisoned sweets in Madrid."

"But it is not true."

"That may be. But how can I know? I live in a small village and come into the market once a week. I can only know what I have been told." Probably every town in Spain within three days had heard the story of the poisoned sweets, and old women everywhere were that much more unstable in their trust of organised government.

So things went on until mid-June, a growing sense that a storm would break sooner or later. On June 15th, I had an appointment with Kim. He had warned me that he would have something serious to tell me. It was a day or so after his party, when he had spoken of "these horrible people." I sat and waited in the Plaza de Catalunya at La Luna restaurant. There was a fidgety atmosphere about. Even the imperturbable proprietor, whom in fifteen years I had never seen without a toothpick between his lips, was distraught. I noticed particularly that he had no toothpick, and I stared at him in surprise. It was the last time I saw him, with or without toothpick, for by August he had fled to France. Down the road limousines drew up incessantly at the Hotel Colon, always the centre for military officers and señoritos. Officers kept coming and going; but Kim himself never came. Two days later he wrote to me.

"MY DEAR JOHN,

"I was so sorry to hear that you waited for me at La Luna because I sent a letter to you there. That day something 'big' was being prepared, and I went to Valencia to watch. (Don't think that I am a fascist!) ... We are living moments of great excitement and *sooner or later* something has to happen. I'll try to inform you because, if I can, you know I'll be delighted to help. As far as concerns myself - one gets convinced of how difficult it is to be absolutely indifferent to what's going around. I have a sense of curiosity and a certain patriotism (Spanish), nothing old-fashioned or 'reaccionaire' (*no!*), modern, but a feeling in which materialistic reasons have more weight than purely idealistic motives... Be sure that I am a good friend of yours—friendship is about the only feeling which lasts throughout the natural ideological changes.

" KIM."

I went on to say good-bye to T. T. said he was sorry for Kim because he was very unhappy. T. thought that it was a love-affair. I knew better. I knew that Kim was playing with fire. He had told me a few days earlier that a friend of his, in Zaragoza, had said that it was with difficulty that the officers could be restrained any longer. In Barcelona barracks, too, there was something going on.

During the next three weeks, I was in England waiting for news. Only one thing was certain, that there would be no socialist revolution. The Popular Front had everything to gain by supporting democracy, and everything to lose by a coup d'état. It is necessary to realise this, for much later the fascist rebels were to claim that they acted to forestall a red uprising. There was never any question of a red uprising. To begin with, the Popular Front was the political power behind the government, and so long as it continued it had the forces of law and order on its side. It could constantly keep the liberal ministers up to scratch because, without the voting strength of the people, there could be no liberal government. Every day that passed increased the strength of the forces of law and order known to be loyal, that is the Guardias de Asalto, and decreased that of the doubtful army and Guardia Civil.

In the second place there was never any thought of red revolution because by keeping the political *status quo* the worker was able to get everything he wanted by economic action. In theory the workers were divided politically into the diametrically opposite philosophies of the U.G.T. and the C.N.T. The U.G.T. stood for socialist political action along the lines that the British Labour Party defended in the early 1920's before the great betrayal of 1931. The C.N.T. stood for syndicalist and anti-political action, and had time and again stabbed the socialists in the back in the political field. But, when it came to a matter of strikes in the economic field, the U.G.T. and C.N.T. were a solid and invincible force.

It was precisely because there was no danger of a red revolution that the fascists were preparing their own disloyalty. Every week that the liberals were able to remain the legal government meant a weakening of age-long privileges. Moreover, as time went on, it became clear that the words of Largo Caballero on May 1st had been no idle boast: "The greatest terror of reaction," he had said, "is a perfectly disciplined proletariat." The discipline was not perfect, but it was growing better every day. By outrage after outrage the fascists tried to undermine that discipline. Remember that the Spanish workers and peasants were simply trying to rid Spain of those social indecencies that Cromwell and our Puritan fathers finally destroyed in England. Remember, too, that they knew what to expect if Gil Robles and Calvo Sotelo came into power again;[1] they would experience exactly the same white terror as followed October, 1934. Nothing to me so vividly shows the mentality of what the London *Times* has called "the anti-red revolutionaries" as the fact that when the Robles-Lerroux people last came to power, they sent police out into the allotments that the peasants had been given by the agrarian reform institute to pull up and destroy the half-grown crops and so make the rescued land desert again.

---

1. José Calvo Sotelo (1893-1936) was a monarchist and the right's leading spokesman in the Cortes. He was a harsh critic of the Popular Front and had spoken out against what he viewed as escalating religious terror and hasty agrarian reforms which he considered Marxist-Leninist in nature. He advocated the creation of a corporate state and urged the military to seize power. His murder led directly to the military uprising led by Generals Mola, Franco and Sanjurjo.

Such people would stop at nothing. They *have* stopped at nothing, thanks to "non- intervention."

When we remember this it is surprising indeed how well-disciplined the trade unionists and organised workers remained through those heartbreaking weeks from May to July 18th. Every provocation was given them and, except for a few burned churches and a few isolated acts of violence, they remained loyal to the principles of democracy. No one has a right to lay even these burned churches to the charge of the Popular Front any more than a burned haystack in England can be given a political significance. Usually incendiarism is best understood in Freudian rather than Marxian terms. They burned a church in Cadiz and the incendiarists are said to have taken off their caps as they entered the building. Their leader turned out to be a watchmaker whose shop was opposite the church. He said he was "tired of seeing foreigners pass his door on their way to see the El Greco." The Marquis is my authority.

Meanwhile preparations were hurried forward for the fascist betrayal. At first as Kim had warned me they had hoped to make June 15th "der tag"; but it had to be put off until October. By the beginning of July the government, groping in the dark, unable to distinguish friend from enemy, had begun to build up an effective opposition. The loyal Guardias de Asalto, republicans to a man, were going from strength to strength, their discipline and power began to eclipse even the Guardia Civil; the anti-fascist cells in the barracks were closing in on the rebel plotters. The hand of Franco was being forced.

It was on July 12th that the tinder caught fire. A leading Guardia de Asalto, Lieutenant Castillo, was shot in the back in a Madrid street by a car-load of fascists. Within a very few hours Calvo Sotelo was found murdered.

Before examining this vital incident let us remark that it had nothing to do with the "reds," this deciding incident. Whatever the truth about details (and accounts differ), there can be no doubt at all that the immediate cause of the Spanish civil war was the murder by fascists of one of the republican liberal government's armed police, and the murder, in turn, of one of the fascist leaders known to be involved in that murder. It seems that Castillo, in the execution of his duties, had earned the personal enmity of a relation of Calvo Sotelo. There can be no doubt that this is why he was assassinated. There is also no doubt that Calvo Sotelo was immediately arrested by some of Castillo's brothers-in-arms, who were determined that he should not escape. It is not at all certain whether they meant to shoot him in any case, whether they shot him to prevent a rescue, or whether the whole thing was an accident or whim of the moment. Anyway, Calvo Sotelo went very suddenly to his grave with a load of social crimes upon his shoulders.

Who was Calvo Sotelo? He was the ablest leader of reaction in Spain. He had made the grand tour of all the fascist countries and learned method at the feet of Hitler and Mussolini. He had been very busy "establishing relations" with the fascist international. Above all he was the close political ally of Juan March.

And who is Juan March? The Americans might call him the sugar-daddy of the fascist rebellion; the Spaniards themselves call him the Last Pirate of the Mediterranean.

Juan March is another of those "poor boys who made good." For some reason his earliest dealings with trade in his native island of Majorca did not agree with him, and he sought an outlet for his talents farther afield.

He landed up in North Africa and was soon manufacturing tobacco. In those old bad days most Spanish officials could be bought, and Juan learned to gauge their price with detailed accuracy.

Moreover, the coasts of his native Majorca are much indented with little harbours, and many of his boyhood friends were glad to help their fellow islanders avoid the unpleasant formality of paying the Government a tax whenever they smoked tobacco. Soon Juan grew more ambitious. Primo de Rivera had come to purify the land, and give it nice clean trains-on-time dictatorial government. Juan knew some of the puritans, including Calvo Sotelo. Juan and Calvo had some talks, and Juan explained that he would very much like the tobacco monopoly in Morocco.

From the Government point of view there was a great deal to be said for the plan. It would save the money that was being spent on preventing, or rather on failing to prevent, Juan March smuggling the tobacco. But it was a little awkward to announce to the public that piracy was to be stamped out by setting the pirate to catch himself.

Juan had a bright thought. The Queen was interested in tuberculosis; he would give her a seven-million-peseta sanatorium in his own island of Majorca, and so ride to power by hauling down the Jolly Roger and hoisting the Red Cross in its stead.

Even then Juan March did not altogether live down his past, for there were other things in it besides tobacco. There was the very awkward affair of Tomás Llausot.

Tomás had been murdered in 1916. Perhaps because the dead man had been a particularly intimate family friend of Juan's, the magistrate sent for him and interrogated him for several hours.

Immediately afterwards the magistrate rashly announced that the murderers would be known to the general public within two days. In less than half that time the magistrate found himself transferred to a distant district.

His successor seems to have been bored with the case; not so Juan March, who found in it a possible outlet for his well-developed sense of patriotism. He began a little private investigation into the Llausot family history and found himself able to denounce the dead man's father and brother as guilty of treason to their country. They were imprisoned.

In 1919 Juan March's patriotic researches received a set-back, and the case was quashed by some meddlesome higher judicial court. In 1923 the brother José, who must have been as innocent as he was unforgiving, sent his documents to the newly-arrived national purifier, Primo de Rivera. Primo put a judge in charge of the case, but no sooner had he begun to investigate than he was relieved of his office.

Juan, who happened to be in Paris all this time, was bound over in a large sum pending further investigation, and to show how little he feared justice he immediately returned to Spain to take part in person in whatever was to happen next. But nothing else ever did happen, since all the papers in the case had mysteriously disappeared. The dictatorship had done a lot of spring-cleaning, and doubtless the charwoman had thrown them away by mistake. Thus Juan March never succeeded in his patriotic effort to solve the Llausot mystery.

Cackling people said very nasty things. Even the great hospital gift did not silence them. So Primo de Rivera came to the rescue in one of those speeches which made him famous. There were doubts, he said, as to the way in which this Spaniard had got his money, but what had that to do with it? Wasn't he doing his best to use it well now? Besides, and far and away above all other considerations, the scheme had the blessing of a Government so clean that anything that it touched was *ipso facto* purified of all dross. If his Directorate were to touch stinking money, Primo implied, it would be able to endow it with the odour of sanctity—and there is every reason to think that Primo believed every word that he said.

In due course came the Republic. In its kill-joy way it set up a secret commission to sift the responsibilities for the graft of the days of Primo the Pure. It is said that Juan March took very good care to post his friends at the keyhole. But he could not prevent the Republic taking his Moroccan tobacco monopoly away.

Doubtless, in their materialistic way, they hoped to make a better bargain; but a very curious thing came to thwart their intentions; the Spanish armies and the Moors apparently gave up smoking. Perhaps the soldiers, good-hearted men that they were, had given up smoking to pay out the Government for its ingratitude to Juan March.

There is another theory, that there had been a sudden recrudescence of smuggling. After all, Juan March could not be expected to keep smuggling down once he had lost his monopoly, especially as, for all we know, he may have been friendly with the chief smuggler! In any case, there was a debate in the Cortes, and Juan found a firm champion in the devout Jesuit-taught Catholic, Gil Robles. The Government, said Gil, should give back Juan's monopoly so as to put an end to smuggling. Doubtless Gil Robles, prominent Christian that he was, was thinking of a modern equivalent to turning the other cheek.

The Socialist, Indalecio Prieto, as one might expect, thought otherwise. Without caring how deeply he wounded Juan March's feelings, he said that the money represented in the decline of the tobacco revenue had been stolen from the Government by Juan.

The Minister of Finance, Jaume Carner, went even further. "Either the Republic will put an end to Juan March," said he, "or Juan March will put an end to the Republic." Next day they put Juan into gaol.

It is not nice to think of Juan, open-air fellow that he is, confined; but he seems to have had a good time even in prison. He had such winning ways. He smoked the best cigars; he had almost complete liberty to do what he liked; he had very nice furniture indeed.

He was removed to the Reformatory at Alcala de Henares, where the records show that he continued to carry on his traditional generosity. He gave the chief-cook a thousand pesetas a month, and two other culinary officials five hundred a month each. When in due course Juan succeeded in escaping, he took his warder along with him, which shows once more the extraordinary facility with which he attached to his cause whoever came near him.

Meanwhile Juan's interests had grown. Of course he had bought a couple of daily papers; rich adventurers can never really enjoy life without doing that. He also devoted himself to politics. He may be said to have been the "angel" of the election of 1933.

There followed the bath of blood in October, 1934, when Juan's friend gave the Moors and Foreign Legion in Asturias their dress rehearsal for 1936. In February, 1936, the Gil Robles-Lerroux government discovered that even with Juan as "angel" once more, they could not induce the comrades and widows of Asturian miners and the people left alive elsewhere to vote for them. Only Juan himself kept his seat. Majorca remained faithfully venial.

It was a great disappointment to Juan. It was a shock to find that he could no longer buy votes, so he resolved to buy other things instead. Long ago he had found that tobacco smoke was not the only smoke that could be made to pay. He dabbled in armaments, and when votes were off the market once and for all, he settled down to buying airplanes and shipping them to Morocco. Now as he watches the Moors, transported across the Straits in his planes, advancing to the capture of Madrid, if he has a regret perhaps it is that Calvo Sotelo is not by his side watching the triumph of all that they have laboured for. Calvo has to be content to watch from his seat among the gods.

The death of Calvo Sotelo was a great blow to the fascist rebels, first because he was politically their best leader, second because they expected it to be the first step in a planned attempt to leave them leaderless. But for other reasons also they determined to act at once; the government knew too much. Their complete plan was as follows:

1. General Franco was to proclaim a Fascist Republic in Morocco and transport as many Moors as possible across the Straits. Presumably it was expected that the Spanish Navy would rebel, too, but in this they reckoned without the lower deck. Although the position is very obscure still, it seems that some Naval officers were loyal, and that others who tried to bring their ships over to the fascist side were executed by the loyal crews. That this has happened is suggested by the unskilful navigation and gunmanship shown by the loyal ships.

2. The Guardia Civil were to be withdrawn from every town and village to the capital of each province, where they would seize the administrative buildings and proclaim themselves defenders of the republic against a red menace. This partially failed. Indeed, at first it was thought to have completely failed, since the Guardia Civil did not scruple to pretend to be loyal so as to gain tactical advantages. Thus in Pueblo de Valverde, in the Province of Teruel, the Guardia Civil who had not had time to get to Teruel itself fraternised with the anti-fascist militia who were being hastily organised and then shot down several hundred of them in the main square. But in Toledo, for example, the plot was very successful, even to the stealing of all the ammunition from the Arms Factory. It now appears that one-half of the Guardia Civil joined the rebels.

3. Meanwhile strategic points like Seville, Zaragoza, Burgos, were to be seized by their garrisons. This was completely successful at those three places, but at Valencia, a most important point, the loyalists won the day, thus keeping Madrid's lifeline secure.

4. Madrid and Barcelona were to be seized by the garrisons in those places. If this could have been done the whole rebellion would have been successful in forty-eight hours; but the astonishing determination of the people, together with the loyalty of the Guardia de Asalto, and in Barcelona at least of the Guardia Civil, saved the day. This was the weak point in the plans, and the plotters knew it. By October they had hoped to remedy it, but they could not wait.

5. There can be no doubt that the fascist international of Italy, Germany, and Portugal had already promised aid. Directly it was seen that Franco's transport of Moors was impeded by the loyalty of much of the Fleet, Italian airplanes swarmed to Spanish Morocco and took its place. Ships are known to have left Hamburg loaded with airplanes and pilots in the first few days. German airplanes were captured in Spain as early as August 9th. On July 31st the *Usarama* left Hamburg for Lisbon with 28 modern bombing-planes and a cargo of bombs and artillery and machine-gun ammunition. This is not the place to describe in detail the foul shame of the "non-intervention pact," which will be discussed later.

The government were not taken by surprise, but they seemed to have thought that when Madrid and Barcelona had been saved for them by the almost miraculous bravery of the common people, the whole thing would blow over very rapidly. Almost at once they must have become preoccupied with the possibility that once the workers' organisations had crushed the military they would seek greater political power also. After all the Republicans were only a government on sufferance; they existed by reason of the statesmanship of Largo Caballero. Now, thanks to the fascists, Largo Caballero and the rest might reasonably be expected to become more arrogant.

"We support your policy," Largo Caballero had often told them, "but if you fail, as we think you will fail, we shall take over and then it will be our policy."

The Republicans must have hoped that all was over when La Montaña barracks were saved by the bravery of the people, and when news came that Barcelona, too, was loyal. But very soon it became clear that in other parts of Spain the rebels were meeting with success. The first actions of the government show that they hesitated as to which was the most likely to be dangerous, the growing strength of the Anti-fascist Militia or the doubtful loyalty of their remaining troops. On the one hand they declared Martial Law illegal wherever it might be proclaimed, and called on workers' unions to declare general strikes as a counter step to any attempt to impose martial law; thereby strengthening immeasurably the Left forces within the Popular Front. It was a necessary action, since only in this way could loyal recruits be released from allegiance to their rebel officers.

Moreover, the fear of the military was shown in other ways; all troops in Madrid, however loyal they might seem, were confined to barracks, while the Marxist Militia were mobilised and the Popular Front deputies sent to their constituencies to organise resistance. But the government Andromeda would have preferred some other Perseus than the Marxian militia.

It was the Guardia de Asalto that the Government relied on most. How wise it had been of the Republic to organise this counterblast to the Guardia Civil. Indeed, if the fascists really desired, as they pretend for foreign consumption, to "save the Republic from the Marxists" their better plan would have been to wait a year until the republican Guardia de Asalto had achieved the same reputation and tradition of loyalty to the Republic, as the Guardia Civil had had to the ancient regime, and then if illegal rebellion had broken out *even from the Left* this body would have been loyal to the democratic order. But nobody but a fascist or a fool believes the Spanish fascist excuse.

While the capital was saved by the People's Militia, the miners had risen in Asturias and were closing in on Oviedo. Farther along the coast the democratic government received support from another source, about which the reactionary and especially the Catholic press in England have remained notably silent. Except for Navarre, the most truly Catholic region in Spain is the Basque country. So Catholic is it that the Basque Nationalists have fought consistently since the coming of the Republic for a sufficient independence from Madrid to allow them to ratify a separate concordat with the Vatican.

The Basque Catholics remained absolutely loyal. Indeed, when later Largo Caballero became head of the Government with a cabinet that our right-wing organs have called 'a communist rabble,' a Basque Catholic was included in it. In San Sebastian and Irun, in all the Basque provinces, it was devout Catholics who defended the Spanish government against the darlings of *The Universe* and of Lord Rothermere.[1]

In these early days *The Times* had no doubt whatever about the government being the popular side. "The attitude of the civil population," so its correspondent reported on July 20th, "seems in fact to be proving decisive. All over the country they have turned out with rifles, shotguns, pistols, and any other weapons to hand in defence of the Government, and in many places have succeeded in smothering attempts to join in the revolt." In those days *The Times* reported that the anti-fascist militia women searched ladies in the streets "with scrupulous politeness," and on July 23rd it told us that "our escorts and the Republican crowds in the towns, all armed to the teeth, were the most amiable and solicitous revolutionaries one might wish to meet." It went on to say that "apart from the burning of the churches, Tuesday morning seemed to dawn on a quieter note. Indeed there was something of the carnival spirit in the way in which the crowds surged out into the hitherto deserted streets."

Then, on August 1st, the change came. We read in *The Times* that "the anti-fascist revolution in Barcelona and Catalunya has become a reign of terror." From that time on the campaign of hate

---

1. Harold Harmsworth, 1st Viscount Rothermere (1868-1940) was a British newspaper proprietor, whose titles included the *Daily Mail*. A strong supporter of appeasement, he tried to use his newspapers to influence British government policy towards Nazi Germany and for a period in 1934 his papers championed Oswald Mosely's British Union of Fascists.

and filth has never stopped, although *The Times* itself has never stooped to the extreme calumnies of most of its contemporaries. To-day most English people have been convinced that the government supporters are not only 'reds' but ghouls; that the reason why they have not defeated the fascists is that they spend their time raping nuns and watching them dance naked.

Apart from the sending to Spain of irresponsible journalists who were able to fly airplanes but not to speak Spanish, the press made great play of stories from returned English residents. Many of these lost their heads completely, and one can sympathise with them, seeing that the British officials, supposed to look after them and help them, lost theirs. One such official, perhaps out of guilty conscience for having openly wished to God that the head of the government to which he was accredited, had been shot after October, 1934, became so childishly terrified that he refused to lend a conservative newspaper-man a car to go out to the local airport, saying that it was too dangerous, and that he would not risk the lives of his chauffeurs. This was in mid-August when everyone else was settling down to normal existence. The British correspondent finally got his car from the consulate of a minor South American country, where they were less frightened.

What with the atrocity stories at home and the peculiar way in which British officials interpreted their duties in Spain, added to the arch hypocrisy of "non- intervention," it has been hard for an Englishman to hold up his head. But this is not the place to dwell on that side of the picture. It is far more pleasant to remind oneself of the conspicuous example of the British tradition of fair play not being forsaken because of a craven fear of "Moscow," or a tacit conspiracy to betray democratic principles to the fascist international.

Malaga has been particularly quoted for outrages, atrocities, disorders, anarchy and whatnot. Now Sir Peter Chalmers Mitchell, a distinguished scientist, Fellow of the Royal Society, ex-director of the London Zoo, was in Malaga from long before the fascist rebellion until October 9th, 1936. His story, published as a letter in *The Times*, is that of a courageous and truthful English gentleman, moreover, it is the best possible objective description of what civil war is, and as such I shall, with his kind permission, quote it before continuing my own narrative. Here it is:

"I left Malaga on Friday last, having been there during twelve weeks of the rebellion, which began on July 18. During that time the lives and property of private British subjects who took no part in Spanish politics were in no danger, except from rebel bombing. I received much kindness, and, where possible, assistance, although I was openly trying to protect Spanish friends under suspicion as wealthy monarchists and closely related to persons actually implicated in the rebellion.

At first that assistance was given to me as an Englishman. Spaniards defending a Government elected by the people were sure that democratic England would be on their side. From the first I tried to disabuse them. I told them that at the mere echo of the word 'Communism' the British Government would shrink in horror, and that the official Labour Party would acquiesce with professions of reluctance.

According to plan, some Army officers went to the Civil Governor on Saturday afternoon, July 18th, and demanded the declaration of military law. The Governor refused, and the Assault Guards unexpectedly took the Government side. There was a good deal of random firing in the streets, but no one was killed. The rebel officers were captured or surrendered. The plot had failed. But the town, like an angry hive, swarmed into the streets, all the wilder elements of the populace joining in. Incendiarism and plundering began, most of the houses set on fire belonging to persons who had already fled from Malaga or who were known to be active opponents of the Republic.

By Tuesday afternoon order was restored, trams began to run, shops were reopened, and the Civil Governor, a moderate Republican, was cheered as he drove through the streets. I myself went through the streets alone and found nothing but relieved exhilaration. It was nonsense to talk of Malaga's being or having been 'in the hands of the Communists.' So far as political organisations were concerned, it was in the hands of middle-class bourgeois Republicans, the Anarchist-Syndicalist Federations who are bitterly opposed to international Communism, especially that of the Soviets, and the General Union of Workers, which is largely a trade-union with only a Communist tail.

But on Wednesday it became known that the plot had been successful in many other towns. Authentic information came that the rebels, where they had succeeded, had shot Left politicians and large numbers of persons with the badges of the confederations and unions. At once the temper of the town rose. Armed patrols searched for rebels in hiding and houses for evidence implicating individuals. Except where armed resistance was encountered, detained persons were not shot, but were taken to the Civil Governor's offices, and after interrogation were released or sent to prison where, until food became short, they had a canteen in which they could buy tobacco, chocolate and fruit.

But, as the fortunes of the Government wavered, as Moorish troops poured in from Africa, as munitions and armaments and trained officers poured in from Fascist Powers, and as it became clear that not even moral support was coming from England and France, the Civil Government of the town became weaker and control passed more and more to the Left, the Trade Union-Communist group (U.G.T.) and the Anarchist-Syndicalist group (F.A.I. and C.N.T.) took the most active part in affairs. Both sets organised militia; the former were more active in trying to regulate supplies and unemployment and in housing refugees. The latter specialised in arranging new hospitals for wounded soldiers and in propaganda for the future. The former attempted to bribe men into the militia by promising them permanent service in the standing army when the war was over. The latter were bitterly opposed to all standing armies and even their leaders refused the rank of officers in the militia. The former thought chiefly of raising wages at the expense of what they supposed to be the capitalistic fund. The latter were trying to organise a new Spain based on creative work of all kinds. Among the latter I made the acquaintance of some of the most constructive idealists I have ever met, some of them miners and carpenters, others of knowledge and culture.

The aeroplane raids did more than anything else to exasperate Malaga. They began on July 27, and, with occasional respites of from a few days to over a week, occurred all my twelve weeks of the war. One or two had direct objectives such as the Government warships, the petrol stores, and the aerodrome. But usually the planes crossed at a great height and dropped their bombs casually. A warship was damaged once and a heavy oil reservoir set on fire. But many civilian houses were wrecked and many women and children killed or mutilated. It was after the first of these that evil things began to happen. But let me say at once that there were no outrages in the ordinary sense of the word, no torturing, mutilation, or other horrors. It is a question-begging term to speak of 'hostages' in Malaga. The prisoners there were:—

1. Military and naval officers caught in open rebellion. These, after Court-martial, were shot.

2. Military and naval officers suspected of implication in the rebellion. These were being tried by a popular tribunal presided over by trained lawyers, with the accusation properly stated and the prisoners allowed to give evidence and to cite witnesses.

3. Persons accused of sedition. In the early days the latter had a summary cross-examination on arrest, and a subsequent examination by an assessor in the gaol. In the last few weeks these also have been coming before the popular tribunal. I myself have been cited as a witness, shown the evidence for the prosecution, asked for my views on any matters within my knowledge, have had a concise précis of my evidence typed and submitted to me for my signature. Naturally in every case I was for the defence.

But in a long middle period men were taken from their houses, hustled into cars, and thrown out and shot by the roadside. After an air raid in which people had been killed, prisoners were taken out and shot, either in the prison yard or in the cemetery. There was some pretence of selecting as victims persons more certainly guilty of sedition, but the choice was often casual. The Civil Governor, rather ineffectively, and the Committee of Public Safety (a joint committee of the Left organisations), more effectively, suppressed these crimes. But they were the worst things, the only really evil things that happened in Malaga. On the closest estimate I can make, there must have been some 500 odd of them in Malaga and the province. But at least it may be pleaded that in Malaga they were fighting a rebellion; the crimes of the Right were the crimes of rebels.

Yours faithfully,
P. CHALMERS MITCHELL."

CHAPTER 3

THE ARMY IN OVERALLS

It was the first time that I had ever crossed from the Gare du Nord
to the Quai d'Orsay in a motor truck with a gendarme, but I had
come without papers, and France had to be mobilised to see that
I did not ride the motor bicycle anywhere betwixt Calais and the
Pyrenees. We hung on to it as it slid this way and that, and chaffed
back at the tramcar conductors in the traffic blocks. We handed
it over to the proper authorities; we found our train; we slept; we
reached Toulouse and changed for Latour de Carol, the French
frontier town.

From Foix through Ax-les-Thermes to Latour de Carol Spain
is always only just the other side of a mountain. I had climbed into
Spain at several different places around about and I knew every
bit of the valley up which the train was passing; I had walked
through these very tunnels before the line was laid. There is something exciting about any boundary; I always expect to find myself
in a new world even when stepping from Kent into Surrey; I am
prepared to meet men carrying their heads under their arms. I am
certain that over there, there are dragons. And of all boundaries
none can be more definite, more full of promise of a new world

on the other side than the Pyrenees. On the other side of that wall, one says, is Africa at least.

Here in the valley of the Carol is France, green, cultivated to the last patch, parsimonious, careful, civilised; over there is Spain, deserts and oases, colour, blood, bulls, passion, sun. Of course it is not true. The interminable wall of mountains does not even separate linguistic groups; they speak Catalan everywhere south-east of Toulouse and they speak Catalan everywhere almost to the Ebro. Some vague undrawn line north and south leads to French and Castilian; the sharp, impressive barrier of the Pyrenees keeps no one apart as far as talking is concerned. We have to agree with Q. there, and if people did nothing but talk, Q. and his friends might make a go of their efforts to unite the Provençal French and the Catalans into Occitania.

Moreover, the material culture is the same on both sides of the Pyrenees, so long, that is, as you do not penetrate too far beyond the foothills. If you live on a mountain side, with plenty of water, fertile soil but not too much of it, you will develop the same sort of agriculture, the same uses of water power, the same habits of marketing, the same timetable and calendar, the same attitude to your daily experiences; and it will make very little difference that the map says that you are a Frenchman and your neighbour a Spaniard. It is when you consider the influences that penetrate from the north and south that the differences begin to appear. Up the northern valleys of the Pyrenees penetrated the Renaissance, the Revolution of 1789, the nineteenth century National Idea, the Industrial Revolution; while up the southern valleys came, or rather in them there remained, the Middle Ages, the Inquisition, local patriotism refusing to be unified into a nation, feudalism. It was scarcely until the Great War that the industrial revolution seized on the waters flowing southwards and used them to turn wheels, to light lamps, to forge machines.

But now all that similarity, all that flimsiness of mere boundaries had disappeared. At Latour de Carol we still had the modern substitute for a truce of God which we call the democratic compromise; over there they had heaven knew what. The Pyrenees were almost as real a barrier as if they had been barbed wire entanglements rather than soft snow on crumbling rocks thrust skywards.

But could we get there? Normally the train after a short pause for a glance at the passports would have gone on to Puigcerda, crossing a river into the new country. We would have looked out to find olive-green carabineros and guardias civiles in patent-leather hats. But now the frontier was closed; we must go to Bourg Madame, once more under guard, lest I should start up the motor cycle; and push ourselves across the international bridge. The customs' agent overcharged; the sun blazed down; and tired and angry we struggled to the border. Little crowds stood staring up the road, where beneath the long avenue of plane trees you could see a low, half-hearted barricade.

If one compared to-day with more normal times, one was conscious of a subtle change of atmosphere. The officials were correct in all they said, the little crowds said nothing, but still one seemed to hear on every lip a whisper; "For God's sake go over there and help as much as you can." The little crowds were not just idle gaping groups; they were waiting helpless, while over there their battle was being fought. For every peasant and worker in the south of France was fully conscious, even then, of what some of us have not yet learned, that democracy was winning or losing a decisive battle, that it was not Spain's affair, but our own that was being settled one way or another.

Over the international bridge at Bourg Madame there struggled all day long, Germans, Italians, Russians, French, Belgians, even English, going to help as best they could without arms to beat the monster of Fascism. Those who did not cross stood as if listening for news.

Formalities concluded; my son and I and the motorbike crossed out of peace into war. Behind us the crowds stood silent; in front two armed men rose from the barricade and strolled towards us. One glance at them made me see why the Spanish government is so unpopular with the sons of Colonel Blimp whom we send out in aeroplanes to report on the Spanish civil war. Not only did they not wear the Old School tie, but they had not shaved for weeks; and worse still, instead of a recognizable uniform, one of them was dressed in a thing that Colonel Blimp would never recognize, in either sense of the word, the honest dark blue overalls of a working mechanic. The one that could claim to be wearing a regular uniform was a carabinero; the other was an anti-fascist militiaman, the first, and perhaps not the finest, specimen of the great Army in Overalls with whom we were to live for weeks.

They led us to the normal frontier police station where I had of course to produce my documents. Everybody knows the sort of thing that happens; you produce your passport; somebody stamps it, and on you go. But now it was different. I opened the document; there, large as life were the magic words: "We, James Ramsay MacDonald, a member of his Britannic Majesty's Most Honourable Privy Council ... request and require ... all these whom it may concern to allow the bearer to pass freely without let or hindrance…" But by passing out of the world of democratic compromise into one of cruder realities and more real crudities I had out stepped the limits of James Ramsay MacDonald's magical efficacy. The official looked at my Passport and shook his head. I pointed out that not only was it a nice British Passport but that the Spanish Consul-General had given me a special sort of visa, a "visto bueno" which was said to be not only free but potent. I capped even this with a special document signed by the Spanish Consul saying what an excellent man I was, what a noble paper I represented, how friendly to the democratic government of Spain. The official shook his head. All the officials, the carabineros, the anti-fascist militiamen shook their heads.

It was true that I seemed to be *muy bien documentado*, but all this *no vale nada* wasn't worth the paper it was written on, unless I got a pass from the local Committee. Here was the sort of thing that puts Colonel Blimp off his food for the rest of the day. J. Ramsay MacDonald representing His Britannic Majesty himself, backed up, for what it was worth, by a Consul-General, were to be of no use to me unless five working men, unshaven, caps on their heads, smoking rotten cigars, saw fit.

Everybody was perfectly polite about it; far more polite than frontier officials are in more usual circumstances, but until I had the Committee's safe conduct, I should experience both let and hindrance. An anti-fascist militiaman with rifle and bayonet, in blue overalls, was detailed as guard and guide to take me before the Committee.

We found it in the Mayor's office very busy stamping authorisations for people to do all sorts of things, to buy gasoline, to go to La Seu d'Urgell, to send a package of food to Alp, to sell a house, to sleep in Puigcerda for a night, to telephone to Barcelona, to carry a rifle, to commandeer a pistol, to cut a field of wheat. And who were the Committee? They were the local authority of Puigcerda entrusted by the central government at Barcelona with the task of carrying out martial law. In normal conditions the authority which carries out martial law in a country is the Army of that country; but when the Army itself, disloyal to its military oath, rebels, clearly that cannot be. Martial law must be carried out by whatever forces the government can turn to for aid. In Spain to-day the legally-elected democratic government deserted by its normal guardians, has turned to the workers and peasants to protect it. These formed the Anti-fascist Militia, the Army in Overalls, and set up Committees in every town to administer law and order. The men before whom I now stood were the Committee of Anti-fascist Militia in Puigcerda.

It is very important to understand this, since so many of the sons of Colonel Blimp, finding themselves forced to get safe conducts from unshaven working men, have rushed back over the frontier and telegraphed to their papers that there is no established government left in Spain, that everything is in the hands of workers' councils—'soviets' is the word they like to use, since though it is inaccurate it is charged with the right emotional overtones—that half a dozen different organizations working against one another have reduced the whole place to chaos.

In sober fact the central governments of Barcelona and Madrid have never ceased to function; but, since in a country under martial law it is the functions of martial law that are most likely to be noticed by visitors travelling rapidly from place to place—especially when the whole country is virtually a war zone—many casual observers have mistakenly assumed that there are no executive bodies in Spain to-day except these local Committees.

After a little backchat between me and the chairman of the Committee and an assurance that I was an Anti-fascist I was given a document that read:

"The Popular Front Committee of Puigcerda. We authorise the English subjects, Juan Landon, and his son to transport themselves to Barcelona using the motor bicycle No. BKP 665. Puigcerda, 6 August, 1936."

It had four stamps of the four bodies whose representatives formed the Popular Front Committee. From top to bottom they are the Left Republican Party of Catalunya, the C.N.T., the Communist Party and the U.G.T. We cannot do better than explain these parties here and now. The Left Republican Party of Catalunya is a bourgeois political party to which the members of the Barcelona central government largely belonged at the outbreak of the rebellion. It is the party which virtually won the elections of February, 1936, in Catalunya. It is the party to which my good friend T. belonged. As far as social and economic programme is concerned it might be compared with Lloyd George in his 'three acres and a cow' days.

The C.N.T. is quite a different matter. We have seen it in conference at Zaragoza. It is not a political party but a trade union organization, and its leaders are opposed to the idea of a state or of workers' participation in politics; although the rank and file doubtless voted for the Popular Front at the elections, it is theoretically outside it because of its political philosophy. The C.N.T., in short, is the great syndicalist organization of Spain. Next comes the seal of the Communist Party about which we all know everything. Let us say, in passing, that the syndicalist philosophy of the C.N.T. is as far removed from Communism as Capitalism is from either. The C.N.T. is an anti-political trade union organization, the communist party is political. Moreover the people who represented the C.N.T. point of view in Russia were 'liquidated' as ruthlessly by the victorious communists as the capitalists themselves.

Finally comes the seal of the U.G.T., the Union General de Trabajo. Here we are once more dealing with a trade union organization, but instead of it being a syndicalist affair, like the C.N.T., it has a Socialist philosophy. That means that the U.G.T. believe in a socialist state, whereas the C.N.T. do not believe in any state at all; the U.G.T. follow the doctrines of Marx while the C.N.T. follow those of Bakunin.[1] Finally the U.G.T. is the organization headed by the most important man in Spain, Largo Caballero, sometimes called by friends and enemies alike, the Spanish Lenin.

It is worth while considering the significance of these four seals on one piece of paper. They are a symbol of the sort of unity that can only come from an overshadowing common danger. Nothing could be more diverse than the philosophies that are represented, but the threat of fascism has brought them all together in one Popular Front. When, on July 18th, the news was broadcast that the Army had risen against the government it had sworn to defend and that that government had turned to the people to defend it, every little town like Puigcerda at once set to work to organize itself to resist the enemy. The left bourgeois political party within the Popular Front and all the workers' organizations got together, forgot their grievances with one another, and prepared resistance. First they got whatever arms they could; and we should remember that every Spaniard has used a firearm at some time in his life, as a conscript, or as a poacher, or in the heat of argument. They formed anti-fascist militia and a Committee to put the town on a

---

1. Mikhail Bakunin (1814-1876) was a Russian revolutionary and is considered to be the father of modern anarchism. He was a critic of Marxist theory believing that the dictatorship of the proletariat would lead to a party dictatorship that would enslave the masses. While both anarchists and Marxists aim to create a free, egalitarian society without social classes and government, they disagree on how this should be achieved. Anarchists believe that it should be established by direct action that will lead to social revolution and reject any intermediate stages such as the dictatorship of the proletariat. His ideas caught on quickly in Spain and soon had many followers. Some historians believe that the deep traditions of co-operative communities, mutual aid and anti-centrist feeling made anarchism attractive to Spaniards.

war footing.

The first question in everybody's mind on that day was: will the Guardia Civil and the Carabineros remain loyal? In Puigcerda for the most part they did; but there was some 'cleaning up' of fascists and an officer or two shot; also a doctor and the local tailor, doubtless known to be fascists, though there are other reasons why men might take a good opportunity of shooting their tailor. Moreover, loyal as they seemed, it was thought wise that a militiaman should go along with each carabinero in the performance of his duties, which explains why I had seen the two types together at the International Bridge.

Meanwhile barricades were built across all the entrances to the town, and the incendiary squad, coming perhaps from elsewhere according to plans we shall consider in a later chapter, set fire to the church furniture gathered in the church square. Timid newspaper correspondents armed with field glasses saw from Bourg Madame, across the border in France, churches, convents, schools, public buildings go up in flames well greased with monks and nuns; but those who were actually in Puigcerda saw less. Actually no single structure was damaged, though vestments, furniture, images, confessionals were all destroyed. On the convent walls I saw a notice saying that the Catalan Generalitat had taken it over for the use of the People. In the Church Square small boys were scratching amid a pile of charred fragments.

By the time I had proved my motor cycle to be as anti-fascist as myself it was too late to think of crossing the Coll de Tosses that night, so we went off to the Terminus Hotel and the first thing I saw there was a retired English banker drinking brandy.

He had been on holiday in Andorra when a terror-stricken British official had ordered all British subjects out of Catalunya, and he had not heard the wireless message; and now he was hanged if he was going at all. He and his wife were perfectly comfortable; the anti-fascist militia were unshaven and rather unpleasant, but damn it, look at the fascists; Moors and all that; he hoped the government would win; anyway, have another brandy.

At another table there sat an enormous patriarchal family trying to conceal their gloom and their fascist sympathies. The father was a rich local doctor who had been warned that he might be safer in a small hotel than in his somewhat isolated house in the valley below. He hurried up to me for news. Nor was it extravagant for him to suppose that a man so lately arrived from England should know more than he, since the isolation of one district from another in Spain is such that you can only find out what your own parish is doing about the revolution.

The doctor showed immense satisfaction at the good account I was able to give him of the government's prospects and it was not until he had returned to his own table that he buried himself behind a daughter or two and relapsed into gloom. The British Banker chuckled: "What you said was gall to him," he said; "what he wanted to hear was that you thought the rebels would be in Barcelona by next Tuesday." It was the first evidence of what later I saw to be a general rule that anybody with money, however little he might approve of armed rebellion against the democratic government in the first place, hoped to heaven now that the fascists would win. It is only men of spirit and social sensitiveness who continue to loathe all that fascism stands for, even after fascism has become the sole protection of their stocks and shares.

"See that table over there," said the banker, "last night there was the hell of a rumpus.

Half a dozen anarcho-syndicalist anti-fascist militiamen armed to the teeth arrived and arrested the hotel keeper. His daughter was sure he'd be killed, and went about screaming that she would soak her handkerchief in the blood of the man who killed her father. (She had just served me with a lettuce salad and looked pretty calm.) It wasn't necessary however to spoil a handkerchief, as they let him go. Well, everybody said that they knew nothing about the reasons for the arrest, but I found out it was about the two people who used to sit at that table. They'd registered as man and wife, but we all noticed that the man never spoke to the woman at all, and it seems he was really a Canon from Toledo implicated in the revolt and trying to escape in disguise. I suppose that's why the table's empty to-night. Have another brandy?"

Next day we started on the journey. I was to leave my fifteen-year-old son with T., at a small village in the valley where we had all lived a dozen years ago. We had made the arrangements before the news came and it had not seemed necessary to cancel them, especially since T. telegraphed that all would be well. We had not known then that T. was almost beside himself with terror in spite of the telegram.

There is no more beautiful valley anywhere in Europe than the Cerdanya. You climb out of it along a road that runs parallel with it, and you look down on squares of yellow and green and orange, upon rose-coloured farms and pearl grey villages, with the white Andorran mountains on the far side and ahead of you the impenetrable rockiness of the Serra del Cadí. It was eighteen years since I had ridden a motor cycle; but all went well as we steadily mounted to the snows.

We looked down on the little village in which I remembered to have taken shelter in a thunderstorm years ago. I remembered the huge supper of mashed potatoes and raw eggs and how for the only time in my life I slept between sheets of flowered muslin. Now I could see the anarcho-syndicalist flag floating from the tower of its burned out church.

On the top of the Coll de Tosses, in a pine forest, we were challenged by the frontier guard; four young men as happy as could be with their guns and their responsibilities. Two were C.N.T., one was U.G.T. and the other Left Catalan Republican. They showed us a specially good spring of water, and handed us their leather wine bota and talked of England and the curse of fascism. And then we descended into the next valley, and the little villages among which we had lived.

We came to Ribes. I always think of an evening in 1921 in Ribes. T. had brought me to hear a wild-haired poet stir up the inhabitants to a frenzy of Catalanist nationalism. I can see him now exhorting them to use their own language and not Castilian: "Your language is your spirit, and your spirit is your race," I think he said and we all applauded. Two years later this same young man disguised as a monk escaped over the Pyrenees from Primo de Rivera; later still he had tried to lead a Catalan expedition over from Prats de Mollo by the pass that Hannibal once took, but fortunately for everyone the French gendarmerie were told all about it and no one got into Spanish territory. And now Ventura Gassol, the wild poet, was Minister of Culture in the Catalan Generalitat; and Ribes was barricaded at both ends. Ribes, where Richard Ford had found the best trout fishing a hundred years ago, Ribes which leads to Nuria, in the snows. Nuria is hours away, a hermitage turned into a winter sports hotel, and yet the incendiary squads had not forgotten it, and had gone up there also to burn the symbols of the fascist church.

The people of Ribes passed me through their barricades and on down the road to the next village. More barricades and armed youths, one with a pistol, which I think he must have stolen from the local museum of folk art. It had a wooden handle and a funnel shaped mouth to be stuffed with odds and ends, a sort of sawn off blunderbuss, in fact. You could laugh at it, if you felt like it, or you could think; this is all he can find, but he is going to take his place with the rest of the village at the barricade in their common determination that whatever happens in the rest of Spain They Shall Not Pass This Way.

We had so far only seen half a dozen villages, each with its piles of sandbags and stones, each with its ill-armed young men, each with its Committee, no doubt; but already we were beginning to understand the underlying current of feeling; and as in the next few weeks I motor-cycled through nearly a thousand miles of fields and deserts and came to village after village each bravely barricaded, though with ill-armed guardians, I realised what had happened; how a whole people with spontaneous determination, had freely risen to destroy the horrible possibility that the old evils of Spain might once more raise their heads and make life worthless for the common man.

The spiritual force of Spain has never come from any central organ, it comes from every cell and tissue; it has to be conquered village by village and so long as one village remains with its barricades intact Spain will not be fascist. It is hard for us to realise this; we live in countries so well supplied with central nervous systems, with blood vessels and lymph vessels joining all in one, with railways and telegraphs and roads and telephones that the life of the parts has been dominated by the co-ordination of the whole. It is hard to imagine the Kent and Sussex villages barricading themselves, organising themselves, arming themselves without a single message from Whitehall. Decisions are made somewhere in London, all that we can do in Horsham is to accept them with a grumble.

It was in this village that I was to leave my son armed with a safe conduct signed by anarcho-syndicalists, one of whom in true Spanish manner told me that if anything happened to my son I should have the pleasure of shooting him. And then having saluted the Committee we went down the road a few miles farther to visit Ripoll, where we had once lived for nearly three years.

Ripoll is typical of what the electric age does to mountain valley towns: on all sides you see arched aqueducts carrying smooth-sliding waters to the leap out of which comes power. Cotton factories, machine factories, paper factories, forges, each mile or so of the river affords them life-force. The workers live in colonies built near each factory, or are concentrated in over-crowded quarters in the small towns. Many of them are peasants one generation and less removed from the soil; many go back to some remote medieval mountain farm when work is slack, many are "foreigners" from Aragon and Murcia and Castile. When I lived in Ripoll it was towards the end of a period of post-war strikes: the mushroom industry of a wartime neutral was collapsing; want and unemployment existed everywhere and rival unions shot one another's leaders in the general demoralisation. Round the factories you could see in those days barbed wire entanglements. T. himself used to boast of how he lay all night side by side with the faithful porter waiting to shoot any worker who tried to attack the factory. I imagine that it was memory of those days that was giving T. such bad dreams now.

Our landlord had been the sole surviving royalist of the town; I had visited him when the Republic came and he had shaken his head with tears in his eyes and said: "Alfonso is good enough for me." A pathetic little old man, his only child dead, he used to stand all the morning feeding pigeons and calling them "my little ones," and then he would wander round examining his property for new cracks, his property, the possession of which gave his life its sole meaning.

But old Senyor Vidal, too, had his hour of glory. There came the dictatorship of Primo de Rivera, and since nearly everyone else in Ripoll was a republican, a Catalanist or a syndicalist, Senyor Vidal was summoned into public office. He became an inspector of sanitary conditions in Ripoll with a right to take his place at the head of processions with "the authorities civil and military." One of his jobs was to inspect the general conditions of the local brothels, three in number. His report caused great joy among the philistines; "two of these houses which I have personally inspected," he wrote, "are bad in every way; bad drains, bad closets, bad smell, bad ventilation, but in the third I found everything really excellent and, if I might say so, almost to be recommended."

And now this public servant, this feeder of pigeons, cowered in an upper room terrified lest he be shot. He was not shot. Indeed, the fact that he was never molested in spite of his known views, was the clearest evidence that his life had no importance whatever; that he might just as well never have been born.

We went before the Committee of Ripoll, partly for old time's sake, partly because I was already an inveterate collector of documents. You remember that Puigcerda had a Popular Front Committee. Well, Ripoll had a Committee of Defence. That is another example of the great difference between the source of inspiration of action in our countries and in Spain. During the war we had all sorts of local committees whenever Whitehall told us to have them, but since they were inspired from the centre they had the same names and ways of working wherever they were. Here in Spain on July 18th-19th the order went out over the wireless to every village, "Arm yourselves and Organise yourselves against the Rebels," but everything else was left to local patriotism. Puigcerda formed its Popular Front Committee, Ripoll its Committee of

Defence, Granollers, its Anti-fascist Revolutionary Committee, -every local centre did what seemed good to it towards the common end.

In the Ripoll document you will see at the top between the communist stamp and the U.G.T. stamp, the small, clear stamp of that great mystery, the F.A.I., the Federation of Iberian Anarchists.

It was the F.A.I., you will remember, that, according to Q., had killed Badia; it was the F.A.I. that was supposed to do all the notorious political assassinations that have kept Spain on tiptoe for generations; it was the F.A.I. that was supposed to be only a few hundred strong, and yet owing to its secret organization and determined ruthlessness able to dominate the C.N.T.

According to Q., the F.A.I. were all Murcians, ignorant, illiterate degenerates sent to chastise the Catalans for being content to allow a flint implement to be called *neolític* instead of *neolítico*.

A republican Catalan journalist had written some time back a series of articles calling on the Catalan government to suppress the F.A.I., as a criminal secret society. A few days after this stamp was put on my document, men came by night to that journalist's house, took him from his bed, and later left his corpse on the lonely Rabassada road. Everywhere the F.A.I., working secretly and very efficiently; according to Q. a few hundred criminal pistoleros; if so, then remarkably omnipresent for their numbers, and with eyes and revolvers all over Catalunya. Under a member of the F.A.I.'s protection I left my son; the Ripoll Committee were cordial and helpful; they remembered us when we lived in their town; certainly I might go where I liked, buy gasoline, or anything else I needed; as for the boy he would be an honoured guest. He was; but two weeks later and on the day after he left, this same Committee in a fit of irritation walked off to a certain house down the road and finding thirteen fascist sympathisers met together killed them all. Several of the victims were priests; I had taken their photograph one Holy Thursday fifteen years ago as they climbed the hill along the Via Crucis, sweating and arguing and chewing grass. Doubtless there was very little good to be said of them; but as I thought of those superb, simple-hearted working men and peasants in overalls, organizing as best they could to keep the Moorish invasion from saving Christianity by killing Spanish Christians; as I thought of their gentleness, their zeal, their courtesy, and how in spite of it all they had been moved to get up and kill thirteen fairly harmless men, my heart hardened against those who had brought to Spain the most horrible atrocity of all, civil war.

Think for a moment of this Committee of Defence of Ripoll. They were the heirs of all the hundreds of years of black oppression that had made the Spanish people the most ruthlessly exploited of the sons of men; they had seen for the first time a mild, liberal, well-intentioned government come into being in Spain, the sort of government that Mr. Baldwin would find to his liking in most particulars, a government with a social conscience almost overlaid by caution; they had seen this government at once attacked by illegal armed rebellion relying on foreign hordes of Moors and criminals; they had the job of seeing to it that whatever happened in the rest of Spain They Shall Not Pass Our Barricade; they knew that, thanks to Italy, Germany and Portugal, the Moors were well armed, while they themselves had little better than museum pieces to protect their barricades; they heard that thirteen fascist sympathisers, who doubtless spent their days praying that the Moors should come, had met together and were planning to escape; they took their guns and shot them in cold blood. Ugly? Yes, but how natural; thanks to those who let loose the supreme horror of civil war. Do you condemn the harassed workmen on the Committee of Defence of Ripoll? It was not through them that the offence came.

In Ripoll, I went to see an old friend who was likely to be in trouble. I had met him years ago on a wild boar hunt, which had been a curiously inept and tiring affair. We had started in little groups at dawn, with a number of mongrels and a mule to bring home the boars. The theory had been that the mongrels should be let loose at the foot of a precipice, a thousand feet high and five miles long, while the huntsmen climbed to the top and took up their positions at the water-courses which here and there broke the perpendicularity of the cliff. Then when the boars had been disturbed, they would have to mount the precipice by one or other of these water-courses, and if it happened to be yours you would have a three seconds' view of them before they flashed past to security in the hinterland. However, there were no boars. I had no gully of my own to watch, being armed solely with a camera, and so I spent the morning talking to Josep, sharing our wine, chocolate, and cold omelette; and in the evening he invited me home to hear him play the César Franck violin sonata. Now he was in trouble. He was a notoriously religious Catholic, and also a capitalist. He had several sisters who were nuns, several brothers who were priests, and he had two or three businesses.

"Yes; they had put him in prison on July 18th"; "they" being a group of revolutionary enthusiasts up from Vich come to help "organize" Ripoll. But within two hours half the workers of Ripoll had marched to the prison to get him out again, and had brought him in triumph back to his house.

"I really don't mind," said Josep. He has a way of filling up the interstices of his smile with a mixture of humility and surprise. "If the fascists win they will put me in prison for much longer than two hours because I am too good to my workers. And anyway it was pleasant to find how much they loved me. I should not have known had they not put me in prison first."

We talked of the burned churches. Josep goes into retreat every other year; and in the Christmas miracle play at Ripoll he has taken every part, beginning with a cherub with a wig of yellow straw and ending as leader of the orchestra; and as I looked at him I remembered that interminable four-hour entertainment with the great moment when the three Kings come to the Manger and take the opportunity to throw handfuls of sweets at the children in the audience. It was strange to think that Ripoll had said good-bye to all that.

"I am a Catholic," said Josep, "but I believe my church needed to be purged with fire. It has been betrayed by the bishops and archbishops who have turned their cathedrals into armouries and fortresses."

I asked him what was happening to the businesses. He laughed:

"I am a worker now; I draw a wage; everything goes on otherwise as usual." Josep was one of those fortunate people who are not only capitalists but technicians also, and therefore equipped to survive violent changes because they are always useful.

Amid the gathering of a storm and at the coming of night I left Ripoll and rode down the valley. I passed the "English Colony," where a British cotton firm, finding that they could make more profit out of using Spanish than British labour, had set up a large factory. Over its colony of workers' dwellings fluttered the anarcho-syndicalist flag; at each end of the neighbouring village stood the Army in Overalls at their barricades: somewhere in England no doubt people were already writing up their claim for compensation against whatever government survives the wreck of democratic capitalism by the fascist rebellion.

You go down the narrow valley with its aqueducts and channels and factories and electric power stations until suddenly you find yourself in the drained out bottom of a mesozoic lake. The petrified mud banks rise on every side, some of them like round, swarthy breasts with a nipple of topsoil giving contrast to their smooth nakedness. In the centre of this district lies the cathedral and garrison city of Vich.

Fifteen years ago, I was rash enough to give a lecture in Catalan, in Vich. It was on the Irish Sinn Fein movement, and it was given in an exhumed Roman Temple. The audience of three hundred was two-thirds priests. In Vich there had been priests everywhere. The great main square of Vich, the streets, the cafés, all had been thick with priests whenever I had come that way. Priests and sausages were the sole local products. And now as I rode into the town it was hidden in a black cloud, and every now and then it leapt out of its obscurity as a flash of lightning played above the surrounding mud-hills. The rain damped the ardour of even the Army in Overalls and I passed along the Barcelona road, skirting the great Square, as through a dead city. Not a soul challenged me; scarcely one terrestrial light revealed the outlines of the innumerable churches, only the blinding lights of the sky, showing in a fragment here and there the torn up roads, the piles of sandbags, the broken walls of burned out churches; all lying amid a great silence which made me glad of the companionship of my noisy motor. Once out on the other side with a straight avenue before me, I stepped on the gas and hurried into the empty night.

On July 18th, when the news of the fascist rebellion came, the incendiary squads assembled in Vich; obscure, bitter men, living beneath the shadow of the Cathedral, in an excess of anti-religious mysticism joined together to fight against the dark powers of heaven. How and why they acted I shall tell in a later chapter, at present I shall only tell the story of Cristina, T's wife.

It was with Cristina that I had left my son in the mountains above. I have known her for many years. She lived all her child-hood in a mountain farm three hours from the nearest road; her father was a maker of wooden shoes. I have watched the old man chipping the blocks into shape, hollowing them out, and varnishing them; all done with tools that were used centuries ago by his ancestors.

For some reason, Cristina's parents desired, above all things, to educate their daughter, and she learned far more than is normal for a peasant in those mountains. One day they held a Catalanist political conference in Ripoll and Cristina came as a delegate from her village; the only woman delegate of anything that had ever been seen in Ripoll. T. saw her, fell in love promptly, and told us all about his feelings. I can see him walking up and down the Paseo with Cristina and a chaperone on that first day.

They married. Cristina learned to drive a Hispano Suiza car at an intolerable speed. She had a baby regularly once a year. She would go ski-ing in the morning, decide she was about to be in labour, say good-bye to the party, descend to the car, drive herself home, have the baby, and next day when the rest came back have a meal ready for them. A week later she would drive the car two hundred miles in five hours through the Pyrenees with the infant in her arms.

There was an English workman in the factory, and from his wife Cristina learned English. She edited the woman's page of the local progressive magazine. She made the children's clothes. She spoke at the republican meetings round about.

On July 18th Cristina was at the seaside by herself recuperating from a not unnatural attack of fatigue. Directly she heard of the outbreak she decided to get back to her children. She got as far as Vich when night fell and there the train stopped dead. She heard that the Cathedral was burning and her first thought was for the museum of ecclesiastical art next door. It is one of the finest collections of primitive church furniture in the world. "They" would be bound to burn that also.

She ran to the Cathedral square and found an excited crowd standing and watching the flames. Vich Cathedral, attractive outside, is horrible within, save for some murals in sepias by Sert which are, or rather were, better at least than his later hotel work in New York. They no longer exist. Their most superb moment must have been their last, their gigantic golden brown figures lit up by flames and hovering amid gusts of smoke—nothing could have been lacking but an orchestra of fiends playing music from Amor Brujo.

The anger and mystical inebriation of the crowd reached a climax when it was found that, hidden in the vaults, there was a treasure of sixteen million pesetas in gold, as well as firearms. Everyone knew all about the bishop of Vich and his sympathies. Here again, as in so many places, the church was proving a fascist treasury and armoury. On to the Bishop's Palace; down with its gates: burn it down.

It was then that Cristina flew into action. Within the Palace was the priceless museum. She must save it. Tearing down a piece of red cloth from a balcony, she bound it on her arm and in the light of the burning cathedral, she climbed on a pile of rubbish and faced the crowd.

"You must not burn the museum," she cried. "It is the People's. It belongs to our Past. It is not religious. It is ours." They shouted to her to get down; she threw herself against the iron gates. They told her she must let them pass; she must get away so that they could smash the gates. She stood her ground.

"Burn every church in Vich," she cried. "Burn the crosses and the images; but you must not touch the Museum. It is the People's. It is Ours. I, too, am of the people. Look at the colour I have bound on my arm. Destroy the religion of the priests, but do not touch our Inheritance."

Astonished by her passion, the crowd paused to scratch its head; the spontaneous gust of fury was stayed. One man said, "Let's leave the museum and take the treasure to Barcelona." And very soon the same men who had set fire to the Cathedral had loaded sixteen million pesetas into a lorry and were taking it to hand it over intact to the central government in Barcelona.

Having saved the museum of Vich, Cristina felt she must get to her own village and her children. There were no trains and no cars, and so she walked on foot through the night, thirty miles into the mountains.

As I pierced the long avenues of plane trees towards Barcelona, blinded by rain, conscious of invisible streets and buildings rising up behind me, I did not feel that I was leaving a town, but that I was running away from a dark corner of the human spirit.

And then quite suddenly and quite finally my motor ceased to function. Without even that blustering sound to keep me company, I was sliding alone between half visible trees down a long straight road to Granollers. I had neither the skill nor the energy to discover what had gone wrong. I knew that the road continued to go downhill until the long single street of Granollers was reached; I was soaked to the skin; the night was black: I was hungry. As I pushed on I kept remembering an astonishingly good lunch I had had on market day in Granollers ten years before. My children had been given an extra helping of prawns by the plump proprietor, who was all smiles and pats on the back. I would like some prawns and a large rice at that hotel, then a bath and a good bed. I plodded on towards that cheerful proprietor's face as towards a beacon- light.

Far down the road at last a few lights appeared, and then the greyness of heaped paving stones beneath electric bulbs. I think I must have looked, as I felt, forlorn; for the Army in Overalls advanced almost tenderly towards me without even asking me for a countersign. Of course they had seen my light crawling towards them for two miles of a Roman road and one cannot appear very dangerous after that.

"My motor cycle has gone wrong," I said. "It is very late to go to Barcelona to-night; can you help me find a garage and a hotel?"

They seized on the offending machine and pushed it into a garage; they summoned a car from a side street and took me off to the Committee. It was just such a Committee as those I had seen in Puigcerda and Ripoll and Campdevanol, working on through the night, organizing, determined that They Shall Not Pass Our Barricade. I had only to say that I was a decent human being; that is to say an anti-fascist and all was well. "Might I stop the night at the local hotel and go and get something to eat?"

"No," replied the Committee. "If you are an anti-fascist you shall be the guest of our Popular Kitchen"; and a guard and a car were ordered to take me off to the Granollers Anti-fascist Committee's Cuina Popular.

The building itself had been the residence of a wealthy man now gone abroad for his health. He had transferred it in some unspecified manner to the new authorities for its new purpose. I arrived to find the militiamen just finishing supper. There was a large dish of something perilously like Hamburgers lying on the table, along with loaves of bread and glass porrons of red wine. Rapid explanations from the militiaman who had brought me, and a general sortie to get Carlos out of the kitchen.

Carlos was the inevitable speaker of English; throughout my journey I was to meet the English-speaking comrade, whose English was rarely as good as my Catalan or my Castilian, and of course he had always learned to speak English cooking or waiting in a hotel in New York. That explained the Hamburgers. Carlos was imposing American culture on the Army in Overalls in Granollers.

They wanted to put me at a table in a room by myself and all wait on me at once, but when I protested that I also was a comrade and an anti-fascist, they agreed to let me sit with them, and Carlos was instructed to tell me that the anarcho-syndicalists there present were ashamed of their discourtesy in not speaking my language. They gave me a huge dinner ending with roasted almonds. I said that my wife liked roasted almonds and they tied up a pound of almonds for her in a bag. Later they were actually eaten in a room overlooking Clapham Common a few doors away from the school whence Harriet Westbrook eloped with Shelley. They gave me a dozen cigars.

Then at least twenty of the Army in Overalls, all talking at once, all asking questions—you do think we will win, don't you? and I not knowing what "non- intervention" would in due time achieve, said yes, with conviction—all showing their guest the honours of the house, took me round the kitchens, the store rooms hung with hams, the dining-room—we have no beggars in Granollers now; we feed them here,—the sleeping apartments. They found clean towels and gave me a shower. And at last, very late, they took me off to find a room at the hotel whose genial proprietor had a face like a beacon light. But when we got to the hotel, the shutters were up, the chairs were all on the tables, the lights were low, and the one man visible said that the hotel was full. The militiamen were not put out; the committee would look after me and to the committee for a second time we went. We found them examining arms that had been collected to help defend the legitimate democratic government of Spain from the Moors and their paymasters, and one weapon in particular was to leap to my mind's eye weeks later as I sat in the Friends' Meeting House in the Euston Road. It was an old flintlock, mostly made of wood, which might have frightened a thief on a dark night in the early eighteenth century. In the Friends' Meeting House I had to hand round to a Committee investigating evidence of German and Italian aid to the rebels the most modern aerial incendiary torpedo bomb. It had been dropped from a German plane on to the workers and peasants of Spain. I saw the pistol of Granollers; I wished that I could have held it up in one hand and the aerial torpedo in the other and said: "This, gentlemen, is what our government's effort at a neutrality pact comes to in reality; this against this; museum pieces to defend the democratic government of a friendly power, and the latest gift of destructive science for the rebels."

The committee were told that there were no rooms at the hotel; but that was a matter that could easily be settled. They got my genial proprietor friend on the telephone. "You are ordered by the committee to find this man a room." We returned to the hotel; the one man left in charge led me down empty, deserted corridors and opened a bedroom door, and soon I was sleeping, utterly alone in a guestless, forgotten building.

And next day as I drank some coffee I saw the man who had given my children an extra helping of prawns. Ruin and fear had sagged his cheeks, and all his affable self-sufficiency was gone. He was the first example of what I was to see often enough, the havoc that violent change plays in a few weeks with personal appearances, with jovial obesity, with dapper neatness, with bourgeois imperturbability of feature. Everything that this man had loved was gone: the orderly running of his hotel, his reasonable profits, his right to dismiss whom he pleased, to superintend, to make decisions, to show special attention to the local bigwigs, to crack a joke with a visiting swell; all was gone and his tissues had shrunk. He needed a massage, he needed a wash, he needed a good night's sleep, he needed a return to accustomed routine. It was as if the camaraderie, the vigorous hope, the fun of being on the winning side at last that shone in the features of everybody at the Cuina Popular, had sucked dry the life and spirit of his hotel and of his body also.

I went back to the Cuina Popular for breakfast; hunks of bread with olive oil for butter and pieces of uncooked ham and wine out of the porron. They all wanted to have their photographs taken. They all wanted to show me the church next door, and the priest's house, and the convent school. I stood and looked at a sight which reminded me of something, quite different you might think, in New York City two years before.

I had been walking up Sixth Avenue vaguely watching a knot of people ahead of me. Presently I heard "Here's one," and a rush towards a taxi slowly driving our way. Then I saw men tearing the taxi doors off, smashing glass, gashing the leather, scratching the enamel. Another taxi turned in from a side street: the same rush of men, the same smashing, gashing, scratching, the same wrecking of work which men had sold precious hours of their only lives to do. It made one sick to stand and watch deliberate destruction; deliberate effacement, it seemed, of parts of human lives.

Then I remembered that there was a bitter taxi-strike on, and that these were scab cars. The destroyers were taxi men fighting for their economic lives, for more food for their children, more home decency for their wives, and like destroying angels they were obliterating the men who were taking advantage of their dangerous warfare to make a few extra dollars for *their* children and wives. Nature red in tooth and claw; shattering glass, broken hinges;—and here burned out churches. The motley tinsel and imitation marble made of wood, the futile extravagance of a decadent baroque, had lost their substance save for a floorful of twisted iron, charred wood, blackened plaster. The angels of destruction had passed that way also.

I asked my friends who had done it and why. "Well," one answered, "in every movement there are men who are in the movement for good motives and others who are there for bad; and ours is no exception. We have our bad men. When they set fire to the churches we went and pulled out everything of value that we could." "They," always "they"; who were "they" who had thus purified with fire the house of prayer turned into a den of thieves? Nobody ever seemed to be willing to answer that question.

And so I went on to Barcelona past barricade after barricade, giving the countersign every few miles to members of the Army in Overalls. I was approaching the strangest city in the world today, the city of anarcho-syndicalism supporting democracy, of anarchists keeping order, and anti-political philosophers wielding political power.

CHAPTER 4
RAMBLAS AND PARALLELO

I shall not easily forget my entry into Barcelona at the beginning of August, 1936. At the best of times, the sprawling suburbs are sinister. It is partly the mixture of centuries—ponderous mule-drawn carts winding along at walking pace; noisy Hispanos only sometimes slowing down to forty miles an hour; overcrowded trams never keeping on the same side of the road for very long; hordes of children seeking in traffic-perils a natural check to population that contraception has not yet affected; old women marketing and shouting through the roar; lean cats; dogs, blind or amorously careless; piles of granite cobbles and unexpected holes that the cobbles may someday fill; tramlines and light railway lines sticking six inches above the road surface; unexpected traffic lights, and traffic police disguised as generals or G.A.R. veterans and Chelsea Pensioners; beggars displaying their sores in the middle of the road; vast quantities of itinerant vendors. Most of this you can find in the East End of London or in any other great city, but as you approach Barcelona you are aware also of a crude intensity of living, a menacing activity, a human energy which quite plainly gets little or nothing of what civilisation can give as a reward—an overpowering sense of something about to explode.

As you drove through all this a year or so ago in a modest Ford you used to hear now and then the single word 'rico' shouted after you; and I, for one, have more than once ducked my head from the sound as if it were a missile. It is the wonder of Barcelona that in its plan you may see very distinctly, without the slightest attempt to obscure the outlines, those ugly divisions into economic classes at war with one another that are somehow carefully hidden here in London. Of course we have Kensington and Shoreditch, but the Kensingtonian, unless he deliberately wears a black shirt, can pass through Shoreditch without feeling that he is in enemy territory. In Barcelona the man who is motoring to put up at the Ritz has to run the gauntlet, shoot the surf, pass the enemy's lines, before he can get there.

I was not going to the Ritz, but to the little hotel opposite. Last May we had swept out our room, gone without our baths, bought our food and eaten in the bedroom, all because of the FOSIG. I looked over the road at the Ritz. Across its door was a huge new red lettered sign:

HOTEL GASTRONOMIC NO. 1
U.G.T.—F.O.S.I.G.—C.N.T.

The Hotel Ritz was nowhere to be seen. In May its waiters and cooks had refused to serve anyone at all; now they were serving thousands of poor men and women daily, for they had taken over the hotel and turned it into a Popular Kitchen. All along the beautiful wide Corts Catalans the windows of the ex-Ritz were flung wide open. Within, the huge chandeliers were a blaze of light. Outside was a queue hundreds long of men and women from the Fifth District, the *barri xino* waiting their turn to sit at the table of Dives, who had gone abroad for his health. I made a note to visit Hotel Gastronòmic No. 1 at my leisure.

But for the moment I was exhausted. I had had my first experience of practical anarcho-syndicalism. For Barcelona had done away for the time being with traffic lights and traffic policemen, and as far as one could see every human being had commandeered a motor-car from somewhere and was learning to drive and to beat records at one and the same time. It seems that in a city in full-flooded revolution it is necessary for everybody to get somewhere else in the shortest possible number of seconds. Every young man in Barcelona had procured a car, a uniform of overalls, and some sort of gun, and so long as there was still gasoline everyone was going to make the best use of the rare opportunity. Yes, the Fifth District, the Parallelo, the suburbs, had broken through to the inner magic circle and made themselves masters of the Ramblas, the Paseo de Gràcia, Mayfair and Belgravia. It was none the less pleasant for them that they had come in the other people's cars.

My Pension-Hotel occupied the top stories of a large corner building, and at the street entrance were a crowd of militamen belonging to the Esquerra Catalana.[1] They captured me promptly and took me before their Committee in the floor above; it meant one more nice document for my collection, a document with the four bars of the Catalan national flag. Years ago T. had told me that when the original Count of Barcelona was dying of wounds, Charlemagne congratulated him on his excellent behaviour and asked if there was anything he could do for him.

"I haven't got a coat of arms," said Count Wilfred the Hairy. Whereupon Charlemagne dipped his four fingers into the dying man's wound and smeared four bars of blood across his shield, which was how it came about that my paper from the Esquerra Catalana Anti-fascist Militia had four red bands upon it. T. had always told me with scorn that the Castilians hadn't even got a flag of their own; that they had had to take half the Catalan flag, that is, two red bands on a gold background; and in those days the most exciting thing you could do, if you were a bourgeois Catalan, was to run a flag with four bands up a pole and wait for the Guardia Civil to come and threaten to arrest you unless you immediately hauled it down and put up one with only two bands. Now most people had forgotten all about Wilfred the Hairy and

---

1. Lluís Companys's Republican Left Party of Catalonia.

Charlemagne and had gone over to Bakunin and Malatesta and the black-and-red flag of the F.A.I.-C.N.T. It seemed somehow pleasant and domesticated to have one document with medieval symbols upon it to add to my collection.

But when I found that even T did not feel any very great faith in the efficacy of my scrap of paper, I hurried to re-inforce it elsewhere; hurried, I say, but in fact I "hastened slowly."

First T. took me to a professor, a delightful man who asked me in perfect good faith to come with him next week on the expedition to retake Majorca. That was very early in August and the war was to be over in a couple of weeks and the Esquerra Catalana, leaving Zaragoza largely to the F.A.I.- C.N.T. were chartering a few odd craft in order to run up the "Four Bands" on the public buildings in Palma.

The professor took me to the School of Marine Arts, the headquarters of the Barcelona Anti-fascist Militia. There I met Jaume. Jaume was one of the young men who years before had tried to blow up Alfonso at Garraf. The others had come to a bloody end; Badia, I had watched as he lay dead; Comte had been killed in October, 1934 at a balcony at the end of the Ramblas, which had been left in its shattered state ever since as a memorial; another had just killed himself in a motor accident. But Jaume was very much alive, l'homme moyen sensual – I thought of him later in Toledo when I looked at the Captain. Jaume ordered his car, a Rolls-Royce, to be brought for us, and with three armed guards we started off on a voyage of discovery. I felt safer now because I had Jaume's material support and also a new piece of documentation. It is written in Catalan, which was a surprise to the Army in Overalls when I showed it at the barricades in Castile. Besides the stamp of the office of origin you can see three other stamps. There is the stamp of the Valencian Anti-fascist Militia of Workers and Peasants, a communist body who barred my free passage to Valencia but made up for it with a glass of wine – what customs' official in England or America ever treated a victim to wine! – and free

---

1. Errico Malatesta (1853-1932) was an Italian anarchist theorist.

garage service, for ten days. The weak stamp over the signature is
the Popular Front of Madrid's and the other to the right is the Madrid Railwaymen's Union's, which came to me pleasantly enough,
as I shall tell in due course.

Having got into the Rolls-Royce we set out on a chase after
certain documents of quite a different character. Somewhere in
Barcelona were hundreds of documents seized by a search party of
Anti-fascist Militia in the early days when they raided the German
Nazi headquarters. I knew where they were, but I did not tell Jaume because I thought a few false scents would show me more of
Barcelona and I liked Jaume's company and his car. We went first
of all to the Hotel Colón. Right across its huge front on the Plaza
de Catalunya you may read in Catalan Partit Socialista Unificat
de Catalunya. Now I do not wish to make a hasty judgement, but
I have never before seen such a pandemonium as existed within
the walls of the Hotel Colón. We went from one hive of activity to
another and finally went and sat out on the balcony overlooking
the Paseo de Gràcia. Out of almost every window poked rifles,
more murderous looking than they were, each manned by a grim
youth in a scarlet shirt. One felt that they were taking life too seriously by half.

We stared at the tops of tramcars passing below. There were
many arms around waists, a sight common enough in Hyde Park
or on Hampstead Heath but charged with revolutionary significance in the Plaza de Catalunya. Jaume enjoyed what he saw.
"Revolution is a great aphrodisiac," he said.

But as nothing was likely to come of the Colón we left and
cruised around the town for some time, passing the unfortunate
monument to the Count de Guell and a dozen other evidences of
exuberance.

At last I told Jaume that the place to go for my documents was
the C.N.T.-F.A.I. headquarters in the Via Laietana. He accepted
the suggestion politely but made no bones about leaving me,
when I suggested it, at the door. The "Four Bands" quivered a
little, I thought, at the close approach of the more modern magic
of C.N.T.-F.A.I., rather like a needle that has just entered into a

magnetic field.

I found myself in the hub of the universe, an anarcho-syndicalist emporium of law and government. Not so long ago this had been the huge office of Camb , the great Catalan financier, the founder of the older school of political Catalan nationalism, which could be summed up as all Spain as a field for Catalan capital and particularly for Camb 's capital.

In the appropriate office sat the director of Propaganda in the English Language. He had pale blue eyes, an expression identical with our modern poet, Mr Stephen Spender; he was a Lithuanian and came from Rochester, New York. And in passing I might say that if I were a smeller-out of conspiracies, I should blame not Moscow but the U.S.A. for all the trouble in Spain. Wherever I went I found an American, or at least a Spaniard clearly corrupted by a stay in that famously revolutionary country. The Lithuanian from Rochester, New York, eyed me very suspiciously. He had heard me broadcast the night before and had found me pessimistic.

"Are you a Stalinite?" he asked with intense feeling.

"No, I am not a Stalinite," I replied honestly enough; "nor," I added, "a Troskyite. In fact, I am nothing much."

"So long as you are not a Stalinite," said a hitherto unobserved comrade with one arm and no hair, in French.

"So you are French," I said hoping that at last someone could be positively classified.

"No, I am a Russian," he said with the same sort of mysterious intensity as the Lithuanian. I began to long for a good healthy Spaniard.

"Then you must be a communist," I said with a vast degree of innocence.

"On the contrary, I am a Russian anarchist; one of the few who escaped." And then I remembered how the anarchists had been liquidated as violently and as completely as the capitalists in Russia; and I was gladder than ever that I was not a Stalinite.

"Here are the documents," said the Lithuanian, "and all I ask in return is that you never say anything untrue about the F.A.I."

I wish to be perfectly honest: I went home and slept quite badly that night. Had I said anything wrong about the F.A.I.? I was conscious too that all over Barcelona my broadcast talk was being equated with Bakunin, and I resolved not to accept a lift in any car whatever after nightfall. And then as I fell asleep in the early morning I was awakened with a start by the "Melody of Broadway" bellowed from a wireless across the way.

Having calmed my moods I sallied forth into the city. Barcelona is my well-beloved mistress, and to love her has been a liberal education. Let us visit her, Baedeker in hand.

The tourist arriving at the railway station from France turns to the left and finds himself in the Paseo de Colon. The Paseo de Colon is a gloomy place with the most dusty and ill-groomed palm trees anywhere in Europe. On one side lies the ocean and on the other a dark wall of architecture. The ocean is hidden by the ugly necessities of a harbour, warehouses, railway sidings, customs agencies; the wall of architecture is execrable; the street between is dusty, the palm trees dying. We do not like the Paseo de Colon. But we notice that the chief building is pockmarked with bullets, and that here and there the window-ledges and architectural features have been badly chipped. Outside this building are two steel sentry-boxes, rusty and ugly, their opening facing the street, and in their sides to left and right are embossed two women's faces with open mouths, through which the man within can spit revolver bullets up and down the Paseo.

This building is the Capitania General, the place from which every ruthless government has done its best to throttle all that is free in Barcelona. It was here that the famous 'ley de fuga'was organised, a neat way of breaking strikes. I once saw a number of workers marched into its quadrangle roped together; they had been holding a meeting, and the military had taken the opportunity to round them up. If among the mixed bag there was found a Trade Union leader who was regarded as a particular nuisance, it was ten to one that later he would be found to have been shot "while trying to escape."

On July 18th, the rebels made the Capitania General one of

their headquarters. When the news spread to the workers' quarters they came from the Fifth District, from the old town behind, from the suburbs, and took shelter behind those ugly warehouses opposite, crawling out of sight until there were enough of them to smother the rifle and machine-gun fire with their own bodies. Then they rushed across the Paseo between the sickly palms and took the Capitania General by assault. They dragged small artillery pieces into position, and shot off fragments of the atrocious facade, and then they ran up the road and attacked the Drassanes barracks. We follow more slowly Baedeker in hand.

The horror in the sky above us is the statue of Columbus, famous Catalan discoverer of America. Q. and T. have given me books proving that he was a Catalan, and not an absurd Genoese. I am expecting to hear at any moment that Mussolini has ordered a general bombardment of Barcelona because Q. and T. say that Columbus is a Catalan. Anyway, the Catalan commemorative column is so ugly as to be itself halfway to an international incident.

From the foot of this unfortunate column we look up the Ramblas, the superb promenade that divides the medieval bourgeois world from the dark-age workers' world of the Fifth District. T. has, I imagine, never been through the Fifth District to the Parallelo. I said as much to Puig.

"That is because T. is not a human being," said Puig. "Human beings visit the Parallelo once a week."

T. is content to leave all that lies to our left as we look up the Ramblas a blank space on his map, with the device, "Here are Prostitutes." T. is a Puritan; but so great is his Catalanism that he gives the impression that he is proud that Barcelona contains a larger number of prostitutes than any other town in Europe. He shakes his head with proud shame when he tells me that Catalan contains more obscene words than any other language. I don't believe him; my researches lead me to believe that Catalan, like all other languages, has exactly five obscene words.

In August 1936, the Ramblas was not full of prostitutes. At the lower end, where one used to be accosted by the strangest derelicts, were lined up three armoured cars, home-made pathetic things, with iron sheets a quarter of an inch thick hopefully fastened round their vitals, death-traps for brave amateurs, created by the steelworkers' unions, bravely flaunting their magic letters C.N.T., F.A.I. It was these armoured cars that finally convinced me of T.'s moral bankruptcy. An engineer who knew all about stamping steel into all sorts of shapes, he stood and sneered at them. Why the hell couldn't he go and make better ones. The awful pathos of those armoured cars, hopefully knocked together by the insulted and injured, ground into one like a Dostoyevsky novel. There they stood between the plane trees, flanked on the right by the burned-out offices of an Italian steamship company, and on the left by a burned-out church, once sacred to Joseph the Carpenter.

Round the armoured cars the confident proletarian crowds swarmed in their optimism. A strange new crowd, as if the Parallelo had come to take possession of the Ramblas. The Ramblas lie sloping gradually upward for more than a mile to the Plaza de Catalunya. From the other end you looked down on an unending harvest of heads. To-day there is not a hat, a collar, or a tie to be seen among them; the sartorial symbols of the bourgeoisie are gone, a proletarian freedom has swarmed in along the Calle del L'Hospital and the Calle del Carmen from the Parallelo. Or, as Puig suggests, the bourgeoisie have disguised themselves for better safety as proletarians by leaving hat, collar, and tie at home.

The *Solidaridad Obrera*, a syndicalist paper, has a splendid editorial against hats and ties. So long as there are no hats and ties seen on the Ramblas the workers may know that the victory is on their side. Hats have ever been a useless symbol of pride and privilege. Pirates, buccaneers, princes, señoritos, priests —these are the hatted folk of history. What has the free worker to do with the outworn symbol of bourgeois arrogance? Away with the infamous unhealthy useless excrescence. No hats, comrades, on the Ramblas and the future will be yours; ties are only fit for the bourgeoisie to hang itself with. All of this seems to me sound good-sense. I almost thought of writing to congratulate *Solidaridad Obrera* for its assault on the futile.

Next day *Solidaridad Obrera* withdrew and apologized. A storm

of protest had come in from the workers in the hat and tie industries, both affiliated to the C.N.T. Where would they be if workers
were never to wear hats and ties? What we needed was to get
rid of the social injustice that denied those things to any except a
privileged class. Not only must we have hats and ties on the Ramblas, but on the Parallelo too.

I remember how, in New York, a year or so ago, when people,
inspired perhaps by Charles Lindbergh, were beginning to eman-
cipate their heads, a big notice appeared saying, "The man who
does not wear a hat is a cissie." Vested interests, always vested
interests.

We walk up the Ramblas again. On both sides great buildings
taken over by anti-fascist organisations, trade unions, Popular
Front parties with a dozen different sets of initials. There is the
Liceu, one of the largest opera-houses in the world, with a magnificent lounge and next to no dressing-rooms for the performers.
It was burned down once, an anarchist exploded a bomb there
years ago. Now it has been taken over by the Catalan government
and has become the Catalan People's Theatre. It is to be re-opened
soon by Casals. In it are the offices of the People's Cinema Industry,
which is hurrying all it can to re-open the cinemas by next Sunday.
The courting couples cannot stand it any longer. T. told me years
ago that what he called a "new vice" had broken out in Barcelona;
girls of really nice families met young men in the bioscopic dark to
seek biologic enlightenment. The cinemas must be re-opened as a
moral safety-valve for the militia girls.

Now we are in the flower market and the bird market. For
a hundred yards or so under huge umbrellas old ladies sit amid
some of the biggest dahlias in the world, poking flowers into the
frame-work of memorial wreaths. Change has come here also;
there are no crosses made for funerals; only wreaths tied with red
and black ribbon, and most of the flowers are red.

In April, I had wandered between these umbrellas and watched
the rapid fingers weaving flowery memorials to the brothers Badia, tying them up with ribbons, four red bars on a golden background; while here and there a cross of lilies and gladioli was

being prepared for some old beata who had gone her way more peacefully, dreaming nothing of what would soon be happening to the Church she had haunted. Now they were making wreaths for fallen militiamen, and tying them with red and black ribbon. A vast loudspeaker blared out encouragement from Madrid. The Calle del Carmen was closed by a barricade; and Betlem, of all churches most like a theatre, with loges and boxes and heaven-knows-what stage effects of scenery and candles, was a shell; a shell that must come down because the stage props within had made such a brave fire that all the arches of the flimsy fake architecture were broken. I tried to photograph the barricade, but the F.A.I.- C.N.T. guard told me to get a permit. A dead militiaman was carried shoulder-high to his grave up the centre of the Ramblas amid a forest of upraised fists, and at the same moment a woman crossed the road with a newly purchased love-bird in a cage. The funeral passed, a tiny crowd, absorbed for a moment in the larger, eddied back around the parrots on their stands. Up above in the trees the thousands of sparrows looked down on their caged idle-rich relatives in the market. I remembered how years ago the Humane Society of Barcelona had marched *en masse* to the bird market and forcibly opened all the cages as a protest. Barcelona has always believed in direct action.

A C.N.T. militiaman hands me a paper. It is an appeal to the *petite bourgeoisie* not to be afraid of the anarcho-syndicalists.

"A la Petita Burgesia," it is headed, "Es francament inexplicable aquesta temença que la petita i modesta burgesia té de nosaltres—it is frankly inexplicable this fear that the petty and modest bourgeoisie has of us— that the capitalists, the millionaires, the plutocrats, the landowners should fear us is logical, because they are the incarnation of injustice and represent the privileged classes. But the modest bourgeois, the small businessman and small industrialist, should clearly see that we are not their enemies... In Catalunya the *petite bourgeoisie* is a large proportion of the community. We do not want to underestimate their social function. We believe that in the building of the new society which is being born, this group will be a most important piece of the powerful

mechanism that the workers have been forging since the very moment that capitalism passed away on July 19th...

"The National Confederation of Labour and the Federation of
Iberian Anarchists invite you to abandon your fears. Learn to be
confident and learn to put yourselves in your proper place—joined
to the proletariat."

At lunch I handed the paper to Puig. He is a petit i modest
burgès if there ever was one, a clerk in a cotton broker's. Puig
smiled and produced another piece of paper from his pocket; it
had some figures on it.

"You see this," said Puig, "it is a telephone number. If at any
time during the night I hear men trying to get into my apartment,
I am to telephone to this number, and within five minutes the
Anti-fascist Militia will send a car of armed guards."

He folded up his paper and handed back mine. "Do you know
what happened last night to my partner in the office? First, you
must know that they have taken all the keys away from the serenos."

(The serenos are the traditional night watchmen. I used to hear
them going round at night in my little Pyrenean town: "Hail Mary,
it is three o'clock in the morning, the weather is serene." That is
why they are called serenos, since the weather is nearly always
good. In England they would be called Wets. At their belts they
carry your house-key and your neighbour's. You clap your hand
twice and the sereno hurries up to let you in to your own house.)

"They have taken the keys from the serenos," said Puig, "so as
to make it more difficult for the F.A.I. to carry out raids. Well, my
friend was letting himself in at the street door of his block of flats
when four armed men pushed past him saying, 'We've business to
do here,' and ran upstairs to another flat."

Puig took up the glass porró, that superb Catalan invention
whereby you pour wine in a thin stream through the air to fall on
the exact spot in your throat where it is really needed, and drank.

"Well?" I asked.

"They took the man away, I suppose, and his body was no doubt
found in the early morning on the Rabassada road and removed to

the Official Deposit. Fifty or sixty every morning, they find."

Now Puig is not in the least like T.; he is able to laugh, and he does not go around groaning like a pessimistic rabbit. He is financially ruined; he is a bourgeois; he does not know what he will do next; but he is not a tiresome defeatist or a crypto-fascist. But all the same he is living under the Terror, the only true Terror that exists in Spain. Let us look at this Terror.

It has nothing at all to do with the sexy pictures imagined in certain newspaper offices for the delight of repressed and perverted readers. I cannot prove anything so negative, but I am sure in my own mind that no nun has been raped or made to dance naked to the red mob. I know that priests have been killed, and in another chapter I have given reasons why this has happened. I am prepared to doubt the stories on the other side of Moors cutting off children's hands because they raised them in a communist salute. Moreover, (were I a fascist rebel), if every nun in Spain had been raped and burned alive, I would do all I could to hide it, since every atrocity must be laid to the account of those who brought the greatest of all atrocities and mother of all atrocities, civil war to Spain. People who gloat over atrocities can never begin to understand the true tragedy; those who see terror in terms of blood and bestiality cannot understand the silent unobtrusive Terror, quite unsensational, quite without sex-appeal, that really exists.

Puig said that fifty or sixty bodies of shot men and women were found on the Rabassada every morning. He was right, except that he had multiplied the real number by about ten. The simple fact is that through July and August and for all I know since, five or six people on an average every night were taken from their beds, pushed into cars, and driven to that lonely road amid the pines beyond Tibidabo, and executed. Five or six in a population of over a million; quite enough to make Q. and T. uneasy for their own future in spite of their relatively blameless past. It is largely the menace of these half-dozen murders nightly that keeps Barcelona so jumpy, although the nearest battlefront is a hundred miles and more away.

Outside the great city, beyond the overhanging mountains of

Tibidabo, and on the way to Sant Cugat, is the lovely lonely road, La Rabassada. It is typical of the fierce mysticism that we shall study later that, when you are going to take a capitalist or a fascist sympathiser for a ride, you nearly always go this way. You could bump him off in twenty different places, or throw him into the sea; for that matter you could let him die in bed; but you don't, you hurry him off to La Rabassada to be killed without hate. I listened to Puig's calm statements and thought. Here, it was clear, was something to be investigated. It was no mere atrocity story dished up for the literary palate of those who go to rubber-goods shops to buy the *Complete Works of Aristotle*, and the *History of the Rod*. Because there was something in it, the C.N.T. were handing out the bills begging men like Puig to stop being frightened. I started my investigations. I went first to talk to Kim. He was looking more like an El Greco portrait than ever, so that already my prophecy was coming true.

"How many people do the F.A.I. murder every night?" I asked.

"Fifty or a hundred," he said.

"How do you know?"

"Because you can see the bodies in the mortuary every morning."

"Have all the corpses been brought to the mortuary?"

"Except a very few, which may be thrown direct into the sea."

"Then the number of corpses in the mortuary is an accurate indication of the number of murders?"

"Certainly."

I went off to the mortuary, armed with an introduction to the Head of the Sanitary Department. "You cannot see the bodies of course," said he, "because they are buried at once, but you shall see the official list of all persons found dead in Barcelona district."

He brought me the typewritten list of entries into the morgue. There were here and there entries such as 'unknown person found La Rabassada.'

I asked him how many bodies are found dead nightly in normal times.

"Between eight and nine, including suicides, natural and accidental deaths, abandoned infants, homeless gipsies, and so on."

Now in the thirty-five days between July 19th and the day on which I looked at the list of deaths, this normal number would amount to 300. I counted the entries; there were five hundred, including the deaths in the first days of the fighting.

And so, allowing for unfound bodies, the Terror in Barcelona has led to perhaps 200 murders in over a month, not 2,000 or so, as Kim or Puig believed, and certainly not cartloads and piles, as the bloodier newspapers wish us to believe. This is of the same order of magnitude that we find in the normal night life of an American city of the same size as Barcelona.

Now a murder is a murder, of course, and 200 murders are 200 too many, even if that is only one-tenth the number of people known to have been shot in cold blood by the rebels in Badajoz within one hour. Two hundred people, mostly factory owners, had been shot in Barcelona. By whom?

By Murcian pistoleros called the F.A.I., comes Q.'s answer, pat. But it is not as easy as that. We can say that these murders, which are almost ritual murders, just as with the burned churches, seem to take place wherever anarcho-syndicalism is dominant, and seem to disappear where socialism and communism are the chief creeds; but I should hesitate to attribute them to the F.A.I. as a whole. It would be safer to say that a few dozen psycho-paths, using extremist political nihilism as a rationalisation, are doing the horrible business. That they have plenty of excuse can be seen if one takes the trouble to imagine the situation in which Barcelona finds itself. That there are a large number of capitalists who hope that the fascists will win goes without saying; I myself know dozens of them; that many of these are doing all that they can to sabotage the government is proved by what the daily raids bring to light in their houses. Anyone who remembers how in the Great War the mere possession of a foreign-sounding name was enough to bring suspicion to the most innocent human being, ought to see how in a civil war, where the other side is relying on mercenary Moors, Italian and German aeroplanes, and Légionaire riff-raff, the possession of guns, money, fascist symbols, must make a man peculiarly obnoxious to the desperately determined anti-fascist. If you lit a cigarette during an air raid in London in 1917, you were at once supposed to be signalling to the Zeppelins. Is it hard to imagine the psychological state that leads to the shooting of a man on the Rabassada, just to be on the safe side?

On the last Sunday in August, Puig and I strolled down the Paseo de Gràcia together. On every tree there was a F.A.I.-C.N.T. 'banda,' or manifesto. 'La Organización de Indisciplina' it was headed, and it told how the workers of Spain had succeeded in defeating Fascism thanks to the glorious life-giving power of Indiscipline. And now there were people so blind as to want to cramp and stultify this power by imposing the deathly influence of Discipline. If the worker was to triumph, he must resist this attempt to muzzle his free spirit, and substitute for it an Even Better Organisation of Indiscipline. I am not a theologian of the Religions of the Left, and I have no idea at all what the exact difference is between Discipline and Better Organised Indiscipline, but as I read the notice on the tree-trunk I realised once again the strange conflict between order and disorder, between reason and exuberance, that rages over the birth of new things. Could the murders on the Rabassada road be stopped best by Discipline or Organised Indiscipline? Would anarcho-syndicalism learn through having to do things, and would it then settle down to a Stalin-like routine? We saw a small group reading another recently pasted-up notice: "Anyone entering a private house," it says, "without written permission of the Anti-fascist Militia will be shot without trial." One more attempt to allay "aquesta temença que la petita i modesta burgesia té de nosaltres." Puig and I read it, and strolled for relaxation into the Circo Barcelonés.

It is a fine old-fashioned theatre, with tier on tier rising to the gods. We found that it was rather too early to detect signs of revolutionary art triumphing over the effete forms of bourgeois entertainment. In fact there was precisely the same set of acts one after the other as usual, beginning with a troupe of performing dogs, so clearly the product of cruelty as to make one feel sick. There was the acrobatic act with an absurdly plump little girl supporting her stage brothers and blowing us kisses. There were the pock-marked monumental gipsies who put over their song-and-dance superbly, in spite of every natural and artificial obstacle. There was a young male dancer who would make a fortune properly produced abroad and emancipated from his chocolate-box partner. There was an absolutely intolerable pair of double-entendrists, the woman fat, the man ghastly thin. There were several other dancers, singers, and entertainers. All without any exception, high and low, were receiving in accordance with the new bases of labour in the theatrical profession a flat fifteen pesetas a performance, with varying supplements if there were profits. The orchestra also and the scene-shifter received their fifteen pesetas. Heaven knows how long it will last.

Outside another theatre nearby we saw flowers on the pavement where an actor had been killed fighting fascism. In Barcelona all actors and actresses belong to the F.A.I.-C.N.T.

Puig and I plunged into the Fifth District in the direction of the Parallelo. If your Baedeker deigns to mention the Parallelo, it is probably under the name of the Calle del Marqués del Duero, but it would be stupid to ask a local inhabitant to direct you to the Marqués. If you look at a map of Barcelona and put your finger on the district between the Ramblas, the Parallelo, the Ronda San Pablo, the Ronda de San Antonio, and back to the Plaza de Catalunya by the Calle de Pelayo, you are touching the most tragic human cantonment in Europe to-day. The tourist is not encouraged to enter these dark alleys, for tourists do not want to see human sorrow unless it lives picturesquely in troglodytic caves. The Fifth District stinks of drains, contains sordid brothels visited by 'human beings,' as Puig said, once a week, filthy little cafés, deformed beggars, advertisements for quack cures of venereal disease, nearly every ugly reality that most of us like to forget. But, like hell, it is famous for better company. I do not believe that such bravery, such gentleness, such unselfish human comradeship is to be found anywhere in the West End of London; I am sure that human nature flowers more exquisitely out of the dung of the Fifth District than out of any Garden Suburb.

I remember the time years ago that Kim took me to see the night life of Barcelona. It does not compare in some respects with that of Paris; for it is not organised for American and English tourists. It is the brave attempt of the Insulted and Injured to laugh and enjoy their brief candle while it burns, with here and there a catering for the señoritos, like Kim and myself. We passed down dark streets ten feet wide where huge men stood in undershirts, their arms crossed, at sinister doors. Kim explained all about them, and I have read about everything in Havelock Ellis and Freud; yet brought up against these particular facts of life in the flesh, my imagination could scarcely grasp their social function. We went into a brothel and drank bad beer while girls in pink celanese petticoats and transparent gauze above the waist pathetically pretended to be spontaneous to sailors drunk and lonely enough to be deceived. We went to a dance-hall which was of a slightly higher grade, and danced with two girls who with exquisite courtesy asked if that was all we required and dropped the subject at once when we said that it was.

"Do you see that girl?" said my partner, between dances, pointing to a lonely figure, sitting at the other end of the dance floor. "She is Concepció. Poor dear, she is pregnant and cannot earn any money. Do you think you could afford to give her a peseta?"

She took the coin to Concepció, who bowed very gravely in my direction and then smiled her thanks. Her mother had called her after one of the seven glories of the Virgin Mary.

We put our heads into little café bars where the most hideous women were serving out anis and rum to habitués who seemed to have grown into the furniture. We watched little children playing singing games at doorsteps, while their older sisters stood offering themselves to the passers-by or talked to their grandmothers back from vespers.

Yes, there is plenty of vice in the Fifth District, but it is perhaps the least interesting of all the things to be found there. Because there is a brothel in the street, one should not forget the hundreds of other houses. Because they have almost nothing in the way of possessions, because they have no hope of ever getting out of this squalor, because they live so close together that no individual can wrap himself away from his neighbours in a veil of hypocrisy and pretence, the men and women of the Fifth District understand comradeship. Because they have so little to be proud of outside themselves, they must maintain personal dignity and make of mere existence something to be proud of. They do not fight against one another in the glorious free competition of bourgeois brigandage, they are united, comrade to comrade, by being victims of social injustice. And because society offers them so little, animal vitality comes to their aid and forces them to find enough joy to make life worth living. On Saturday and Sunday they pour out into the Parallelo from their rabbit warrens, to laugh and drink coffee, to listen to music and to dance.

The Parallelo is very wide; far wider than any London street. It is flanked for a mile or so with cafés and cabarets. Some cafés are so big that several thousand can be seated at once, some cabarets so small that an audience of a hundred feels crowded. I never saw anyone drunk on the Parallelo; I never saw a human being bad tempered; I never saw a quarrel; just tens of thousands of very poor men and women marvellously content with very little.

In the cabarets you pay a peseta or so for a 'consumición obligatoria,' a cup of coffee with some cheap rum in it. You sit on benches with your cap on and without collar or tie, and shout at all your friends in the audience. An amazingly energetic orchestra strikes up; a little blackboard is poked out from the wings announcing in white chalk that Conchita, or Pilar, or Dolores, or Mercedes is about to sing or dance; and Conchita, or Pilar, or Dolores, or Mercedes always proves to be fat, to be dressed in a chemise with a false diamond cross glittering between her breasts, in black trunks with which she tries to be provocative, and to have neither voice nor movement of any artistic value. She goes through her act hurling bright eyes to the farthest corner, rotating her stomach, shivering her shoulders and fatty appendages, presenting a hip to the front row, a row of aficianados, who try to whack at it with the evening newspaper or a teaspoon, whereat Conchita, or Pilar, or Dolores or Mercedes draws back with simulated anger, modesty, and contempt, and huskily starts the next verse. It is a brave attempt to scale Parnassus from below sea-level in the Fifth District.

As the evening proceeds the singers and dancers begin to have a little more to be said for them artistically. The first performers probably get nothing and are only there to display themselves. Some are beginners hoping for a starry career, others gave up all hope long ago but cling on because there is no alternative. You can see them afterwards sitting together in a loge, watching the programme as if it was all new to them. Members of the audience whistle up to them but they treat whistles with a haughty disdain fit for a princess in a fairy tale.

Even here there is a magic at work. Forget all you have ever learned about morals and aesthetics, throw away the prejudices that civilisation has been at pains to give you, and you will find bravery and even beauty in this attempt of the inhabitants of the Fifth District to live not by bread alone. Look at that blue-shirted worker, obviously tired out, yet with his eyes fixed upon the dancer. It is not lasciviousness that shines there, it is the unbroken human spirit struggling for light and air. There are people who expect the next few years to bring the downfall of civilisation. Civilisation, which is after all but a product of life and not life itself, may have to take the count because it has got out of training. But so long as the people of the Fifth District are undefeated, the living spirit of man will not die.

Take your Baedeker and follow me and Puig from the Circo Barcelonès. We have stood at the end of the performance while the Internationale is played and after it was finished a voice from the gallery shouted: "Visca Catalunya Llibertària," an anarcho-syndicalist shouting *in Catalan*. Last May T. told me that he had some hope even for the C.N.T., as workers were beginning to use Catalan. "Long live Libertarian Catalunya," which means by implication down with capitalism, down with communism, and to hell with the rest of Spain.

The Circo Barcelonés is in the Calle de Montserrat just behind the burned-out church of St. Josep. We turn past the Book Market at the end of the Ramblas into the Portal Santa Madrona. The Book Market is devoted to sexual and anarchist literature with a sprinkling of Marxist titles. *Nudism from the Marxist Viewpoint* evidently makes the best of both worlds. Someday I shall compare the attitude of the followers of Marx with that of the followers of Bakunin on this vital subject. The most popular English author is John Strachey.

We are behind the demolished Cuartel de Atarazanas where in the road we see a group of people surrounding a pile of flowers on the pavement. Look at their faces, the faces of 'human scum' trying to upset civilisation as represented by Hearst,[1] Rothermere, Lady Houston,[2] Oswald Mosley, Franco, Queipo de Llano,[3] the Moors, and the Foreign Legion. They are looking at the spot where Ascaso died. Ascaso, one of the three chief leaders of the F.A.I., killed throwing himself against the barracks opposite on the outbreak of the fascist rebellion. Those pots of flowers were brought and placed there by the dwellers in the Fifth District, their gift of beauty to dead bravery. Does it matter that the little pot in front may have been bought with the proceeds of prostitution, or that the little girls so silently staring at the deathbed of their comrade know more than is good for them of the facts of life? Are the two young men in the picture your idea of scum or degenerates? Do you think they waste time stripping nuns naked and making them dance? As I turned the film in my camera, a ghastly woman beckoned to me from the doorway behind, mechanically going through the motions of her trade.

Remembering this, I look at the photograph and think of a speech of a C.N.T. leader last August, explaining why he wished

---

1. William Randolph Hearst (1863-1951) was an American newspaper tycoon, who was regarded by the left as a Nazi sympathiser.

2. Lady Lucy Houston, (1857-1936) was a millonairess and adventuress who supported Mussolini.

3. Gonzalo Queipo de Llano (1875-1951) was a high ranking army officer, who initially supported the Popular Front but was distanced by their policies on agrarian reform and federalism, as well as the outlawing of the Falange Española. He joined Franco and Mola in their plot to overthrow the government and on 17 July 1936 took control of Seville.

to do away with all catholic education and set up free education instead. "They have had centuries to work in," he said, "they have money and privileges, and look how they have educated our miserable generation. Look at the señoritos of Barcelona, now fighting as fascists or secretly sympathising with the fascists. What idea of life have they got from their catholic education? Their idea of life and adventure is to invade our Fifth District and haunt the brothels, where our own daughters weighed down by poverty and social injustice are obliged to serve their pleasures. How can such education, which gives men nothing better in the way of desire, dare to claim to live? "   Oh yes, very unfair, no doubt, very unfair...

We pass on and turning to the right we reach the Parallelo. It is almost empty. The cabarets are shut. The cafés are plantations of empty tables. The men who used to pour out of the side-streets to find relief here are camped on the deserts of Aragon; the cynosure of their eyes is the Virgen del Pilar. I have seen this vast street crammed from end to end with circles of dancers losing their identity in the Sardana. I have watched the tram-cars clatter down upon the circles breaking them for a moment until they can reform behind. The Sardana, the unique expression in ordered movement of a communal spirit, has gone. At the juncture between Parallelo and Ronda de San Pablo is a huge barricade, guarding the Fifth District from any attack from the direction of the Plaza de Espanya and the barracks at Sans. Here was heavy fighting on July 18th and men killed all along the street. "No pasaron" is scrawled up on the walls.

We turn up the Ronda de San Pablo; we pass the Calle de Flores, which could not have been worse named, and are brought up full stop against the horrors of the Middle Ages. It is the Woman's Prison. You must see it to believe it. A red-and-black flag hangs from one of its windows and a notice, "This torture house was closed by the People, July, 1936." It was here that the unfortunates of the Fifth District were dragged for punishment; it was here that the daughters of the workers often learned the tricks of the trade to which they would be condemned for life. The Woman's

Prison had become a symbol of horror, and the very first thing that the C.N.T. demanded was that it should be pulled down and not one stone be left standing upon another. There it stands, deserted; though no doubt THEY will fill it up if they succeed in passing the barricade outside. It is strange to think that in England important newspapers, to say nothing of the gutter press, are encouraging their readers to hope for the day when the Woman's Prison in the Ronda de San Pablo will be filled with those who escape murder by German and Italian bombs or Moorish mercenaries. If only English and American people could see these dungeons and understand what it all stands for. If only they could substitute the three-dimensional human beings of the Fifth District for the puppets of their imagination.

We pass now a whole block of buildings burned out. In all their long frontage only two things remain, half the glass tube of an enormous thermometer, melted by the heat to a cocksure angle of 45°, and the advertisement of a German camera film. Why these escaped while all else perished, it is hard to understand. The building was the church and schools of St. Antonio Escolapios, from which the worthy religious folk fired on the crowd. They too have been purified by fire. They looked down the street too long with complacency on the Woman's Prison. We pass the market of Sant Antoni, remarkably busy considering that foreign newspapers assure us that there is a food shortage in Barcelona. We reach the University, where the rebels obtained entry by pretending to be loyal, and so we get back to the Plaza de Catalunya. We have encircled a black spot out of which comes a threat to our civilisation, but also an ultimate hope for the human spirit. It is impossible to take in the Fifth District honestly and with sympathy, without beginning to understand why some heroic men are nihilists.

I paid my visit to Hotel Gastronòmic No. 1. I went up to an extremely handsome red-shirted communist guard at the door and explained that I was an English anti-fascist who would like to see over the hotel.

"Well, comrade," he replied, "if you are English, let us talk English. I learned when I was a waiter in Washington, D.C." I stood and watched the long queue of poor people filing in to get their free meal. Each was supposed to have a card signed by the union responsible in the district where they lived. Some had no card.

"Now, comrade," said the guard to an old man who was hoping to get in without a card, "you have seen that notice which says you must have a card. Don't come to-morrow without one or I shall not let you in. You may pass now, comrade, but don't forget."

The old man hurried in. "You see," said the guard, "we must not be too severe. They have never had any education. But every day I pitch out two or three, who are obviously too well-fed to have a right to eat here. That old man was hungry." I caught sight of a big notice above my head. "Comrades," it read, "remember that you are serving your own people. Respect them." What a change from some weeks back! I had once stayed at the Ritz, the guest of an English archaeologist. He had been told that you must always ask if the fish has been caught this morning before eating it in Barcelona. He used to ask to speak to the head waiter.

"Was this fish caught this morning?" he asked at every meal.

"Yes, sir," the waiter replied and my host turned to me with great relief, and said, "You know you must always ask that, because otherwise the fish may not be safe to eat." An amazing exhibition of faith. I was not in the least surprised to find, when we drove out into the country, that my friend took off his hat whenever we met a magpie.

I thought back to those days; a few dyspetic overfed, over-rich people, served by many waiters. Now, thousands of half-starved folk served by exactly the same waiters; cooked for by the same cooks, members of the victorious FOSIG. We went inside. In the winter garden several hundred members of the theatrical union were being fed on boiled eggs and garbanzos. These were the girls who had worked so hard in the cabarets of the Parallelo, and the families for whom they had slaved. Gone were the grease-paint, the absurd arch looks; hidden the breasts, the chemise, and the trunks; a roomful of hungry working girls eating with great modesty and using the Ritz plate, the Ritz dishes, with delicacy and care. Remembering my American bourgeois friends who boasted of furnishing their one-room apartments from Pullman Cars and hotels, I was interested to hear that not one spoon had yet been lost from the hotel.

We went into the Ritz kitchens and into the wine-cellars stacked with innumerable bottles of vintage brands. A notice hung above the bins, "Comrades, anyone stealing what belongs to the People will be punished with revolutionary vigour." I thought of the tales of looting with which our papers regaled a hopeful public.

My guide, whose name was Borrull, brought up a little man of some sixty years, myopic, wizened, in the black and red cap of the C.N.T.-F.A.I.

"Here," said Borrull, "is Tomás. He speaks English, too."

"Yeh, I spik English," said Tomás, "I learn him when I cook on English steamer."

"Tomas is a member of the Sailors and Workers Committee for the Navy," said Borrull, whacking the newcomer on the shoulder. I liked the idea of Ship's-cook Tomás' promotion to more important duties.

"You're just the man I want to meet," I said. "I hear that a French battleship's crew mutinied in favour of the Spanish Popular Front, and they had to steam away to Toulon in a hurry."

"Yeh, I dare say," said Tomás, "we'll go for to see. You come back here at midnight and we will all drive together to the Port and ask the comrades there."

We did. At midnight I got into a fast Buick with Borrull and another communist, Tomás, and a Guardia de Asalto sitting on the hood. With rifles and bayonets sticking out of all windows we charged down the Ramblas at a sickening pace. Just before hitting the barricade opposite the burned-out church of St. Josep, we charged into the car in front shooting it sideways towards the armoured cars.

"By God's—" said the leader at the barricade, "what do you think you're doing?"

"We chanced to hit that car," said the driver.

The leader, a F.A.I.-C.N.T. militiaman, stared after the car in question. "Oh well," he said, "it's only a Pim-Pam—POUM car, that's nothing to worry about.[1] Pass comrades." We visited the Port and found that there had been no mutiny on any ship.

"And now, comrade," said Borrull, "you are an Englishman. You must have some whisky."

"Yeh," said Tomás. "And we have show you the best we have in Barcelona, the Ritz, now we show you the lowest of the low. Is that right?"

It was; so we plunged into the Fifth District. There we found a horrible café-bar, with a woman who had trachoma, and a cloud of smoke out of which appeared vague forms of militiamen who made room for us at their tables, while Tomás went behind the bar and fished out a bottle of Johnny Walker. "It's good whisky," he said, bending down to my ear, "it came from the Ritz."

We drank and talked. Someone asked me if I could dance. Yes, I said, both jazz and sardanas.

"I wish I could dance the sardana," said Borrull. I started to tell them how my wife was a professional actress and dancer and had made up a dance based on the Santa Espina in which a wayside image comes to life and gives a crucified peasant a sickle with which he destroys his enemies—fascism, militarism, and superstition.

"Gee," said the representative of the Sailors and Workers Committee for the Navy, "that's fine. She must come and dance it at the Ritz."

"If you like the sardana," said Borrull, "there's a book by an Englishman you should read called *Dancing Catalans*."

"I *wrote* it," I said.

"You wrote it," cried Borrull. "Comrade, comrade, shake hands. When I was in Washington D.C., I was very lonely for my country, and I read that book and it made me so happy that

---

1. POUM, *Partido Obrero d'Unificación Marxista*, the Workers' Party of Marxist Unification, was led by Andreu Nin, who had previously been Trotsky's secretary although they were by this time disassociated. Trotsky frequently condemned the movement. Although the party was labelled as Trotskyite by Stalinists it in fact had more in common with the left opposition in the Soviet Union. These divisions again weakened the left. It was anti-Stalinist and that was all that mattered, as Stalin was out to destroy all opponents on the left. It made a unified Popular Front impossible to achieve in reality.

I gave it to my three American girl-friends, all teachers, when I left America. And only the week before the rebellion I had a letter from one saying, 'I've read that book you gave me, and it made me understand the Catalans are very wonderful people, and I am sure they will do something great some day.' And, look! aren't we doing something great?" It was my greatest moment as a writer. My previous pot-boiler had sold 30,000 and this that I had put my soul into sold less than a thousand. But now in the Fifth District I found I had written it not only for myself but for Borrull.

There were no sardanas now in the Parallelo, for the men had gone away to the Front or were too busy at barricades. But, on the last Sunday in August, the People's massed bands played the Santa Espina in the Plaza de Catalunya and everywhere raised fists were tangled up with naked statues as the crowd listened and applauded.

There was the Santa Espina to please the Catalans, the Anarchist Hymn, the Syndicalist Hymn, the Internationale, and the deplorable republican Canción de Riego. I don't think the POUM have got a hymn.

And talking of music brings me to Chloe.

It would be irrelevant to explain precisely how Chloe got herself mixed up in the Spanish revolution. She is a singer of perhaps forty summers, and as a musician she is in the first rank, but her grasp of the rest of human experience is fragmentary and vague.

From the moment I reached Barcelona the certainty that I should run into Chloe hung about me like an impending doom; and sure enough, when I had ended my first telephone conversation to London, the operator rang the bell at once and said "There is a senyora here who wishes to speak to the senyor who has just spoken to London." When Chloe gets into touch with one, one does not stop to inquire how she does it.

She had merely rung up the Ministry of Culture because she felt I would be there, and she wanted my wife's address. Moreover, could she help me in any way whatever?

I went to see her. First impressions were good; she had lost a hundred pounds and had learned to dress well. Quite simply, but not very grammatically, she told me her tale, and I swear to repeat it without tampering with it.

On July 18th, she was warned by a friend that there was trouble starting. It seems that Chloe thought it would be in Morocco or somewhere like that. When they told her she must not go out of doors, she replied, "Don't be absurd; of course I am going to see my friend." Her friend lived in the Calle de Casp. She went to see him.

She found a line of cavalry across one end of the street looking down towards the Plaza de Catalunya. They had machine guns. "Go indoors," one shouted. "Why should I?" said Chloe. "Look, there are two of them," said another, as he sighted a couple of rebels in the Square.

Chloe marched up to him. "What do you mean?" she said. "Two what?" This was too much for the officer, who dismounted and pushed Chloe against the railings so that his companions could fire. Someone hauled Chloe indoors and she recovered consciousness later in the day, while perfect strangers explained that she had got between the opposing forces at the very moment they were firing the first shots.

From then on life had many surprises for Chloe, and I would add for almost anyone who came into contact with her. Early on while shooting was still fairly frequent, Chloe decided she could not stop indoors any longer, so at midnight she went for a walk up the Calle de Balmes.

The Calle de Balmes is even now a jumpy sort of place where militiamen stop you and ask questions, but in the first week it was a communication-trench rather than a city street. Chloe strolled along towards the mountains. She reached a barricade. Two militiamen challenged her.

"Where are you going?"

"Nowhere, I'm just walking.

"And do you know," Chloe said to me, "I think they thought I was mad."

"What do you mean, just walking? What are you doing here?"

"Why, I've always enjoyed walking in the Calle de Balmes whenever I have been in Barcelona before, and as they haven't allowed me out for days because of all this revolution, I thought I'd go for a stroll to-night."

"Let us see your papers."

"Papers?"

"Yes, haven't you got any papers?"

Chloe searched in her bag. "The only paper I've got is this programme of Catalan folk-songs I sang in London last year."

Silence fell over the barricade, jaws and rifles dropped, the militia, anarchists, syndicalists, communists, socialists, and republicans looked at one another.

"Well, madam, we are very sorry for troubling you," said one at last. "You must allow us to take you back in a car."

So Chloe found herself in a car, with rifles sticking out of all windows and militiamen still wondering if they were dreaming.

All went well, though conversation was difficult, until they got to the next barricade. The car was challenged. The militiamen showed their papers. "Who is the woman?"

"She is a foreign lady we are going to take home."

"Well, that may be true. Where are her papers?"

"She hasn't got any."

"Hasn't any papers! What do you mean? How are we to know that she isn't a prostitute?" I might say that strenuous efforts were being made to prevent the use of cars by militiamen for immoral purposes. Chloe came to the rescue. "No, I'm not a prostitute," she said, "and I can prove it. Here is a programme of Catalan folk-songs I sang in London last year, it's the only document I've got, but won't that do?" Silence fell on this barricade also. Eventually, with infinite courtesy, they took her home. I was a little bit worried about Chloe, lonely, distraught unhappy creature. But when I went to say good-bye, she asked me for the name of a good lawyer so that she could make her will in case she wanted to commit suicide. That was a relief; no one who has asked my help in arranging it has ever committed suicide yet.

How will it all end? As I write, at the close of October, Catalunya is the only region of Spain completely free of fascists.

Last night I had a Spanish meal in London. The waiter, a Catalan, said to me anxiously: "What do you think will happen? To Catalunya, I mean, I care not for Spain."

This morning a communist said to me, "Isn't it true that the Catalans are only interested in saving their skins? Surely they could have helped Madrid?"

A week ago at a meeting for Spanish Medical Aid a questioner, probably a communist, asked: "Why don't you send the ambulances where they are needed, instead of to Catalunya?"

What will happen to anarcho-syndicalism? Will Italy take on the job of pacifying Barcelona from her new colony and naval base, Majorca? When all these questions come I find myself thinking of the man whom I believe to be the greatest man in Catalunya today, President Companys.

I had never liked the look of him. He is too much like those caricatures of the German Crown Prince that helped us to win the war to save democracy.

A weak man, I thought, and a sentimentalist. I was completely wrong. I went to see him in his private reception room at the Generalitat. I waited for an hour while a fussy French journalist with two movie operators and a still cameraman and an interpreter fidgeted and perspired. At last the whole cavalcade rushed off to develop things. Companys leaned back in his chair and smiled. A foreigner who could speak to him in Catalan. He relaxed. The conversation that followed seems to me to contain a statement of certain political truths of the first importance to any student of politics in this changing world, and I will repeat it as I wrote it down.

Myself: Is it possible, in the event of Madrid falling to the Fascists, to imagine a Fascist Spain under the influence of Italy, and an anarcho-syndicalist Catalunya opposing it and holding its own?

Companys: I deny absolutely that the Fascists can win anywhere in Spain. (These were the days before 'non-intervention' had had its conspicuous success.) We have the industrial wealth, the supplies of

LA NUEVA HISTORIA DE ESPAÑA

CON EL GOBIERNO DE AZAÑA

Political strip cartoon, Madrid, May 1st 1936.

Extremaduran peasant, May 1936.

Port de la Selva, May 1936.

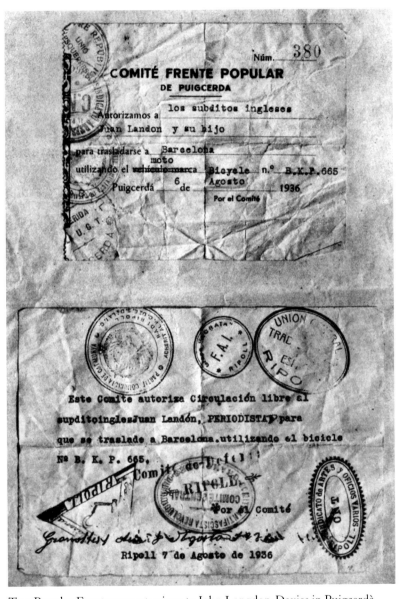

Two Popular Front passports given to John Langdon-Davies in Puigcerdà, northern Spain, and Ripoll, August 1936.

Armoured car and the men
and women who made it,
Barcelona, August 1936.

Assassinations, Barcelona, 19 July 1936.

The retaurant at the Ritz,
Barcelona is transformed into a
worker's canteen, Gastronomic Nº1,
August 1936.

Proclamation against murder, Barcelona, August 1936.

Robin Langdon-Davies, Barcelona, August, 1936.

Paco with John Langdon-Davies, August 1936.

The Alcazar, Toledo, August 1936.

The Plaza de Zucodover, Toledo, August 1936.

Firing from the barricades, Toledo, August 1936.

The last Republican barricade, Toledo, August 1936.

arms, and the morale. But for the sake of argument suppose Madrid were to fall, it would never in any circumstances be possible for Fascism to win here except by the death of every man in Catalunya. I say this because there is no economic class left to help Fascism. The capitalist bourgeoisie is ruined through its own folly, and it is impossible to sow dissension between us, the *petite bourgeoisie*, and the proletariat.

Myself: Is Catalunya now in fact and in law independent of Madrid?

Companys: No. The common front of anti-fascism has drawn us closer to the rest of Spain than ever before. In face of the common danger of Fascism the Madrid Government has given us independence of action, but we are making no attempt to make capital out of it. When it is all over we shall, however, expect to retain the greater freedom that the moment has put in our hand.

Myself: Has the increasing intervention of the C.N.T. in government diminished the power of the Catalan democratic bourgeois government?

Companys: No. The C.N.T. has taken over, along with other bodies within the Popular Front, the duties forsaken by the rebel army of policing and protecting society, and has turned itself into a weapon in the hands of the democratic government. Betrayed by the normal guardians of law and order we have turned to the proletariat for protection.

Myself: But are you not afraid that the proletariat will turn on the bourgeoisie and destroy it after Fascism has been defeated ?

Companys: You must remember that Catalan bourgeoisie of to-day is not the capitalist bourgeoisie of other democratic countries. That has been expropriated by us in co-operation with the proletariat. Capitalism as we understood it before is dead. It committed suicide by illegal rebellion. Therefore there is no vested interest represented by my bourgeois government. We are that part of the middle class which the capitalists try to destroy by fascism. We are therefore at one with the proletariat. We may as individuals have private interests to lose, but our mission is one of service. We do not expect to retain a separate set of privileges. We hope to direct the evolution of coming changes and to maintain democratic individual rights in doing so, but we shall never attempt to oppose progress in economic and social questions.

Myself: Have you a programme of economic reforms mapped out?

Companys: No. We believe that we must accept facts as they arise and help necessary change along the smoothest channels. We have already facilitated the collectivisation of industry, beginning with the public services, and our sole function as a government is to express the Catalan people's will in whatever form that will may be cast. The days of national emotionalism are gone, and we must represent the Catalan people not by fighting for Separatism only but by carrying out their economic demands.

Myself: Perhaps the Catalan will is to be anarcho-syndicalist. Will the Catalan bourgeois government accept this?

Companys: As I see it, bourgeois democracy, cleansed of capitalist vested interests, has no right to oppose anything that is the will of the people. It may be Anarcho-syndicalism, and if so the bourgeoisie must accept it.

Myself: It would be true, would it not, to say that the present situation is due to the arming of the Proletariat on July 9th. Was it you, as President, who armed them?

Companys: No. They armed themselves. We had no store of arms to give them. They conquered their arms, and we were glad that they should do so, because only so could the Catalan Government be saved.

You must remember that it is easy to exaggerate the number of workers who are really armed. There are not enough arms to go round. I doubt if the anti-fascist militia have more than six or seven thousand rifles.

Let us give that conversation its proper background. President Companys is head of the Catalan Generalitat occupying the same position in relation to it as Azaña does to the Madrid Government.[1] When the Fascist revolt broke out, the presidency and the office of prime minister were identical, and Companys was the head of a party government. In order to preserve the sense of unity, the constitution was changed and Companys became a president freed from party governmental functions so that he might be a symbol of national unity. This change was heralded in some English newspapers as the kicking out of Companys by the extremists.

Companys is ideal for his position since he understands anarcho-syndicalism as no other bourgeois can. For many years he acted as a lawyer for the C.N.T. and defended the Trades Unions in legal disputes over strikes, labour conditions, alleged acts of terror. He is entirely trusted and respected by the worker. Ever since the rebellion Companys has insisted in having the C.N.T. take part in the responsibilities of government. Of course, short-sighted people have thought that this meant that the Generalitat was become a mere shadow in the hands of the C.N.T. But the wisdom of Companys has borne fruit. He has tied down the anti-political philosophers to the job of having to organise and to govern.

If he had not vigorously supported the policy of making anarcho-syndicalists responsible for what happened, they would have blamed the bourgeoisie for anything that went wrong; as it is they are themselves forced to justify their existence by learning how to keep public order; they have to control their own extremists. If ever a split comes, all the responsible elements in the C.N.T. will be on the side of order and organisation.

That in itself is an achievement, but Companys has something else to his credit that is even more significant. He has led the lower-middle class, the shop-keeper, the office worker, the professional man, the small fellow generally, to a position where their political and economic interests are seen to be on the side of the workers. When we realise that Fascism has succeeded elsewhere in using all these groups as pawns for the larger capitalists, we see how

---

1. Manuel Azaña (1880-1940) was a liberal, anti-clerical politician founder of the Republican Party and the Popular Front. As Prime Minister 1931-1933, he introduced agrarian reform, regional autonomy, and curtailed the influence of the Church in education. More significantly he cut the number of generals in the army and closed the military training school at Saragossa, which was headed by General Franco. His appointment as President in May 1939 seriously alienated the right and polarised the country. Immediately after his appointment Spanish army officers began plotting to overthrow the Popular Front government.

important such a political event is for European civilisation.

We were becoming used to the idea that the middle class could always be used to destroy democracy; in the fog of civil war Catalunya is conducting an experiment which may produce a different result. When we realise that Catalunya produces half the industrial and agricultural wealth in Spain, and that Barcelona is the chief port on the Mediterranean, we realise the value of this. Upon the ability of Companys to organise a destiny for the Catalan bourgeoisie, which shall land them in precisely the opposite direction to that taken by the same economic class elsewhere, depends the future evolution of democracy in the Mediterranean. For every thousand that has heard of Hitler and Mussolini probably only one has heard of Companys; but that does not alter the fact that he is one of the key-men in Europe to-day.

Next day I went to see Kim off to Marseilles on an Air France plane. The office is in the Paseo de Gràcia just round the corner from the headquarters of the Women's Anti-fascist Militia.

Kim was not there, of course, and I stood and watched the anti-fascist WAACS. I suppose many of my readers do not remember the WAACS or the jokes about them. Well, just the same jokes are current about the women militia. The brothels of the Fifth District are half empty, and their occupants are assisting at the Zaragoza front, and in consequence nearly all the militiamen have syphilis and cannot take Zaragoza! That is one way of looking at things, and not a very sensible one either. It makes no allowance, for example, for the length of the period of incubation. It also makes no allowance for human nature, logic, or facts. On the other hand, memories of the War, the one and only real War, made me unsympathetic with many manifestations of female belligerence in Barcelona. I thought of the whores on the London music-hall stage singing recruiting songs, the hiring of Aphrodite to help the work of Ares, which I had always felt to be hitting below the belt, and I stared at the recruiting poster with the young idealised militia woman pointing her scornful finger at the slackers in the Paseo.

She was a likeable girl, this recruiting poster lady, in her blue overalls, with little round breasts, well-painted lips, and plucked eyebrows. I tried to think back to the British Bellonas of 1914; how out of date their appeal would be to-day; how cold their figures and clothes would leave us.

Just then a detachment of militia marched by. They happened to belong to a communist column and carried the sickle-and-hammer. In the middle of the column

marched thirty or forty girls, not in the least like the poster lady; dressed identically with the men in blue overalls, a few with rifles, but most with cooking utensils strapped to them.

Here was the reality, which is astonishing enough in its own way without romantic frillery. For the reality is that the fascist rebellion, by putting civilisation in the keeping of the workers, has brought real sex equality to the streets of Barcelona. These girls were not asking for any special treatment on account of their sex; they had forgotten the he and she; just as syndicalist, socialist, and republican had scrapped their differences, so maleness and femaleness had gone into obscurity as irrelevant to the moment.

It is not only the existence of women in the militia that has brought sex equality to Barcelona, it is the invasion of the Ramblas by the Parallelo. The workers understand sex equality, because to them a woman is not a form of property and she is not a parasite. If the Parallelo could express itself, it would tell you that there is very little difference between a prostitute in the Fifth District and the wife of a wealthy man who does nothing but grace her husband's bed and board; the commodity both sell is the same; and the prostitute rather despises her respectable sister for having to be such a hypocrite and for so often deceiving her pay-master.

As I thought about the women militia I saw a lady with two little dogs walking up and down outside the Air France office. There was much to dislike about her from the dogs upwards; but to see anyone wilfully bearing the signs of wealth, jewels, luxury clothes, luxury puppies, in the midst of anarcho-syndicalism triumphant appealed in a way that it would not have done, at least to me, in Regent Street. The left hand puppy sniffed at a militia woman's overalls and had to be dragged away. When Kim did arrive, the lady with the dogs at once went up to him and asked him a question, and he beckoned to me to come and be introduced. "This is Senyora X., and this is my good friend, John; he is an Englishman and very anti-fascist." Senyora X. bowed. "But you can have complete confidence in him." Senora X. bowed again, and invited me to visit her. "I had five members of the F.A.I. visit me last night," she said.

"I hope they behaved well," I said.

"At first they were rather rude. They wanted to find out where my son was, and, of course, my son is on the *Uruguay* (the prison ship) though I did not tell them. One of them said that the mothers of fascists ought to be shot. 'Very well,' I answered, 'if you want to shoot me it ought not to be difficult, you are five armed men and I am one unarmed woman.' Then we all laughed, and I gave them a drink, and when they left we were all friends and they apologised for having troubled me." There was a certain insolent pride about the lady which one respected. Kim and I walked up the street together: "She is one of those horrible people," he said, "but she is quite nice in a way."

"Why are you going to Marseilles?"

"I have business for some of my clients who have gone abroad. There is a decree that any property not reclaimed by émigrés before August 15th will be expropriated, and I must try to get power of attorney to act."

It was not until later that Kim told me that he had received warning that he was on the list of those to be taken out to La Rabassada. He had supported a movement a few months before to make a coup d'état and appoint Indalecio Prieto as a sort of liberal dictator. I do not know whether Prieto ever even heard of the plot; but it was enough to forfeit Kim's life, since some of those responsible had since gone over to the fascists. Kim was going into exile, and none too soon. He was arrested at the airport and bluffed his way through. We had waved good-bye to him, and the lady with the dogs had marched off head in air, smoking a cigarette; every line of her body expressing contempt. Her son was on the prison ship and they could shoot her if they liked.

I saw Kim next in London, more like an El Greco portrait than ever. He was busy doing legal work for fascist émigrés.

"What can I do?" he said, "I am a Spaniard, and I cannot forsake my people in this terrible moment. I am not a fascist and I hate these horrible people. But I cannot go back to Barcelona, for they will shoot me, and as a Spaniard I cannot do nothing. So I will see if I can help some individuals. I must do something. I cannot run away.

"One thing, when it is all over, I shall live in England and sell pictures. If the anti-fascists win my work is finished, and I will not live in Spain if the horrible fascists win."

"But why not start a picture business now in London and leave all this misery alone?"

"That would be running away from my people."

"But you cannot help fascists if you have no sympathy with them."

"I hate them, but I will try to protect some of them from being killed. I mean the innocent ones. Some of my relatives have been shot already by the F.A.I., my cousin for example; but I do not mind that; he was a very bad employer and he deserved it; but perhaps I can help some of the others who are innocent."

"What will you do?"

"I will fly to Paris and see what I can do. One thing I am glad for; when this is over I shall never be a lawyer again. Last year in Barcelona I earned more than three thousand pounds; I was becoming a wealthy man and I hate myself. Now I am free. I will save my pictures and books, and I will never be a lawyer again."

And then I had a letter from Kim in Portugal. "I consider you one of my best friends and human enough not to be hard on my actual stupidity. One thing is sure, and that is that once I shall have helped my people—I shall go abroad to start a new life and to be what I want to be. But do not misjudge me, and when I see you I shall tell you everything and I expect you shall forgive me."

What a horrible mess it all is. But we had all better get used to the fact that when our trouble comes many of our best friends and some of the finest among them will go over to the other side. I do not know where Kim is, or what he is doing, but if he has joined the Moors, and Juan March, and Queipo de Llano, and Franco it is one more ghastly atrocity, a spiritual rape to be laid against those who brought civil war to Spain.

CHAPTER 5
THE BURNING OF THE CHURCHES[1]

The astounding truth is that in all loyal Spain—and that is nearly all Spain—there is not one Catholic church open, and in some parts there may never be a Catholic church reopened unless the Moors save Christianity.

Spain, more Catholic than the Pope, has rooted out the sacred symbols. Let us consider the matter in a manner free of cant.

Who burned the churches? Why did they burn the churches?

Not Moscow. They burned churches in Spain long before Moscow was invented. Moscow has as much to do with it as with Oliver Cromwell's men when they knocked the heads off all the saints in Norfolk churches. Indeed, one feels in Spain to-day that there is a wind abroad which blows from the same quarter as that which inspired our Puritan ancestors.

"They," whoever they are, burned the churches, not because

---

1. The passion with which John Langdon-Davies writes here may surprise contemporary readers but it is important to remember that the Catholic Church had been one of the pillars of the Castilian monarchy. It played a role similar to that of the Orthodox Church in Russia in the run up to the revolution which was a bulwark of Tsarism and autocracy. For many Spaniards, the only way to reform Spain was to literally smash the power of the Church.

they did not believe in the symbols painted and plastered all over them, but because they did believe most terribly in them, and considered them to be enemies to be overcome with their own magic. Remember that black magic is the other people's magic, and that if you believe in any magic at all you believe as much in the other people's as in your own.

In my own village, high up in the Pyrenees, the patron saint was an unfortunate mortal named Eudald. On his day we had a procession in the morning, and dancing, movies, picnic, and fireworks in the afternoon. We were lucky to possess a considerable portion of the saint's incorruptible earthly abode. We kept it, of course, in his church, and I have no doubt that old ladies and others with well-developed mystical sensibilities have derived great comfort from its protective presence. Some of these may have loved him, but the majority only feared him; more feared him, it is very certain, than disbelieved in him. I am talking, here, of the workers and ordinary folk in the village and the peasants round about. No doubt the properly-instructed people, who had been well grounded in correct religious attitudes, were able to put St Eudald in his proper place as a religious fact.

But I am sure that when it came to organizing a workers' union, or preparing a strike, or any other act against what priests and their chief supporters are apt to call law and order, the simple workers felt that they had the magic of St Eudald working against them. And further, they did not see their organizing simply as a method of increasing their power of collective bargaining with their employers; they saw it as the organizing of a counter-magic against the Eudaldian magic. They set up their own symbols against his. Instead of greeting one another with "Adiós," they greeted one another with "Salud".

Now I have never heard an English or American socialist or communist object to saying "good-bye," or demand that a corruption of "Marx-be-with-you" should take the place of a corruption of "God-be-with-you"; but precisely that seems a point of real importance to an anarcho-syndicalist. (Of course, he would approve as little of Marx as of God, and he would favour Bakunin-be-with-you, if Salud were not so much more euphonious.)

It is as much as one's life is worth to use the symbol of the other people, "adiós", to an anarcho-syndicalist. It is the sort of thing that brands you forever. Poor Joan had my full sympathy when he arrived at luncheon one day quite out of humour. We knew that, socialist as he was, he was saddled with the job of protecting his monk brother. He used to bring him to our table sometimes, looking like a fundamentally healthy plant suffering from lack of light and air. The monk was naturally a little dazed, and never added much to the conversation. But on this day Joan had parked him somewhere else and came alone very much disgruntled. What was the matter?

"I was walking down the Ramblas with my brother," he said; "and what do you think happened? I sneezed, and Mateu said, ' Jesús!' 'My God,' I said, 'don't you know you have to say "Salud" nowadays?'"

There you have it. For hundreds of years a sneeze has been regarded as dangerous, especially if it has meant the loss of a little moisture, for some evil spirit may get hold of the moisture and do you wrong. So your friend protects you as you sneeze with a holy name. To-day the holy symbol is Salud. In Spain, I have seen many a person cross his mouth with a finger to prevent a devil entering the wide gate of a yawn. Those people to-day have not merely ceased to believe in the efficacy of the sign of the cross and left it at that; they have substituted the sign of the sickle and hammer. I have not seen any people "cross" themselves in the shape of a sickle and hammer, but it would not surprise me in the least to hear that it is done.

But to return to St Eudald. On earth he had had some unpleasant experiences culminating in a carefully thought-out martyrdom. They had taken a handful or so of penny nails, knocked them into the sides of a barrel, placed Eudald inside, and rolled the barrel downhill. It was a popular trick in those days, and was often used to discomfort the true believers, but it must have been particularly striking in the minds of our villagers by reason of the very long and steep declines that surrounded their Pyrenean abode. You gazed up at the Chapel on Catllar on one side and on the green slopes of Taga on the other, and felt for St Eudald more and more.

It seems that Eudald, who, one must feel sure, forgave his enemies, could never quite forgive a nail; and, on one of his feast day processions, as the holy coffin was being carried down a street in which there was a nail-shop, the sight or smell of nails proved altogether too much for him, and he reacted in a way which surprised everyone present. To their dismay the reverent bearers suddenly found the coffin become so excessively heavy that they had to drop it then and there. The event is common knowledge. If the opinion of a multitude of old women, *ratas de iglesia*, is to be believed, there can be no doubt about it. St Eudald did his little bit of magic, and thereby, though his action had no great value except as a demonstration, went up in everybody's estimation.

There came in due course the tragic night of July 18th. The battle of symbols was at its height. The men of the new symbols had come to destroy the old. It was I.X. . versus F.A.I. This village, being more intelligent than some, resolved to save the structure of its church and to take the furniture elsewhere to burn. My friend Puig was there watching.

Six triumphant anarchists bore St Eudald on their shoulders to his second, but probably less painful, martyrdom. The appointed place was approached by way of the street with a nail-shop, and, as they passed the shop, Puig saw six anarchists put their disengaged hands to their belts, draw six revolvers, point them threateningly in the direction of the Saint, while one said: "If you dare get heavy, we'll shoot you." The new symbols proved definitely in the ascendant, and St Eudald, disheartened, tried no experiments with mass or density.

This story is true; it is also very helpful if we wish to understand the attack on the Church which has been so incredibly complete. Eudald, the capitalist-fascist magic-maker was caught at last; burn him as quick as you can and put a stop for all time to any chance of his using spells again. The priests are your enemies, they work evil against you with their magic and their symbols; burn their symbols and leave them impotent to harm you anymore. You have been told a thousand times by the priests that rebellion is as the sin of witchcraft. Very well, the witchcraft of your symbols can prevail at last against the witchcraft of theirs; burn their magical aids. You cannot have a revolution without destroying the spiritual sources of their power. The fascists have arms and gold, but they have also got as allies the powers of the air, principalities and dominations; burn the crucifixes, burn the altars, burn the relics, burn the images, for it is these that are being used to keep you under the thrall of the fascist. Let F.A.I. and C.N.T. and Salud and Sickle-and-Hammer defeat the supernatural allies, and you will be able to destroy the fascist with your own strong arm.

It was not the ordinary villager in the Pyrenees who on the night of July 18th set fire to his church. Nobody really knows who did. It seems that the mystical anti- religionists had planned the attack on the symbols, and that they were at first concentrated in the larger towns. When the news came that the fascists and the military had risen to destroy the democratic government, they mustered their burning squads and drove to every village exhorting the inhabitants to destroy their spiritual enemies as well as their material.

Sometimes they met with resistance and sometimes with hesitation. In one small mountain town they persuaded the villagers to pile up all the church furniture in the market square, but nobody quite liked to put a match to the pile. The villagers were convinced that they must fight the fascists, and that they could only do this by making their own revolution, but it was a brave thing to risk the chance that even now the symbols they wished to destroy might have the power to hit back.

In the gathering dusk excited groups tore down the stucco and imitation-marble chapels and piled gilded angels upon gilded virgins, while the loudspeaker at the village café blared forth exhortation and news from Barcelona and Madrid. But when the time came for a match to light the flames everybody drew back; it was all very well, this concerted action of the whole community, or at least of a solid group within the community, but when it came to

one individual action which might possibly bring down an aveng-
ing fire from heaven, that was another matter. The villagers were
nonplussed; they wanted to make their revolution, they agreed
that you could not win a revolution without destroying the things
with which your opponents made witchcraft, but—where was the
one supremely brave man needed?

At last a wise suggestion was made. "I know what we will do,"
said a city father, "we will pass round the hat, make a collection,
and give it to a gipsy to light the pile." They collected six pesetas
and forty-five centimos, they hired a gipsy, and stood round as he
lit the fire. In the morning nothing was left of the priests' black
magic but charred fragments; the rest was dissipated to the upper
air, leaving the lower branches of the trees in the market-place
scorched and brown.

If you wonder, why a gipsy? You should remember that a gipsy,
not being a Christian, not being bound and delivered over to the
priests' magic by way of water in baptism and the laying on of
hands, need not fear contact with the symbolic baubles. They had
no power for evil or for good over one who did not belong to la
raza blanca, la raza cristiana, scarcely to *la raza humana*.

In the larger towns it was possible to stop the fanatical holocaust. In Gerona, for example, the sacred objects were saved by
the armed authorities, to be used later for a more intelligent attack
upon degenerate religious ideas. In Gerona is a better saint than
Eudald, a saint with a remarkable military career as well as a useful record of endeavour in certain social problems. San Narcisco,
whose body has long been the glory of the splendid Gothic church
of San Feliu was bishop of Gerona sixteen hundred years ago. "San
Narcisco," says the irrepressible Richard Ford, "with his deacon
Feliu, when at Augsburg, put up by mischance at a 'Burdell,' and
there wrought his first miracle by converting Afra, his hostess,
and three of her frail ladies, Digna, Eumenia and Eutropia, 'worthy, well-behaved and well-speaking' damsels, who afterwards
swelled the list of Mrs. Jameson's 'Bienheureuses Pécheresses.'"

He came back to Spain, was martyred, and remained hidden
to human eyes until angels revealed the whereabouts of his body

to Charlemagne, who presented it to the frontier town of Gerona which, from its exposed position, needed as good a network of fortifications, spiritual as well as material, as could be arranged. San Narcisco proved a veritable godsend, and on more than one occasion helped the city against invaders more successfully than its living defenders. One of his most signal successes was on October 5th, 1285. Philip le Hardi invaded Catalunya in order to avenge the Sicilian Vespers, and had no difficulty whatever in getting through the walls and ramparts and actually into the church where the Saint reposed. Turning his attention to the first relaxation of military invaders, he began to pick off the silver from the saintly tomb. At once there was an angry buzz-buzz, and a plague of flies issued forth from the sainted tactician within. "The clerical authorities differ as to their colour, some affirming that they were white, others that they were tri-coloured blue, green and red, while Father Roig is positive that they were half-green, half-blue, with a red stripe down their backs." Whatever the colours, they flew; their effect was devastating: 24,000 horses, and 40,000 Frenchmen died at once, and Gerona was relieved; except of the task of disentangling itself from the mass of rotting corpses.

In 1653 the French, under La Mothe Houdaincourt, were once more at the gates of Gerona, and once more *las moscas de San Narciso* did their duty; twenty thousand horses died in agony. When, thirty-one years later, the French army came again, San Narcisco changed his tactics. He concentrated all his magic into one huge horrible fly, whereat the whole army either died or ran away.

This last miracle was in some ways the most important of the three, since it was duly authenticated by the town clerk, and Pope Innocent XI decreed a national thanksgiving to Narcís, the saviour of Spain.

Napoleon came; an adversary fit to try the mettle of this insectiferous saint. "The local Junta in 1808 declared this Hercules Muscarius, this Beelzebub, to be their captain-general; and on his tomb was laid the staff of command, in order that this *glorioso y invicto martir* as *especialisimo protector y generalisimo* might infuse *luces y valor*, intelligence and courage, into mortal Spanish generals." The whole decree was republished in 1832 (!) and it was signed by the man who opposed the giving of the supreme command to the Duke of Wellington. But if Gerona preferred to trust to the saint who could produce such gaudy aerial squadrons, she was not alone in her distrust of an English military genius, for at the other end of the Peninsula the Junta of Cadiz rejected the Duke and gave its vote to Santa Theresa.

It will be seen that San Narcisco was a particularly powerful wizard, and I have often watched the devotion accorded him by the townsfolk, especially the grandmothers. To have an incorruptible saint capable of destroying French armies is all very well, but on the night of July 18th it was not so satisfactory to think of that body cogitating perhaps an emission of fascist flies. But Gerona, being a capital city, was more educated than some smaller places, and the authorities saved the captain-general from the flames for a better end. They appointed a committee of doctors and lawyers to prise open the lid and to report on the condition of the tissues preserved within. They turned out to be mostly parchment, leather, and wood. Thus the fascists lost a valuable moral support; the anti-fascist militia of Gerona breathed again.

Now there is a type of person who feels that, although he does not believe in the hanky-panky of San Narcisco, it is very bad form indeed to show it up. It was the same during the Great War. An honest man advertised in the papers that he would give a large sum of money to a war charity if anyone could bring him a Belgian child who had had his hands cut off by a German. Nobody ever came with the desired exhibit, and a howl of protest went up at the unpatriotic pro-German behaviour of a man who loved truth enough to want to unmask a foul piece of propaganda. Ought San Narcisco to have been left alone, or ought the opportunity to have been taken to clean out another corner of the human mind long left dusty with superstition? Unfortunately for religion in Spain, it has relied too much on conjuring tricks which can be exposed.

New magic letters for old. The rival witchcrafts in a final struggle. Some years ago I was in Santiago de Compostela, the rainiest and one of the holiest cities in western Europe. Outside a church

I bought a little pocket of coloured cloth containing a paper on which was printed a cross. In the cross you will see letters, magic letters, V.R.S.N.S.M.V.S.M.Q.L.I.V.B.C.S.S.M.L.N.D.S.M.D. Near the bottom is the "Explanation of the letters of the Cross."

"Get thee behind me, Satan, never canst thou persuade me to vanity, thy libations are evil, thy potations verily poison. May the holy cross be my light, may the Serpent not be my Leader."

This 'explanation' is in Latin, and the Compostelans who bought this paper and hung it round their necks can read very little Castilian and certainly less Latin. Though the words are utterly meaningless to them, they can understand the shape of the Cross and they can spell out the letters written on it, and they are led to believe that, by having this paper on their person, they will acquire merit of some sort.

The magic paper is sold them *con la aprobacion eclesiastica*, with ecclesiastical approval. Beneath this statement is a "Notice."

On giving his authorization for the circulating of these WRITINGS, by decree of June 11th, 1894, the most excellent and most reverent Archbishop of Santiago deigned to state the following: "Let the faithful take note that to carry reverently this Cross and Ejaculatory is an act of devotion; but to attribute to it the status of *infallible act* or to use these for evil ends, is an act of superstition, and therefore a sin."

It is added that the paper "has no effect without the competent blessing."

To put it concisely and bluntly—the people of Santiago are encouraged by their Archbishop to believe that, if they wear these magic letters round their neck, it will do them some sort of good, always provided they have paid a local priest to confer magic power on the letters in the appropriate manner. It is clear that the purchasers will be illiterate and uninstructed in Latin; all they will know is that the letters are magical, that they have been blessed by the priest, and that they have supernatural powers, just as a piece of steel rubbed with a loadstone has magnetic powers. They have been left in the same frame of mind as the African savages who, on being given a piece of paper which we should call a receipt for their produce and finding that they could exchange this piece of paper for goods at the company store, concluded that if only they could learn to write the magic signs themselves they would be able to get the goods without having to bother about hunting or collecting ivory.

Well, thanks to the fascist revolution, these people have found that the letters F.A.I. and C.N.T. are much more efficacious than the longer rigmarole on the cross about their necks, and they have hastened to make the appropriate changes. There is, of course, another way of looking at things. Q. did not bother much with the mystical anarchism, the war of symbols, he saw things racially.

I met him by chance in the Portal de l'Angel; a brown little figure, in brown suit, brownish-red tie, and no hat, a frightened little mouse of a man. I suggested a drink at the large café at the end of his road. He thought it was taken over by the C.N.T. and guided me to an obscure little place where we could not be seen.

"I can sum up what has happened in one sentence," said Q. "The Spanish military, by making a rebellion, have made it possible for a bunch of Murcians to destroy a thousand years of Catalan art." A burning desire to tease surged between me and my *amer piquant*. If Q. looked like a mouse, I certainly felt like a cat.

In June I had still been a patient man; now in August I felt different. The realisation that the days of talking were over and that, now that action was demanded, men like Q. and T. had no place in the world, was infuriating. I had admired them and listened to them and I had been deceived and I felt a fool, and therefore cruel. But even the feeling of cruelty was fleeting; a sudden realisation that these men were bores of the deepest dye discharged any more violent emotion.

Round the corner from the café where Q. was drivelling sat a man of a very different type, Ventura Gassol, Minister of Culture. Before the fascist revolt there had been no way of proving that Gassol was any better than Q. or T. when it came to emergencies, but his courage and commonsense, along with that of his chief, President Companys, have done much to save the dignity of the bourgeois, which has been let down by the frightened twitterings of so many.

I went and saw Gassol. "I want to write a true story of the *destruction* of the churches in Barcelona," I said. "Will you talk to me about it, as Minister of Culture?"

"Why worry about the destruction of art," he said, "why not write the much more important story of the art that has been saved from oblivion?" And he sent me to see the chief of the Office of Works.

In the building occupied by that official there was great activity. In every corner piles on piles of saints and virgins, crucifixes and paintings and carvings; men going this way and that with new boxes of objects just arrived; women at tables typing lists of treasure sent in to the government for safe keeping. From burned churches and convents, from private mansions and palaces, came the plundered deposits of all the ages to be sorted and finally placed in public museums. The authorities reckon that the art treasures that have been taken out of dark seclusion where nobody saw them; the books that have hitherto been imprisoned for life in private libraries where perhaps one man read them, or looked at them, or had them catalogued and priced for insurance or probate, far outweigh in value the comparatively few things lost by burning.

Let us forget for the moment the religious question, let us suspend our judgment on the matter of sacrilege, and consider what art has suffered and what art has gained by the "plundering" of the incensed people's forces. Of course art becomes doubly dear when it can be used as propaganda. Precisely those English people who never enter the National Gallery or look twice at St. Paul's became frantic with rage when Rheims Cathedral fell victim to the mother of all atrocities, War. The people whose idea of France is the Folies Bergères fainted when they heard that Rheims had been shelled, and recovered to "give" their sons more readily since art must be saved from the Hun. Setting these human pests on one side, what has humanity lost in the Barcelona burnings?

It is a strange sight to look at the shells of dozens of churches and to realise the havoc within. Usually the only way in which you can see what has happened is by noting the bricked-up entrance, the notice that the structure is dangerous and that no one must enter, the triumphant signature "F.A.I." scrawled up, the slight smoke discoloration in an upper window. Speaking broadly, the great Gothic structures can be completely salvaged, and the Baroque structures will have to be pulled down.

I stood outside Santa Maria del Mar, one of the noblest Gothic buildings in Catalunya, strangely virile, utterly un-French. True enough an "expression of the Catalan spirit," but an expression of that spirit when the Catalan bourgeois was still a revolutionary in the forefront of social evolution. Santa Maria del Mar is of course an expression of religious sentiment, but also of sound practical commonsense; it may have given comfort to angels, it certainly gives satisfaction to engineers and to those who see architecture in terms of functional correctness.

Santa Maria del Mar was built practically and for use, a true meeting-place of the community, where they might approach the spirit of creativeness. As such it commands our respect.

But, as the centuries moved on, the class that made it and other buildings like it, decayed; the merchants, the guildsmen, the middlemen, the bourgeoisie, lost their creative urge. Instead of doing the work themselves, they allowed themselves to subsist more and more on the product of their money let out to stud. He whose money bred most took the spiritual lead of the community, and a new architectural aim began to appear. Instead of a functionally perfect engineering job, in which the minimum of material was put to the most practical use, so that modesty, directness, and honesty led to grandeur and dignity—instead of this, came a demand for show. That building was best which looked to have cost most; the structure was no longer the principal concern but rather the surfaces. They sought to redeem vile bodies with gaudy dress. They lost the power to appreciate a splendid body when it existed. They filled up places like Santa Maria del Mar with execrable trash, tinsel and gilt and marble made out of wood.

All this tinsel and gilt and marble that is really wood were but symbols of social civilization as a whole. The bourgeoisie, once the engineers of a new civilization, had become the counterfeiters. In due course they have been found out. The civilization which produced the vile absurdities which have been burned in the Barcelona churches was the same civilization which inevitably had to produce fascism, illegal revolt, from the spirit its ancestors had fought nobly to produce when they were still able to build Gothic churches.

Now the structure alone is left, tons and tons of trash have been burned. Any artist who thinks of the opportunity this has given to artists in Barcelona must be glad.

It is true that there were some good things inside these old churches, and that some of them may have been lost, but we should not forget that from the very beginning an effort was made even by the mystical firebugs to sort out the good from the bad. Ralph Bates has told amusingly of his own experiences as part of an improvised technical commission at the door of a condemned church.

"It was a grand bonfire. A little technical commission (to which I was elected) stood at one side of the door, passing judgment on the saints as they were carried out. Companero Sagasta relies on my judgment.

"This one, compañero?"

"Revolting, burn him."

"Very good, compañero."

"The bearers run to the fire and St Peter throw up a billow of sparks."

"This one?"

"H'm looks rather old, the carving's direct; probably deserves a second thought."

"Very good." The saint is dumped on his back among the silver-plate candelabra, the books with parchment backs which may make binding for school books, the electric bulbs, the linen, good for bandages, and, in short, anything that possibly has artistic or secular value. This not-gaudy candelabra, for instance; when it came out I yelled, 'Eh, bring that here.'"

"'It's only iron.'"

"'Only iron!' Christ Jesus, it's pure Catalan work of the fifteenth century; look, no rivets, no clips, everything is welded and drawn under the hammer."

"The iconoclasts reverently placed the candelabra to one side, reverently I say, for the compañero has said this is art and, feeling out of it, they rush into church for another trophy."

That last paragraph is very well worth noting, for it contains the key to the attitude of the F.A.I. to art. We have seen that the religious question can only be understood as a battle between two magics; the church symbols must be burned in order to immobilise the witchcraft of the fascists. But in the face of art another matter altogether comes up. Art is itself 'magic,' something not understood, awe-inspiring, but only when it is in the hands of the priests is it black magic. 'Art' has within it a power which must be rescued from the priest, then it can be used for one's own white magic. It can be used for enriching man's life rather than for blighting it.

One day I was in Santiago de Compostela where, as we have seen, witchcraft of all sorts abounds under the blessing of the very princes of the church. I had been looking at the sublime Pórtico de la Gloria, that epitome of dogmatic theology set down in stone for illiterate men to read. Any Englishman can see a plaster cast of it in the South Kensington Museum. It is one of the great achievements of the medieval mind. On the other side of the main column, humbly placed in the gloom of the vast interior, is a statue of the sculptor himself, Mateo. This portrait-bust has many little holes burrowed into it like the burrows of marine animals in rock pools. Undergraduates from the local university come and dig their pencils into the stone, and knock their foreheads against it before sitting for examinations. Pregnant women come and rub their stomachs against Mateo's nose as an aid to safe delivery. Why? Because deep down in the gloom of their superstitious minds there is a reverence for the creator of this Pórtico, whose merit they do not fully understand. Mateo created that doorway, he has then a very powerful magic, is it not natural to hope that his magic will prevail against the demons of the examiners, against the torturing devils who endanger childbirth?

"Really," said a distinguished Fellow of the Royal Society to me once, "if I were to describe my religious views I think I should call them the higher phallic worship, a worship of creativeness." It is this same worship that lies behind the feeling for Mateo, the dead but potent creator who worked in stone. It is this that reigns in the mind of Ralph Bates' iconoclasts when they put on one side something which to them is old iron, because they are assured by a comrade who knows more about these things that it contains the creative white magic called 'art.'

In obedience to their sense of reverence for this magic, the iconoclasts, at the risk of not destroying valuable pieces of the priest's black art, have saved and sent to the Catalan government thousands of museum pieces.

Thus art has gained more than it has lost; some buildings destroyed it is true, some few masterpieces also, but on the other side of the balance-sheet we must put things saved from the darkness of cathedrals, from the life-imprisonment of convents, from the selfish exclusiveness of rich collectors, as well as an incredible weight of foul ugliness burned to leave room for the artists of to-day and to-morrow to do better with the space cleared for them.

We have discussed the religious and the artistic significance of the burning of the churches; there remains to say a few more words about the political meaning of it all. There is of course the simple-hearted reader of the English or American newspapers who is told that it is all a matter of Moscow. The open-handed munificence of Moscow is a theme that always makes its exponent ridiculous, but that Moscow paid or instructed people to burn the Catalan churches is more than usually absurd. Communists do not burn churches. In so far as any political party can be considered responsible at the moment in Spain, it is the anarcho-syndicalist party. As I cycled through Spain I came to a place where the burning of churches abruptly ceased. They were burned in the Catalan Provinces, in Castelló, in Valencia, but in the central Castilian

Provinces, no. In other words, where the Marxists are strong, the churches are locked up and the keys deposited in the mayor's office, and where the Bakuninites have the power the churches have been burned. The Communist in Spain to-day is not fanatically anti-religious. In October, just before Ossorio y Gallardo went to represent Spain at the League of Nations, he received a deputation of the Madrid communist party asking him to open the Madrid churches. In spite of his avowed and sincere catholicism, he refused on grounds of public policy; he pointed out the danger of demonstrations and incidents. It is something that should be carefully considered, this scene between a communist delegation and a catholic minister, for it makes cheap nonsense of much of the propaganda in this country. The communists fully realise the implications of the present, they are the defenders of democracy, not the imposers of a materialist dictatorship; and they have the sense to see it. They would prefer to turn the churches into schools and cinemas, but they are not afraid of the sacred symbols. Perhaps it is because they do not believe in magic that they do not want to burn the magicians' stick and robes.

There are, however, certain things that all progressive people in Spain feel against the church as it has functioned in their country. Remember the damning extract from the New Catechism as used until yesterday in all churches in Spain. Ralph Bates quotes it with much effect.

"QUESTION.   What sin is committed by those who vote liberal?
ANSWER.   Usually, mortal sin."

Remember that very recently the church authorities condemned all women's clubs out of hand as being contrary to decency and religion.

Finally, remember the Confessional. It is, of course, perfectly true that there need be nothing worse in the practice of the Confessional, and as much good, as comes from a visit to the psychoanalyst. But does anyone pretend that the confessional in Spain has not been used as a political weapon? Take, for example, the question and answer quoted from the New Catechism. How many thousands of men and women have been intimidated by fears of hell if they have anything to do with any progressive party? Everybody who has had to do with elections in England and America knows that in industrial districts factory owners often announce during the campaign that if the Reds win they will have to dismiss half their employees. Imagine the power of such pressure when, as in Spain, the reactionary can not only threaten misery in this world, but worse in the next. It is mortal sin, is it, to vote liberal? The average Englishman is not particularly afraid of committing mortal sin according to the catholic moral theology, so he finds it hard to appreciate the political value, the vote-catching propensities of those who can disseminate ghostly threats and fears. "Anyone voting for Mr Lloyd George is in danger of hell-fire." We may think it or wish it, but being a free democratic country we do not say it. Nor must we suppose that the priesthood is content with brandishing their spiritual weapons. Half the cathedrals of Spain were built as fortresses also; there is not likely to be one that has not at some time or other been stained with blood. Here is an extract from that exemplary paper, fascist and catholic, the *Heraldo de Aragón*. It is a happy little picture of how priests are feeling to-day in the Carlist territory.[1]

"The priest of a village in our province has joined the Carlist army as a common soldier. He took part in a glorious action and helped defeat the enemy. The socialists left 150 prisoners in our hands, who were condemned to death. While this priest was giving the last holy benediction to one of the condemned, an enemy aeroplane flew over our camp. The condemned tried to profit by the confusion to escape. But the priest-guerrillero joined in pursuit, caught the fugitive, and said: 'My son, I have no right to let you escape; my duty is to give you the last benediction.' And as he was complying with this duty, the Carlists executed the prisoner."

---

1. The Carlists, *Comunión Tradicionalista*, supported a traditionalist ultra-Catholic style monarchy as opposed to the monarchy of Alfonso XIII.

Is any comment needed? Is it really to be supposed that when priests interpret their duties thus, their enemies will not shoot them when they have a chance? The fascists were frankly shooting their prisoners in cold blood, one nearly escapes, a priest stops him, and blesses him as he is murdered. Very nice indeed. No wonder the supporters of such priests have to invent stories of the other side committing atrocities against nuns. When Catholic and fascist papers *boast* of an atrocity like this, it becomes scarcely necessary for the government papers to deny the atrocities imagined against their side.

Or take this clipping from an English Catholic paper which has a personal interest to me:

"Mr. John Langdon-Davies, special correspondent of *The News Chronicle* in Barcelona, has secured another 'scoop.'

He has discovered that 'the Bishop of Pamplona has just granted 100 days' plenary indulgence to anyone killing a Marxist.'

If the value of his 'news' is equal to his knowledge of indulgences, it does not amount to much... What the Bishop of Pamplona said in a pastoral letter—as reported in *The Universe* last week—was that in no circumstances may Catholics unite with Communists—even for objects that are in themselves good."

There never was a more charming piece of casuistry than this. With huge glee the writer jumps on the mistake about "100 days plenary indulgence." I gather that, if any indulgence is plenary, it is not merely for 100 days, and I have added the information, for what it is worth, to what I know already. But the error is not mine. It was copied from a Catholic fascist paper. Leaving out the quibble about "plenary" and "100 days," the fact remains that according to the A.B.C. of Cordoba, the Bishop of Pamplona has been granting indulgences to anyone who kills a Marxist.

The Bishop may not have done so; but he has not contradicted his own newspaper, and catholic fascists are being fortified into further efforts at killing their fellowmen by the hope of a little less purgatory as a reward.

The Carlist case must be peculiarly poor if it can only be defended by descending to quibbles like this.

Not that what *The Universe* says matters. But that the Bishop of Pamplona is quoted by fascists in this sense matters a good deal.

The whole thing opens up a number of fascinating problems when we remember that a Mohammedan gets a free pass to paradise if he kills a Christian. Does one of Franco's Moors get more or less when he kills a Christian than when he kills a Marxist? Not being a moral theologian, I am not sure what the Bishop has to offer beyond plunder and opportunity for rape to his dusky infidel allies, but I think that he had better make it even more worthwhile for them to kill Marxists, or they may turn their attention to Christians instead. If he values his reputation with decent observers, he had better threaten the lying publishers of his words with the consequences of mortal sin, if the spiritual rum which they are thus offering as an inducement to go over the top, is only very small beer after all. Meanwhile, so long as bishops have such poor press-agents, it is hardly surprising that Marxists feel like shooting them.

A friend of mine watched a man demolishing an image on the wall of a priest's house; above it was an inscription which he could not reach. It read: "Now He shall reign." He shook his mallet at it and said: "So you think; but wait until I get a longer ladder, and then we'll see." It is the same spirit that tears down election posters. Who can be surprised when we think of the part played by the priests in the political affairs of Spain.

I was walking down a street in Madrid one Sunday in August, 1936, going to find the restaurant where most of my militia friends foregathered for milk and coffee before going out to do their bit of fighting. I had just whipped out my camera to take a photograph of some minute little girls dressed as hospital nurses marching along behind a six-year-old boy who was beating a drum. Oo archie pay, oo archie pay, they shouted, and I remembered how less than four months ago just such a group of children had marched down the Paseo del Prado, to the great pride of their parents; had been taken out to their annual picnic in the Casa del Campo beyond the Manzanares.

It was a lazy morning in spite of a civil war, and as I saw one little child after another join on the end of the procession my memory jumped back several hundred years to certain children's processions described in Zuniga's *Annals of Seville*. It was in 1613 that civil war broke out in the great Andalusian city. In September of that year a preacher had the temerity to suggest that it might not be certain that the Virgin Mary had been conceived by her parents without normal sexual intercourse. The preacher had come by his arguments in what would seem to us a rather curious manner. He had taken as his text the verse from the Song of Solomon which says: "How beautiful are thy feet *with shoes*, O thou prince's daughter." He told his congregation that this referred undoubtedly to the Virgin, and "that the first steps of the Virgin had been her Conception and Birth, and that they had been beautiful, the first because when she was conceived she was sanctified, the second, because she came into the world more Holy than any other pure creature. But that to signify that she had contracted Original Sin, the Holy Spirit did not (in the text quoted) praise her steps simply, but her steps made with shoes, which being formed of the skins of dead animals, were to be taken as alluding to the skin-aprons which God had made for our first fathers, after that they had sinned." Or, in a nut-shell, that Solomon's verse proved that the Virgin was not immaculately conceived, by describing her first steps as being taken not in naked purity, but clothed in shoes, the symbol of sin. A terrific scandal resulted. The Archbishop ordered a general procession to march through the whole city singing:

Todo el Mundo en general
A vozes Reyna escogida
Diga que sois Concebida
Sin Pecado Original

"All the Universe together, Elected Queen, says aloud: that thou wast conceived without original sin."

From that day on the whole city gave itself up with enthusiasm to expressions of faith in the impugned doctrine. Any child sent on an errand by its parents had only to begin chanting Todo el Mundo for all passersby to join in behind him, so that you constantly saw small lads followed by knights, clerics, friars, and merchants. The local treasury was exhausted in paying for ceremonies. The Trades Guilds played their part in organizing festivals, as also did all clubs, whether of business men or of nationalities. The Mulatto's Club of Seville had a festival in honour of the Virgin's Immaculate Conception, and this was so gaudy that all the rest were well nigh put in the shade. But the Negro's Club of Seville went one better and had two festivals, which completely put the rest in the shade, since no one in Seville had ever seen anything so sumptuous. The only sorrowful organizations were the Moor's Club and the Moorish Women's Club, which both applied to the city authorities for the right to hold a festival in honour of the Virgin's Immaculate Conception but were both refused.

As I watched the Oo archie pay crowd, I thought of the Todo el Mundo crowd and of how whatever happens in Spain happens in a way that could not possibly be duplicated anywhere else. There is always the sense of being brought face to face with things altogether outside one's imaginative experience. It is not a matter of 'local colour' but of local soul.

And as I thought this I heard the unmistakable sound of Moody-and-Sankey hymn-singing.

It was not unnatural that I should at first assume that my English psyche was playing a trick in protest against these too Spanish stimuli, that I had begun a split personality, a fugal existence. Oo, archie, pay; todo el mundo en general; when I survey the wondrous cross. I had just passed a church where the Virgin over the door had been muzzled with a black cloth and decorated with a red tie; perhaps my ego of school- chapel days was in revolt.

But when I heard an obviously protestant organ searching for and finally discovering that famous lost chord, like the sound of a great amen, which is, I believe, merely the common chord of whatever key the preceding hymn was in; when I heard this I was sure that I was faced with a reality to be investigated. I pushed against a rather new but evidently consecrated door, it gave way and I found myself in a normal protestant church with a clergy-man in cassock and surplice, a cross on the altar, hymn-books in the pews, a pulpit, and a congregation.

The congregation was not precisely as it would have been in my dear old Kentish parish church; it was entirely Spanish, the women's heads were covered with black mantillas, on account of the angels, and they were vigorously fanning themselves on ac-count of the heat. Many of the men were in anti-fascist militia uniform, and when the next hymn began the sister of a militia man handed me a book so that I might take a more active part.

The service continued; the clergyman mounted the pulpit and spoke reasonably and quietly on the subject of "Peace," pointing out to his congregation that, in spite of what was going on in Spain all round them, not a single Protestant church had been touched. Then the collection and another hymn, and we dispersed.

I hurried to the café up the road and sought out Tomás. He is an anarcho-syndicalist of an argumentative sort, always busy with Paco, who is a U.G.T. stalwart. Paco had gone off for his bit of fighting in the Guadarrama, and so I had Tomás to myself.

"I have been to church, compañero."

"Where?" said Tomás, looking around as if he was expecting to see an offending church within match-striking distance.

"At the Protestant Church down the road."

"Oh, ah, the Protestant Church. I did not know there was one down the road," and he stirred his coffee in a relaxed sort of way.

"Why is it not closed?" I said.

"Why should it be closed?"

"Then you approve of the Protestant Churches?"

"They don't mean anything at all to me; but we have no quarrel against them. We have no quarrel against the Free Cults because they haven't fought against us. We have destroyed the people who tried to destroy us; that's all." Tomas looked at his spoon. "Be-sides," he added in a sort of growl, "the free cults do not use the confessional." And he stirred his glass with a sort of grim fury.

Once more it was this matter of the confessional that seemed to obsess the mind of my friend. To the English catholic the attitude may seem unfair; I doubt if the confessional is of much importance as a political weapon in our country, and I am very well aware that even in Spain the confessor is not supposed to use information gained in the confessional for other ends. But I do not believe that this rule is adhered to. "Look here," said Tomás, "the priests teach that it is not only wrong for anyone to be a heretic but that no one should have to do with heretics. Of course, a socialist or a communist or an anarcho-syndicalist is the worst sort of heretic to them. So some wretched worker's wife goes to confession and says she has been to a syndicalist meeting. But why did you go? I went with my husband. But do you not know it is mortal sin to be with heretics, and that a syndicalist is a heretic? But what can I do? Well, if you show your good faith by telling me all about what you hear at the syndicalist meetings, I will absolve you and you may go with your husband. But do not forget; unless I know everything you will be in a state of mortal sin. "And so," said Tomás, "the women are made into spies against their husbands. No wonder the priests have done all they can to stop them being educated. Every worker who has a woman in his house who goes to confession knows that he is being betrayed."

You do not believe Tomás?

Let me quote once more from the New Catechism.

"Q. What sin is committed by those who vote liberal?

"A. Usually mortal sin." ...

When I met the Marquis he asked me about the destruction of churches and religious art.

"In Toledo," he asked anxiously, "is everything all right?"

"Everything."

"The San Francis of Juan de Mena?"

"Under lock and key. Safe, unless the rebels bomb the city."

He asked about the churches in Barcelona.

"Except the cathedral, all are burned."

"That is terrible. I love Santa Maria del Mar," and then his face changed. A new expression came into it.

"And, tell me, the Church of the Sagrada Família, is that burned down?"

"No, it proved to be absolutely fire-proof."

"Oh dear, what a pity, I am very disappointed."

I had been introduced to the Church of the Sacred Family fifteen years ago by T. No human being who has not seen it can possibly hope to imagine the full horror of this piece of human folly, this "expression of the Catalan Spirit."

Your first view of it is likely to be from the train, whence appears in the distance a cluster of four factory chimneys apparently viewed under permanent X-rays, so that you see their ribs with empty holes between. Through a pair of field-glasses you will see that each of these objects ends in a gilded top-knot, one of which, if I remember right, is a model, about a hundred times life-size, of a pineapple.

If you wish to make closer acquaintance with this nightmare you find yourself on the outskirts of civilization amid unpaved streets. I remember that T. had explained to me that the spot had been chosen because the architect had "accurately measured" that it would be the exact centre of Barcelona by the time the Cathedral is finished. That looks like one of those prophecies which prove to be true.

But, once you are confronted with the present reality, you are unlikely to bother very much about any possible future. You will be cowed to silence; you will not protest; you may whimper like a puppy, but you will not criticise; the hideousness is so completely enthralling.

Perhaps remembering that the medieval cathedrals never got their façades finished until hundreds of years later, the Catalans began on the façade and there for the moment they have stopped. The four chimneys turn out to be four out of twelve towers planned to represent the twelve apostles and, when they get round to the other three walls, each of them are to have their four towers also. The present four, Peter, Matthew, John, and James, let us say, surmount the main gateway, rising a hundred metres to their gilded pineapples and other fruit-like protuberances.

The façade as a whole betrays several influences, but none of them architectural. One is the machine that makes a certain kind of sweet in the windows of seaside resorts in England. You must have seen it; it has two arms revolving in opposite senses and complicating a rope of sugar between them. There is no mere gingerbread about the Church of the Sacred Family, it is a matter of thick brown icing-sugar poured over something or other sticking skywards and allowed to find its own level. And while the sugar was only partly hardened, they stuck into it like nuts a variety of highly symbolical objects. It would take a hundred years to chip them all out again, and they cannot be burned. Has anarcho-syndicalism met with its great defeat? It has, and it has not. My terror is that the anarcho-syndicalists may get control of Barcelona, and, finding this edifice fireproof, use it as a model for the rebuilding of the rest of the city. For, apart from the symbols being of the wrong magic, this thing is anarcho-syndicalism in architecture. The official guide written in a number of different languages tells us in English that the "19th May, 1882, was placed 1st stone of that

monumental Temple" and that it is "to testify to the centuries the faith that is still beating in our days, and gives to the art a precious jewel by building for the religion a new church, real mystic poem worked in stone."

A reasonably clear idea of the symbolical method of the church can be gained by reading the following extract from the official description:

"They are building those of the north façade called of the Nativity because it is consecrated to the childhood of Jesus, with which they form its bases a sole body, and which makes the wonderful conjunct which says the birth and first days of Jesus earth. The facade has three doors, crowned by lanterns of moderate proportions the two laterals, and of a gigantic size that of the centre. They rest on striated columns which lean themselves on the shells of immense tortoises, and they are ended by a beautiful bundle of palms, which are mixing themselves with animals and flowers of Christmas and the Nile, the crests looking as icicles. In the middle of the principal door protected by a framed grate there is a column as a trunk of a palm tree, on which is going round a ribbon with the genealogy of Christ after St Matthew. The superior part of the capital of the column will be the pedestal of the group of the Nativity with the sculpture of the ox and the she mule and over a group of angels singing the Hosanna. At both sides of the facade and on friezes with symbolic Christmas animals there are the groups of the Adoration of the Blessed Kings and shepherds with angels calling to adore. There is a great detail upon the Nativity to announce the date of that extraordinary event: and this is a band with the signs of the zodiac engraved in the same position that they were on the night of the birth of Christ at Bethlehem. Over the group of the Nativity and as an end of it, there you will find the symbolic star which guided the blessed kings. There is in the centre of the large window a sculptoric group that represent the Annunciation. Over it and on a pedestal of immense proportions will be placed another group representing the Coronation of our Blessed Lady, and over which will gradually close the wonderful lantern that ends in a cypress tree, the incorruptibility, in which track, is nailed bleeding as on the Cross the Sacred Heart of Jesus. Some angels gather in vases the Divine Blood to sprinkle the whole world with it. On a monumental pedestal rest several groups of angels who circle the name of Jesus incensing and singing Hosanna. A rosary (composed of 15 denaries) runs all the open works of the façade."

And that is only half what is to be found on the one façade. I believe that when finished the upper half of the whole thing was to have been painted blue and the lower half yellow.

Now this is the chef d'œuvre of the Church, which did not scruple to use its Gothic buildings as machine-gun emplacements, and which is now howling at its opponents for destroying art! But it is also quite truly as T. said a "manifestation of the Catalan spirit." Anyone who looked at it with his mind alive to the economic interpretation of aesthetic styles must have known that a capitalism that produced the Church of the Sagrada Familia would not dissolve into socialism and communism but into the precise anarchism which appears to have come.

When, in October, 1934, President Companys surrendered to

the then forces of law and order, it was only after he had shut himself up in the exquisite Gothic Generalitat on which they trained the artillery. I begged of him that if he ever again found himself in danger of a like situation he would shut himself up instead in the Palau de la Musica Catalana, a building as bad and in the same style as the church we have been examining. I repeated my *mot* to a syndicalist, expecting smiling agreement, but instead he answered, "Why? I think the Palau de la Musica Catalana a wonderful building, and I would much rather see the Generalitat destroyed than it." I am afraid that there is some danger of the new Catalan civilization taking over the worse aesthetic elements of the present, and that is another atrocity which we may lay at the door of the fascist rebels who have destroyed democratic society. It may even be that a statue of the architect, Gaudí, will be placed on one of the raised beaches that occur at intervals all over his precious façade,and that the anarcho-syndicalist students of the future will knock their heads against it, while the anarcho-syndicalist expectant mothers will rub their stomachs against its nose.

CHAPTER 6
MADRID

Of course there was no way of going to Madrid by way of Zaragoza. The towns and villages through which I had wandered in May were now "The front." As I packed up for my motor cycle journey I looked down on this charabanc of militiamen and their girls prepared to drive along the road past Lerida to do a bit of fighting. They belonged to an Esquerra Catalana republican column and would doubtless be operating around Bujaraloz.

It was a curious war, what there was of it; at that time nobody got killed until after they were captured. To the C.N.T., especially, the whole thing appeared chiefly in the light of a rather special kind of political campaign. You read that Durruti's column had captured the village of Santa María and with memories of the World War you saw a process of straightening out a long line of trenches, of occupying a quiet spot made barren by artillery preparation, of the immediate digging in of advancing men and the laying of more miles of barbed wire. Nothing like this happened when Durruti's column occupied another village on the Zaragoza front. There was no question of military occupation in any recognizable sense; what Durruti and his energetic men thought of was political occupation, and they did nothing at all in most cases, at least while I was there, to get ready for a military counter-attack.

Let us follow the C.N.T. column into Santa María, any typical village of the Aragon desert. It is a gathering together of perhaps two hundred dwellings round a parish church and a local government building and prison. It has a small amount of cultivated land thanks to an intermittent stream which dries up by July; it has some olives and perhaps a few figs. Its climate is "tres meses de invierno y nueve meses de infierno," three months of winter and nine of hell.

The inhabitants of this composite Santa María are all anti-fascist except one rich landowner—rich that is in that he extracts perhaps a hundred pounds a year out of some property—who lives in Zaragoza most of his time and certainly hurried off there in July; one or two officials, either a Guardia Civil, a carabinero, or a local government clerk; a "capitalist" with some little factory, or electric light plant or olive oil refinery; and the priest. One or other of these—not the priest—will have a son or two who buys suits in Zaragoza, sits longer than the rest at the café and pays attention to any girl who comes his way. This señorito may be small beer in Barcelona or Zaragoza but he is arrogant enough in his own village. He may very well belong to the Falange, and, trusting to the forces of law and order, air his reactionary views.

Durruti's column arrives full of enthusiasm but not very well armed. The first step is to limpiar or clean away any fascism that may be in Santa María; in other words to shoot any of those individuals who have not hurried off to Zaragoza in time. If the villagers give one or other of them a good character he escapes. The second thing is to remove all registers of property from the archives to the village square and to burn them. This is both a practical and a ritualistic act. It is followed by the summoning of all the inhabitants into the square so that they shall have the principles of Libertarian Communism explained to them, with a few warnings, no doubt, as to the dangers of Stalinism, which would please even the Primrose League. A general feeling of hope and freedom having been established, the column may turn to their technical advisers for help. Each column of anarcho-syndicalists carries with it some loyal officers or members of the Guardia Civil who are not recognized as officers, (there being no place for officers in a column inspired by Organized Indiscipline,) but are regarded as a sort of mechanic to look after the military machine. If there is real fighting to be done, these men explain how to do it, and if they have time try to organize a field of fire or a bit of barbed wire or something else entirely outside the range of experience of their comrades. Should the rebels attack they often find little but enthusiasm and bravery to oppose them, but as no strategic advantage can come of recapturing Santa María, its inhabitants are usually left to discuss the principles of Libertarian Communism with one another and to feed the militia.

Of course when, as sometimes happens, a position of real military importance is threatened, as between Zaragoza and Huesca, real fighting takes place and terrible casualties occur. Then you see the humiliating sight of loyalists disarmed by the pact of non-intervention opposing with nothing but faith, artillery, machine guns and bombs, aeroplanes supplied by the Fascist International. You see also a few English volunteer nurses and surgeons offering the only help that democracy outside Spain has sent to Spanish democracy.

My motor cycle carried me south through the rich regions of the Mediterranean coast, past one barricaded village after another. Everywhere work was being done as usual, and for a hundred miles one forgot the horror so near in the blue day and the olive trees which 'seem only to live in moonlight.'

The curious behaviour of my cycle began to preoccupy me. I had left it in charge of a garage run by communist militiamen, and I had asked them to overhaul it. This they had done so thoroughly that the controls refused to be gentle, and I found myself rushing at twenty-five miles an hour on my lowest gear at the very bayonets of a barricade.

"Salud," I said, "is there a mechanic in your village who could help me?"

It was an idle question, there are mechanics in every village of

Spain, competent and helpful. When I told the Marquis about my adventure afterwards he beamed with pleasure, for it showed that even an anarcho-syndicalist militiaman in a burned church was a Spaniard, a mechanic and a gentleman. The head of the barricade turned to a lad with a blunderbuss. "Juan," he said, "take the compañero to the Mechanized Transport Industry Centre." Juan and I pushed the bike down the village street and round the corner to the Mechanized Industry Centre. A month ago it was still the Parish Church. Now in each of the niches that had been chapels was parked a motor lorry; two men in overalls armed with pick and shovel were destroying the last fake marble and gilt horror and dimming the air with stucco dust. I stood and watched; and the militiamen watched my face to see how I was reacting.

"They built the houses of their saints very well," at last one said, as the column showed fight still, "and yet the saints never existed. If it were a worker's home that was being pulled down there would be no difficulty, for they did not build living men's homes so well."

"You have a fine garage," I said.

"A very fine garage, compañero."

"Will it always be a garage now, think you?"

"Not always. Only until we have destroyed Them. See outside, compañero." I looked across the village square at a line of men vigorously digging a trench towards the ex-church.

"This is going to be our village market, and we are already laying on the water. Our women have always had to sell in the street, with flies everywhere. Now we shall have a sanitary market. It will be better for the village health."

Meanwhile two mechanics were dismantling the bicycle with all their hearts. A strong, not very beautiful girl came in to watch.

"Compañero," said an overalled humorist, "what do you think of this girl? She would like to come with you to Madrid."

"Why not?" I replied. "She can have all the pillion seat to herself."

"No," said the girl looking me up and down, "the foreign compañero is altogether too young for me. I will not go with him."

"But, compañera, that is not true; why, I have a son of seventeen of my own. I am not young," I protested.

"No, I do not think I will go to Madrid with you." And so it was left. But I wished for a moment that I had been correspondent for the *Daily Dirt*—'Bolsheviks Barter Woman in Desecrated Church,' would have been a fine heading for those who feel that way. Meanwhile the bike was ready. It appears that my over-enthusiastic helpers at the last garage had cleaned everything, including the control cables, with oil, and I gather that this should not be done.

"How much do I owe you?" I asked.

"It is very difficult to answer that, compañero," said the mechanic. "It was such a little thing. I do not like to ask you to pay."

"Ah, compañero, you have given me two hours of your life and that is not a little thing; you must allow me to make a contribution to the anti-fascist militia funds." And so it was arranged; the equivalent of two shillings and sixpence to the village funds and I was away. I am not a sentimentalist, but as I write I see the rare look of trust and friendship from all those men working in that burned-out church, a look which met me many, many times in Spain this summer, and never ceased to make me wonder why it is so rare among us here; and I wince to think what will happen to those faces when the Moors, with our assistance, pass their barricade. And so I went on and on through hundreds of miles of fertility to Valencia, of aridity to Madrid.

The last part of the journey I did by rail. I reached the station. I got out and walked down the platform. A very fat gentleman with the five-pointed star of the esperantist on one side and the ominous word "interpreter" on the other virtually arrested me. With the reflex actions of a confirmed anti-tourist I tried to get out of his clutches, but times were changed. He hauled me before the Committee and got my papers stamped.

"And now what do you want to do?"

"I want to go to a hotel."

"How much can you afford?"

"Oh, a medium-priced hotel."

"Can you afford seven pesetas for a room with bath?"

I considered that seven pesetas was three shillings and sixpence, and that my paper had a circulation of over a million.

"Yes, compañero, I can afford that. But how am I to get to my hotel?"

"You do not have to worry, compañero. Of course the taxis are all at the Front; but I will find a horse vehicle." Outside the station were drawn up six hansom cabs. To an Englishman it meant that Civil War had brought him back to grandmother.

I began to get into one. "But what hotel am I to go to?" I asked.

"Well, compañero, I will accompany you, and we will go together to the Bristol." And so I found myself creeping up the Paseo del Prado behind the thinnest horse and beside the plumpest anti-fascist I had ever met. Now and then the comrade on the roof flicked his horse into a despairing canter. But each time my companion rebuked him.

"Hi, there, compañero; no cruelty to animals, if you please," and turning to me, "That's the one thing I do not like about our comrades here, they have no feeling at all for animals."

"What part of Spain do you come from?" I asked.

"I, compañero, why I am a Russian. This is my third revolution."

"The others were 1905 and 1917?"

"Exactly; and in some ways this is the most interesting. Hi, there, keep your whip away from that horse." We relapsed, in the interests of humanity, to a snail's pace. I looked up and there was Velasquez, his brush still poised in mid-air, looking down on the Paseo intently. But now there were no more parades; no banners; no singing.

"How much shall I pay this cabby?" I asked.

"Three pesetas, and no more, compañero; he is well provided for by the Committee."

We turned up to the left past the Ministry of War. Outside the Café de los Molineros was a feeble barricade. The café itself, at which the Marquis had entertained me, was full of the Army in

Overalls. We reached the Bristol. The Comrade Interpreter got out and handed the cabby three pesetas. I followed him into the hotel. A vast mass of youthful militiamen guarded everything that could be guarded with an enthusiasm that no mere lack of ammunition could damp. I got my room with bath.

"And how much do I owe you, compañero?" I asked my friend.

"Nothing, absolutely nothing, you are our guest."

"But what about the cab? You paid that too?"

"Nothing, I tell you. And if there is anything you need, I, the official interpreter for the Committee of the Railwaymen's Union at Madrid, am at your service."

I went to see Paco. Of all the starry faces. I have seen none shine like Paco's. He was the editor of the chief Socialist paper in Madrid. He was also the Madrid correspondent of my own paper. He was also chief liaison officer for matters to do with air defence. And every afternoon, as I have said, he went to do his bit of fighting, on the Sierra. He did all this with irrepressible humour, an unquenchable gleam in his eye. While I was in Madrid with Paco, Del Vayo, Caballero and the rest I was living, I admit, in the very flavour of the Three Musketeers. It was impossible to feel out of one's teens when Paco was about.[1]

Paco was a Frenchman originally, and had got into prison during the Great War as a pacifist. He had got into prison again after

---

1. In September 1936, Caballero was appointed Prime Minister. He also took over the job of Minister of War. His administration brought together left and right. It was the first in Europe to include communists who only joined after they had had the go ahead from Moscow. He also appointed his old rival Prietro as Minister of Navy and Air. He concentrated on winning the war and did not pursue a policy of social revolution. He said his government was fighting not for socialism but democracy and constitutional rule. He introduced policies, such as conscription, that angered the left.

He made Julio Alvarez Del Vayo (1891-74), a journalist and radical socialist, Minister of Foreign Affairs. In September 1936, Del Vayo appealed to the League of Nations, in Geneva, under Article 10 to provide the Spanish government with military aid. He worked closely with Stalin. Soviet military personnel, tanks and aircraft arrived in Spain in October 1936. His close relationship with Stalin unnerved Caballero who considered removing him from office.

Caballero was to flee to France in 1939. He was captured by the Nazis and interned in Dachau. He survived but died in Paris in 1946.

October, 1934, not as a pacifist. He is one of the gentlest souls I have ever met. It was he who gave me the number of *Octubre*. It has to do with the affair of the Burning of the Model Prison.

One night in August it was found that the Model Prison, housing some thousand and more fascist prisoners, was on fire. At once several thousand militiamen formed a cordon round it to prevent escapes, and in a few minutes the fire engines were working to put the fire out.

What had happened? Apparently the fascist prisoners had been told that General Mola was in Madrid. Accomplices outside set fire to the prison store of fire-wood while the fascists within set fire to their bedding, and in the uproar everyone tried to escape.

The Government were in an ugly position. The anarcho-syndicalists demanded the immediate execution of every fascist; the socialists and republicans determined to prevent judicial murders. A people's tribunal, with legal advisers and representatives of all anti-fascist bodies was appointed to pass sentence on the ringleaders. That night Paco went to bed in his apartment across the road from the prison. Thirteen times in the early hours he heard the unmistakable sound of a firing squad; the volley and the short sharp *coup de grâce*. Then he got up, shaved, and published *Octubre*, the bulletin of the anti-fascist columns, *October* and *Largo Caballero*, an uncensored, private sheet. They show the names of men who had faced the firing squad while Paco lay in bed. No other newspaper was allowed to mention the affair. So absurd indeed was the Spanish official censorship that it played into the hands of the rebel propagandists, and the story, by the time it reached the English philo-fascist press had been prettily rehashed.

In its new form it told of a group of anarchist prisoners who had been imprisoned because they had wanted to form an all-anarchist fighting column which was considered too dangerous by the rest of the Popular Front. The socialists had therefore put the anarchists in the Model Prison.

The imagination of this particular correspondent was so typical of his class that it is amusing to dwell on him for a moment. Of course he arrived in an airplane, and of course he escaped to tell his

tale, "after much difficulty in an airplane evacuating foreigners."
This was just about the time that I was placidly cruising around
on a motorbike.

He describes the censorship conducted by "a camarilla of Post
Office employees." I don't know about camarilla, but the Post Office censorship is carried out by men employed by the Post Office,
and the Telephone censorship by men employed by the telephone
company. If he tried to telephone from the Post Office that might
have explained part of his difficulty.

His censor was "changed frequently to prevent him becoming
too familiar with the journalists." In my case the censor was the
same for three weeks and never got familiar with me once.

He could not walk in the streets of Madrid without "a pass
signed by the Anarchist Committee of Madrid." There is no such
committee and never was. There is, as the reader knows by now,
a Committee of Anti-Fascist Militia, which in Madrid may have
contained a very small anarchist minority representative, but,
apart from the stamp got for me by the Russian interpreter at the
Station, it never troubled me.

Nor did I ever once show the document during all my stay in
Madrid except when I visited the Ministry of War to procure another document.

Well, this air-minded correspondent told the British public that
256 anarchists shut up there by the authorities "for wanting to
form a separate fighting column" forced the other prisoners into
the flames and burned them alive. All I want to know is why, if
there were anarchists in prison, "the Anarchist Committee of Madrid" did not get them out. But one cannot know everything...

I went to see Largo Caballero. A short, stout but active man,
who at first sight you would put at fifty years of age. He bears
no sign of having been in prison. A plasterer by trade, he began
working for his daily bread at the age of seven. In prison six times,
including one sentence to death and another for life.

His outer man is unimpressive, except for very intelligent eyes,
but when you discover that he is sixty-seven instead of fifty, when
you listen to his unadorned, straightforward way of answering

questions, when you watch him dodge the traffic, and cross the road, in spite of traffic signals, and in spite of his years, when you realise that every day he motors out to the Somosierra Front and does his bit of fighting, marches around encouraging his militiamen, who worship him —then you see that this physical unimpressiveness is really a positive quality, a useful economy, a machine-like accuracy of mind and body, that needs no romantic, theatrical or rhetorical frills.

He is almost a composite portrait of respectable English trade union leaders; nothing of Don Quixote, or of Rudolf Valentino; much more of Philip Snowden without the bitterness.[1]

The last time I had talked to him was in a little hotel in Southampton Row, in London. I had reminded him of the fate of Social Democracy in Germany and Austria; did he not fear that the Spanish Social Democrats would go the same way?

"No," said Largo Caballero, "because they are too strong for the fascists."

"Why is the liberal republican government too strong?"

"Because of us." It was quite clear that last June Caballero knew perfectly well with what economic class strength lay in Spain. He summed up his attitude towards that Government: "We are willing to help them work out their programme; we put them where they are with the sacrifice of our blood and freedom: we do not believe that they will succeed; when they fail, we will take over, and then it will be our programme and not theirs that we shall carry out; but, so long as they have yet to fail, we are loyal to the United Front and even to the middle-class republicans."

Since that conversation the middle-class republican government has failed, thanks to the fascist military rebellion. Largo Caballero has taken over, not by revolution, but by lawful succession. But it is no time for programmes. Because he had not expected so solid a fascist international, he did not know that the fascists would be at the gates of Madrid by October.

In August Madrid was calm and normal. According to foreign

---

1. Former Labour Chancellor of the Exchequer.

correspondents food was short and the rebels had cut the water supply; and yet I, who was there, sat and watched fountains playing, cafés full, restaurants crowded, happy crowds.

I sat at a café waiting for Paco to get back from his bit of fighting. I heard a curious half-familiar tongue behind me and turned to see a vast structure of muscles and sinews.

"Aren't you American?" I said.

"Yes, sir."

"Are you here as a correspondent?" All other foreigners according to the scare press in England, had been evacuated in airplanes.

"No, I'm here on business. And I'm waiting for all this to blow over so's I can get on with it."

"May I ask what kind of business?" You can always ask an American that without offence.

"All-in wrestlin'." I looked across the road at a huge hoarding plastered with news of theatrical ventures. I could read the name of Theresa, "the Spanish Shirley Temple," and next to it a big benefit at which would appear the American Tiger. This was the American Tiger.

The Tiger and I had another drink. It seemed that all-in wrestlers could make a fortune in Spain; the local product was brave, but not very well trained; the American Tiger had put by I forgot how many tens of thousands of pesetas in three months; but except for benefits for wounded militiamen there was nothing doing, and it was so darned hard to keep in training. But these goddam rebels would be licked pretty darn soon and then the Tiger would get some more pesetas and get along home for some good honest food. I gathered that all-in wrestlers, like singers of cante flamenco and minor bull-fighters, were all loyal to the democratic government, just as opera singers, starred bull-fighters and Miguel De Unamuno had gone fascist. We drank confusion to the rebels and were joined by a depressed-looking Jew.

I am not sure why he was in Madrid, but he looked like a theatrical manager. I watched him summing me up; if you look like a Nordic nowadays honest people have to be careful. At last he felt reassured. He told me a story; just another miserable disgrace to human nature of the sort that crops up so often nowadays that we hardly notice.

"Do you know Ibiza?" he said.

"No."

"I lived there some time, but I was lucky enough to get away."

"Why lucky, Ibiza has been recaptured by government forces."

"Yes; but before it was recaptured a German ship came to evacuate foreigners. Now there were a lot of German refugees on Ibiza and the German consul took the opportunity, with the help of the rebels, to put them all on the German ship and take them back to Concentration Camps."

I thought of the documents I had seen in the hands of the blue-eyed Lithuanian; hundreds upon hundreds of them addressed from Hamburg to the heads of the Nazi clubs in Spain—" a German named A. has written against Hitler in the *Mercantil Valenciano*, find out how he can be influenced," and so on, and so on. I realised what it was to be a German anywhere in the world; that this little not at all attractive-looking German Jew was certain to be in his proper place in the card index. They've got his number no doubt in Hamburg or Berlin. Moreover, it used to be only the Jew that was exiled and harried from country to country, but now it is rapidly becoming any civilised human being. The Jew went on to tell me the details of how they trapped the refugees in Ibiza, how they rescued them for the spider's parlour. The American Tiger groaned with impatience; he needed exercise; God damn these fascists anyhow. We in America don't hold with Hitler. Another of the innumerable children's processions passed: "Oo archie pay, Oo archie pay." It was a little more than two months before the rebels scored their great success of knocking out a complete crèche in an air raid on the beleaguered city.

There was a noise like a municipal band from the side of the street and I looked up to see Paco beckoning at me from a very spick and span sports Fiat. The driver was a Frenchman who preferred to keep only two wheels hitched to earth, and the musical effects came from a horn whose four notes blasted from one end of

Madrid to another. In the rear seat with Paco was a man halfway between James Maxton and a cinema dope fiend.[1] As usual I found myself being whisked willy-nilly I knew not whither. Actually I was hieing me to a nunnery.

Paco, I found out later, was busy in the rear seat arranging the rest of the war in the air. We stopped in a sheltered square in front of a long modern building guarded by militiamen.

As I say, it had been a nunnery and it was now the headquarters of the French Popular Front aviators who had volunteered for service for democracy in Spain.

We were greeted by a young officer who looked like Rupert Brooke, but with a stronger profile, and Paco introduced me to the man with the white face and black hair. It was M. the famous French left wing writer.

"You look tired," I said.

"Yes, I have been six hours in the air to-day."

Six hours we should remember in an antiquated bomber trying to find hidden Capronis of the latest style.

" M. is the sort of man I respect," Paco said afterwards. "He can write, but when it is necessary he can also do things. He can bum with words, and also bum with bums." Paco speaks English perfectly except for that one word, and always when I heard him use it my mind went back to an old lady at Paignton during the Great War who pronounced the word in the same way and had odd ideas of patriotic morality: "Do you know," she said once, "I understand the authorities are so worried about the number of people being killed that they are going to help the birth-rate by leaving the Cliff Gardens open all night. I suppose it will be all right; so long as the Germans don't go dropping any of those terrible bums."

The captain in charge took us round the nunnery with the greatest possible pride. I have never seen so perfect a Woman's Home

---

1. James Maxton, (1885-1946) was an out spoken pacifist, Scottish socialist politician and leader of the Independent Labour Party (ILP). The ILP broke away from the Labour Party when Ramsey MacDonald formed the National Government in 1931. Once an important force it had by this point been reduced to a small opposition group.

Companion paradise. The kitchen and pantry arrangements were sublime; no necessity for the most up-to-date domestic science had been forgotten; nuns in clover indeed; but now all this was packed up and forgotten; a business-like simplicity befitting mere aviators had been substituted.

"Now I will show you the chamber of horrors," said the Captain, unlocking a bright varnished door. I thought of the things one hears about nunneries.

A gasp of disgust issued from M.'s vivid lips, as we stood petrified. It was the Chapel: in it had been carefully collected every sacred image and object normally scattered about the nunnery; each one laid neatly side by side unharmed. And this was the sacred art that vandals had been destroying! I looked and cursed the vandals who had made it.

"What on earth am I to do with it all?" asked the Captain. "This place would make an admirable lecture hall; but I don't like to burn the stuff. Just look at this, —and this, and this."

"Surely he could have found an attic to store it in," said the Marquis when I told him about it next day. For I did go and see the Marquis. T., in nerve-strung Barcelona, had advised me not to do so.

"You will not find him," said T.; "he will be dead or in prison. And even if you did find him you would compromise yourself seriously." When T. got to Paris later he warned me to be careful how I wrote, because he was not certain of the other people in the hotel. Poor T., the world is a vast conspiracy chiefly engaged in harrying him. I found the Marquis with a grey face. It was not only that he was in a certain amount of danger; nor that he was pining for his wife and plump little daughter now in Portugal; it was much more that the sorrow of Spain weighed down upon him. Always his sense of *españolismo*; Spain, the least united of European countries, split into regions and districts, and yet the all-pervading sense of being a Spaniard in every Spaniard. Not in the Catalans; that is the real reason why they are so hated elsewhere in Spain. They could have got political independence long ago if they had not been so arrogant of their spiritual independence.

"I don't like the Catalans," the Marquesa had said to me in the Café Molineros in June. "They are always trying to pretend they are not Spaniards."

I defended them then because I had still believed that men like T. would defend their Catalan liberties when it came to a show-down. But even in June when I was driving back from dedicating the fountain to the dead poet I had felt doubts as to all this business about "the expression of the Catalan spirit." I had talked to a leading Catalan dramatist and producer.

"I am doing a new translation," I told him, "of Guimerà's *Terra Baixa* and I hope to put it on in London."

Now that play is perhaps the only first rate drama written by a Catalan, and the general theory is that Guimerà is the best of Catalan writers of his day.

"*Terra Baixa* is not a true expression of the Catalan Spirit," said the eminent theatre man, "it is tainted by Castilianism."

"Indeed," I said, feeling a little hurt that my interest in Catalan art was not appreciated.

"In *Terra Baixa* the man regards the woman as his possession. That is Spanish, not Catalan. The Catalans regard a woman as the mistress of the house and home."

"Indeed," I repeated, and left it at that. But I could not help thinking of one or two Catalan married couples who were tainted with what I had supposed a human failing, but what turned out to be a Castilianism.

The Marquis, though he had nothing to do with the rebellion and did not know it was coming, was obviously disposed by tradi-tion to the *ancien régime*. But in his heart there was sorrow for all Spaniards whatsoever. If he had been taken out by militiamen and shot, half his sorrow would have been that he was dying by the hand of Spaniards. Three-fifths of the hatred of the rebels is due to their being mostly foreigners, Moors, legionaries, and as to ar-mament, Italian and German; while the rebels, on their side, keep their passions at boiling point by pretending that loyal Spaniards are more than halfway to being Russians by adoption.

And so when the Marquis took me home to eat a very special

kind of Welsh rarebit and ice-cream flavoured with maple syrup that he had made himself, I told him stories of the friendliness, the courtesy, the gentleness of the militiamen I had met from Barcelona to Valencia and from Valencia to Madrid. I had done the same to T. a week or so before; and T. had answered: "Yes, but you should remember that the man you see being kind to a child to-day, very possibly murdered a man last night."

"Good God!" I had said to T., "won't you sometimes think of him, not as the man who murdered a man last night, but as the man who is being kind to a child to-day?" And T. had answered, "I have decided not to argue with you anymore. We will not mention politics and then we shall get on well together."

But the Marquis' eyes filled with tears when I told him of the mechanic in the headquarters of the mechanised transport industry.

"That is wonderful," he said. "The Spanish people is the best in the world. If only they can be given a chance."

"I have travelled a thousand miles through Spain in civil war, and I have met with friendship everywhere."

"I am very glad. I am very proud," said the Marquis. "I love my people and I bleed for them now."

I thought of him as I had seen him in Extremadura in that peasants' bedroom ten feet by ten, the home of three married couples. I thought of how there had been shame in his face as well as sorrow, shame that a foreigner was seeing this bit of Spain.

And I remembered how he was taking a film of those things so as to show his own class, the absentee landlord aristocrats, what they were doing, before it was too late. And how he had seen the fists go up in the air saluting us as we drove along and had said, "Look at that. It is something new. I do not understand."

While he had been preparing his movie THEY had been plotting. It was too late. And I thought of the tragedy of so many noble men all over the world who, like the Marquis, "do not understand."

CHAPTER 7
TOLEDO

To the marquis Toledo was the wooden statue of St Francis by Juan de Mena. To many of us it is El Greco. We go there to see how he painted hands like cold flames of intellectual passion.

If you drive to Toledo from Ciudad Real and the south you cross a mountain range where several wind-mills stand as they did when Don Quixote passed that way. Then you drop down to a burned out plain in which the sparse villages lie like rocks in a deserted sea. Among them is the village of Orgaz.

It is like a hundred other Castilian villages, poor, undistinguished, pleasant to pass but not tempting you to stop. "Its climate is cold; the prevailing wind is the N.E., sometimes the S. which is very unhealthy, and the inhabitants suffer from tertian and typhoid fevers: it has 406 houses, of one storey for the most part and of little comfort, built in two squares and twenty-seven cobbled streets: a court house: a good, safe, healthy prison: a castle dominating the country round for ten leagues with a good wall and excellent fortifications capable of holding 200 men: a school for thirty boys and twenty girls: a church with seven chapels and thirteen altars: with the furniture and vestments needed for the cults which are celebrated with great solemnity: two cemeteries: the magnificent dehesa of Villaverde of 11,000 acres: bad roads: a watercourse dry most of the year, but nevertheless crossed by a magnificent stone bridge with five arches over which passes the road used by Royalty when it goes hunting: it belonged to the counts of Orgaz." Such was the gazetteer description of Orgaz in 1849, and so it is to-day.

But because of one picture in a small church in Toledo no one can pass through Orgaz without his imagination catching fire. I remember that when I saw the name at the entrance to a brown mud village I expected to find an aura, an atmosphere different from anything else in the world; but I saw nothing but the usual cripples, the usual unnaturally thin cats, the usual women at the wash-pool. The magic could only be felt in the picture. I ought to have known it.

El Greco's Burial of the Count of Orgaz is one of those rare creations which suggest that the spirit of man, dissatisfied with the universe to which it is doomed, can almost break through to another. But what has been happening day by day this hot summer in Toledo shows how partial such 'escapes from reality' must be.

There are those, of course, who would say that the present continuing tragedy of the streets makes talk about a picture a waste of time. I do not think so, for El Greco has caught in his masterpiece something which explains that very tragedy and quickens our understanding of it. And as I walked through the streets of Toledo, listening to the incessant crackle of rifle fire from the Alcázar, certain expressions on the faces of El Greco's characters came to my mind and mingled with the actual faces of militiamen and guardias de asalto. It is more than three centuries and a half since he painted, and fascism had not been invented then, yet he was the historian of this tragic drama of 1936.

This is what El Greco's contemporaries reported of Toledo: "In whole streets once occupied by harness makers and gunsmiths, glass-blowers and other crafts there is not one craftsman left, so that you could not find a harness-maker who could make or repair a horse bridle or a mule bridle in the whole city, nor yet a gunsmith nor a harquebusier, and only one wretched glass-shop. House property, once the most valuable sort of property in the city, is to-day the worst, because there is no one to live in it nor inhabit it, and in the most central and once most esteemed quarters there are very many houses shut up, and those that fall down are not rebuilt, and people are only too glad to give them rent free to anyone who will live in them. Nuns die of hunger shut up in their convents.

"The lords of Toledo are the priests, who have magnificent houses and enjoy triumphantly the best of everything, without anyone criticising them. The archbishop and church in Toledo have more income than the whole of the rest of the city."

In the country round about, the farms were growing fewer every day, and ruin had come upon the peasantry. The great landowners were adding acre to acre and abandoning all to pasture and waste. It was in these conditions that the Vicar of St Thomas in Toledo, sued the village of Orgaz for not paying various taxes which the pious count had willed to the church two hundred and fifty years before, and having won his case he spent two thousand ducats of the money in hiring El Greco to paint the miracle of the Count's death. For the heavenly powers had been so pleased with him as a superlatively good man that they had sent St Stephen and St Augustin to represent them at his funeral. "His body was brought to burial in the church of St Thomas, built by him, and being placed in the middle, surrounded by all the nobles of the City, and the clergy having said the burial service, and desiring to lower the body into the grave, all saw clearly and patently St Stephen Protomartyr and St Augustin descend from on high, in their proper likenesses and vestments, so that all recognized them, and staying where the body was, they lowered it into the grave, in the presence of all, saying, 'Such guerdons receiveth he who serves God and the Saints' and then they vanished, leaving the church full of fragrance and celestial scent."

El Greco painted the scene; but, as with so many great artists, he did not paint the nobles of the City as they had been at the time of the miracle; he painted the nobles of Toledo as they were in his own day, the same nobles who condemned an Italian engineer who came with a good plan for making their river navigable —it remains unnavigable to this day—and then met together in solemn city council and swore to uphold and defend in all ways the dogma of the Immaculate Conception of the Virgin Mary. And in painting them he painted the whole tragedy of Spanish mysticism, of the escape from reality that made some few mournfully content, but left the fields of Spain waste and her peasantry moribund, by withdrawing all genius and energy from the solution of the inexorable problems of this world to a contemplation of the mysteries of the tomb.

For centuries the horror has gone on; the sapping of practical strength by a lust for religious fantasy; sainted paranoiacs taken as the highest delegates of the spirit of man; only now and again a supreme artist showing, like Greco, the insane sadness of it all, or like Goya, the essential vulgarity of aristocracy running to seed. Meanwhile the great unseen mass of peasantry and working men slaved to feed the mystical gluttons, who became less and less attractive as time went on.

The Count of Orgaz, for all his sanctity, was nothing but an absentee landlord held in the power of priests by his terror of the grave. Yesterday you would have found him in Madrid with a Rolls-Royce car, patron of high art and low life by turns; to-day you would find him shut up with his allies in the Alcázar, or carefully escaped to the Riviera, or taken out on a dark night by some enthusiastic nihilist and shot to encourage the others.

For the mystical melancholy displayed by El Greco gradually turned from the gibberings of old women, ratas de iglesia, and fear of the world beyond the tomb to pre-occupation with profits and dividends, and the city lords of Toledo turned from the Immaculate Conception to plans for saving Christianity by reimporting the Moors. Finally, in July, 1936, Toledo entered on its latest and greatest tragedy. And we can turn to Orgaz and a thousand villages like it for the explanation. Through all the changes it has remained the same, with starving, uneducated, comfortless people, with the great dehesa, uncultivated and wasted, with no work and therefore no food, with no hope and no help.

Then came the first awakening; with the Republic there was started Agrarian Reform. Instead of being allowed to let their enormous possessions sprawl useless and sterile across whole parishes, the absentee landlords were forced to hire it out in parcels at a reasonable rent. You would scarcely think that this was "radical."

There was no question of confiscation except in the case of a few men notoriously disloyal to the legitimate republican government. It was merely a challenge to an age-long privilege, the privilege of murdering the land. But as a challenge to one privilege leads on to other things, the forces of reaction struck back. The Gil Robles-Lerroux government ruthlessly destroyed what little had been done; the peasants in villages like Orgaz saw the guardia civil, and armed roughs in the pay of the landlords, march into their allotments and root up half-grown crops, which had been to them a symbol of new hope. Reaction over-reached itself, the elections of February, 1936, once more went against the landlords and their allies; the peasants prepared to take the land again; and this time they were determined never to lose it.

When I was there in May delegates of the "Societies of Workers on the Land" came to Madrid from the villages of Toledo. They were simple peasants who told their stories of conditions and of rough remedies taken; of men without land, and land uncultivated; of communal farms set up; of dehesas parcelled out and ploughed for the first time for generations; of properties whose landlords had been so long away that nobody knew their names; of villages where everything, down to the prison, the well, the dust of dead men in the cemetery, belonged to one man and he away. Everywhere the same story, peasants willing to pay for land, but at any rate determined to have it, absentee landlords, no longer full of the melancholy dignity of El Greco's day, but wasted by the indignities of modern idleness, equally determined that the land they refused to use should not be used by anyone else.

So Toledo has come to life again. It contains other wonders besides the El Grecos; besides El Greco's house itself with a kitchen like an old master; besides the synagogue, with its garden from which the custodian picks you a bunch of flowers; besides the numberless humble whitewashed cottages each with its trailing carnations suspended like red butterflies from the iron balconies; besides the riches of the cathedral and the Plaza de Zocodover and the Alcàzar, and the Puerta de Alcantara, the "Bridge of the Bridge"; besides the river Tagus.

Let us look first of all at the overshadowing unity of Toledo itself.

It is one of those cities which has lost its geographical raison d'être. Perfect as a medieval stronghold, the guardian of the north, one can see very well why men built it. And in this it is unlike Madrid, which ought never to have been built at all, if natural surroundings have any part in the choice of a site for human habitation. Madrid has a river, but you have to look for it very carefully as it sulks between its artificial banks. No one would have made Madrid a city for the sake of a Manzanares. And Madrid has nothing else, neither fertility, nor accessibility, neither genial climate, nor natural defences. It is nothing but the arbitrary centre of the sad wastes of Castile. It became the capital of a centralised Spain for no better reason than that it was not the capital of any one of the regions which must be forced unwillingly to unite into one kingdom.

But go forty miles south across the undulating treeless plain and there you find a natural born city fit to be a capital, Toledo, a lordly place when Madrid was a wretched village; Toledo, superbly embraced by the Tagus and barring the road to intruders from any point of the compass; Toledo, for all its beauty, a sad thing, like a woman made a widow at thirty.

For whereas a medieval city drew its importance largely from its natural strength, from its military value, a modern city must have industries, resources, communications if it is to live. Because there are no economic excuses for Toledo's existence, it remains medieval and a corpse, an incorruptible sainted corpse, but nevertheless simply the dead body of a city.

In Toledo three civilizations lived together and made contributions to human dignity, the Arab, the Jew, and the Christian, but the modern world has passed it by and their once active civic consciousness has become a museum. One looks down on Toledo from the other side of the river and thinks 'if I were an American millionaire I would buy this place, tidy up all those rubbish heaps, and throw it open free to the public except on Monday, when I should charge a peseta.' True, Toledo has, or had until only yesterday, an Archbishop, innumerable convents and monasteries, a provincial government, a garrison, an arms factory; but after all these are every one of them but medieval survivals, they do not make a city. Not even a good tourist industry makes a city.

But for one thing Toledo would be merely a geological formation belonging to the quaternary age. That thing is the incredibly persistent Castilian spirit that survives in its great works of art such as we have been observing at in The Burial of the Count of Orgaz; a spirit I had believed to have survived only there, and certainly not in the narrow streets. To-day I know better; for I have seen Toledo, the common people of Toledo, rise up in their wrath and defend themselves. I have seen them strike a blow to destroy the melancholy mysticism which long ago has degenerated into the vulgarity of fascist reaction.

There has been a good deal of street fighting in Toledo in the last two thousand years, and most of it must have been cut to one unalterable pattern, the pattern I saw one August day in 1936. The city has stained its pages with all the appropriate blood spots. Here in 806 a Moor invited four hundred leading citizens to a banquet, cut off their heads and placed them in a well; here was carried on a constant fight against the emir of Cordoba and his "soldadesca asalariada," who was bitterly hated by the capitalist Jews of the vassal city; here, in 1355, the unpopular Don Henry was refused admittance at one bridge but let in by rival factions at the other, after which one thousand Jews were slaughtered; here in 1449 one faction of the citizens irritated at excessive war taxation not only shut their gates in the king's face but sniped at him from the walls, whereat another faction let him in and captured his enemies, who had taken refuge in the Cathedral; in 1468 the king had to make a night escape, but his faction returned him in triumph in the morning; here, for a change, in 1479 Queen Isabel, the Catholic, gave birth to Doña Juana la Loca or Crazy Jane; the sixteenth century saw the city split between the Silvas and Ayalas, the local Montagus and Capulets, while at the same time a vast accumulation of fascinating relics enriched it. In 1680, owing to depreciation of the coinage, street fighting broke out once again, and finally, in 1808, the city rose against Napoleon's armies and especially Dupont. The populace, alarmed at a rumour that Napoleon was not going to recognise the odious Ferdinand VII, assembled in the Plaza de Zocodover, waving a banner with his horrid face upon it and, "full of a religious sentiment," made everybody bow the knee before it.

The object of their adoration was the king who closed the universities and established schools of bull-fighting in their stead. His likeness has been perpetuated by the ruthless brush of Goya. In 1808 the people of Toledo loved him; screamed for him; kneeled to his image; execrated the French for him; and all without shedding a drop of blood. But when, in December, the French army appeared at the gates, discretion led them to open as widely as possible to a host whom unfortunately they feared as much as they hated. They must have been an unpleasant lot, these priest-ridden underlings crying that they should be given back their chains.

And yet what we are told in the chronicles of Toledo is but the muddled memory of the clash between growing and failing economic classes. If we could sort out the details we should see the aristocrats and the bourgeois fighting one another; one faction stirring up anti-Jewish riots, another burning churches, another calling in the king's party to redress a growingly unstable balance. We should see amid the black gowns of many priests and religious orders the protest of anti-clerical elements; men who had learned to associate the ecclesiastical princes with wage slavery. On all sides we should see a thing as old as the hills with which we today are threatened under the last of its many names —we should see in the thousand-year-old narrow streets of Toledo the undying ruthless bands of fascism, now staring into a tomb, now making a tomb of the good earth of the surrounding plain.

One day in 1838 a curious English vagabond turned vendor of Bibles wandered on a horse into this city. He looked up the chief bookseller and offered him a dozen Bibles. They were readily accepted, and the bookseller guaranteed to circulate them. George Borrow was astonished: "Will not your doing so bring you into odium with the clergy?"

"Ca!" said he. "Who cares? I am rich. I do not depend on them, they cannot hate me more than they do already, for I make no secret of my opinions. My brother nationals and myself have, for the last three days, been occupied in hunting down the factious and the thieves of the neighbourhood; we have killed three and brought in several prisoners. Who cares for the cowardly priests? Many is the Carlist guerilla-curate and robber-friar whom I have assisted to catch. We will make the clergy shake, I assure you."

That was in 1838; a little less than a hundred years after, the Street of the Archbishop had become the Street of Karl Marx; every church was closed; the guerilla-curates and robber-friars were being besieged in the Alcázar. It was thoughts such as these that ran in my head as I motored across the burned-out wastes between the capital and the city on the Tagus.

I had been told that the War Office would give me every facility that I needed in Toledo, and that I had only to go and get a car and an escort, and be off. That was not literally true: there turned out to be formalities, and nobody seemed to know the official in charge of foreign correspondents. When I ran him to earth he presented me with a long list of names, and asked if mine was among them. It was not; but what intrigued me was that this document was, or ought to have been, somewhat private, for against the names of my Press colleagues were annotations. Against most of them, I am glad to say, was written 'bueno' or 'muy bueno,' but against some there was the warning 'muy cuidado.'

A certain correspondent had made me a bit cross by reason of the number of nuns he had seen from his aeroplane stripped naked and made to dance to the mob. I was glad to see that 'muy cuidado' was against his name. "Oh yes," said the official, "we have to be very careful of foreign correspondents," and to show how careful, he ran down the list with me. "By the way," he added, "your name is not here?" I wondered what he would do if I had claimed to be X with 'muy cuidado' underlined in the margin. The simple trust of all Spaniards whatsoever may not make for efficiency, but it is nicer than the ingrown insolence of officials in certain other parts of the world.

When I got my car I was thankful to find that its vintage well nigh secured me against any wish of the driver to break records. My nerves had been shattered in Barcelona; I was perfectly prepared to face a certain amount of misdirected rifle firing on the safe side of Toledo streets, but experience made me fear the journey. We went at a steady thirty miles an hour along the splendid road over which King Alfonso had so often speeded, and I was able to let my imagination wander over the scenery.

At all times of the year the central plains of Spain are deceptive; now in August you would think them a ruthless desert incapable of growing anything. But for the huge golden piles of straw at the threshing floors, it was impossible to believe that the crippled villages could get bread from these stones. And in May, when I travelled the same road, you would have believed yourself in a rich granary and an Elysian field of flowers. The sun gives and the sun takes away; May comes to less than it seems to offer, but August paints the landscape with too grim a palette. If only there were trees.

The driver and the armed guard are not communicative. I do not know if they are soured by experiences with other foreign correspondents, but they assume that I cannot speak a word of Spanish. This idea they convey to the barricades, and save for a mechanical Popular Front salute, I give no sign of life until in a distant hollow below us Toledo comes into view. But within me I am thinking of the Marquis; of the golden age in which most Spaniards believe before the trees had been cut down by the Arabs, or the Carlists, or the French, or the Goths; of the amazing effect of a little water in a dry land; of how the French soldiers must have felt trudging these alien wastes in 1810; of how the soldiers of the Great War, after experiencing horror and fatigue in half a dozen countries, came back, apparently unchanged by all that had happened, to sell milk in Devonshire or to mind a machine.

Toledo was dim in the hollow; a dull brown in a dull brown haze; the four square citadel, the Alcázar, dominated it from the very first glimpse. We stopped to take photographs.

The Alcázar stood up amid the huddle of houses. On the left was the smoke from a small battery in government hands on the other side of the river; on the right was the smoke of the nearest cottages to the Alcázar, set on fire the previous night by the rebels. To me at least it seemed fantastic that men should be working in the fields in the foreground, creating new food to sustain life, and that in the hazy background men were busy with death. To the right of the you can see the Cathedral, while immediately below it and a little to the right is the arms-factory.

When, on July 18th, the preparations for the revolt were completed, the Guardia Civil, gathered from every town and village in the province, went down to the arms-factory with six motor lorries and informed the old gentleman in charge that they were taking the whole store of munitions up to the Alcázar.

"Oh, but I forbid it," said the aged commanding officer.

"We insist," they replied.

"Well I can do nothing," he said, and by so saying probably forfeited his life. If he has not been shot already he is certainly in prison for complicity in the revolt, and his career is at an end. Poor old man! How little there is to save us from fatal mistakes when daily life has become uprooted. I can picture the sort of man he must be, this officer commanding the arms-factory of Toledo; too fat, bespectacled, thickset, not dignified in spite of an unsmiling face; he cared for nothing provided he could sit sufficiently long over his coffee to digest a newspaper and a meal. And then six motor trucks arrived; a rebellion; almost bound to be successful; and in any case how could he resist; and so he is in prison, unshaven, with no newspapers, wretched coffee. And in the Alcázar they have three million rounds of rifle ammunition, scarcely any water, nothing to do except shoot at the walls opposite and hope that the

Moors will come in time.

Now we have come nearer; the houses stand out in greater detail. All those low houses surrounding the great building, are full of militiamen, their wives and children; an armed city waiting, while inside the Alcázar between one and two thousand human beings wait also.

Horrible stories have floated out from the doomed rebels: there are known to be loyal soldiers among them, caught in a trap. I can just hear the rattle of machine guns as I twist the spool in my camera; they say that the rebel officers lean the machine guns on the shoulders of the loyal soldiers, after forcing them to the windows, so that if answering fire comes from the roofs and streets of the city it is a loyalist who receives the bullet; they say that in there three women have given birth to three infants and that all were born dead, lucky innocents; they say that they are feeding on horseflesh and half a pint of water a day, unless, that is, they are able to get water by stealth from the nearest houses at night.

In the picture on the right of the Alcázar (see photographs) is a little gap; notice it, for we shall be going there in the afternoon.

Ahead of me the main road winds into the city; I have often driven that way, but to-day I mustn't do so. You can see the sandbags half across the road on the extreme right. From that point on, the road is near enough to the Alcázar to make the firing inconvenient, so we are going to edge the car under the bags and proceed across waste ground beneath the protection of those cottages.

I cannot believe what they tell me: I look at the triangular danger signal by the side of the road; set up no doubt by the Spanish Tourist interests to show how careful we are in Spain, how civilised, how able to look after our foreign visitors who come to spend money and to see the El Grecos. In normal times I should go up that road, slowing down at the sign, and after passing the gate find myself in the Plaza de Zocodover surrounded by touts and amateur cicerones. Indeed, I remember losing my temper in the Plaza de Zocodover only a few years back and telling a persistent youth that he could go to hell before I would let him lead me to the Cathedral, the Casa del Greco, the synagogue or any hotel whatsoever. It had spoiled my cup of coffee beneath the arches of the Plaza de Zocodover.

Now I found myself edging off to the right, skulking behind sandbags, glancing back at the Alcázar from which I could see little spurts of smoke. They looked like the splashes of raindrops on a misty lake. It seemed incredible that a woman was hanging up linen to dry; that a little boy, in spite of a notice forbidding any-one "hacer aguas mayores o menores," was doing just that; func-tions, social or natural, cannot be held up because a few million rounds of rifle cartridges have to be blown off somehow before death comes to twelve hundred men.

We reached the city gate; a medieval, solid affair, kept, one had always supposed, for tourists, and yet how real and useful it looked to-day. The large Ministry of War placard on our car does not save us from a thorough search from several enthusiasts. A part of the Army in Overalls, the guardians of the gate of Toledo in 1936; descendants of the men who shut this very gate in a king's face and then sniped at him from the walls. They are guarding the gate through which, if the twelve hundred rebels in the Alcá-zar are ever to escape alive, must come the descendants of those very Moors, whom Isabella, mother of Toledo's royal child, Crazy Jane, expelled from Spain nearly five hundred years ago. For ev-ery night the inmates of the Alcázar tune in their wireless sets and to them through the three metre thick walls come stories of fascist victories, of columns coming to relieve them, of the fall of Madrid; hunger and sickness whisper in one ear 'surrender,' the ether waves whisper into the other promises of rescue.

We pass through the gate and begin to climb that road all tourists know past the Gate "with Moorish influence," bearing left until the Zocodover Square is reached. But to-day we do not reach the Zocodover Square; at the farthest corner we once more meet sandbags but for which we should be under fire from the overhanging Alcázar. Militiamen are lying on mattresses beneath the shadow of a dram-shop wall. An old woman milks a goat, thus calling attention to nature's ugliest effort at designing breasts. We are told to swerve to the right and wedge the car into an absurd crack of a road as steep as a cliff path.

I have a letter to the captain of Militia. Paco gave it to me. Paco and the captain were prison companions, having been shut up together after October. Helped by militiamen of every sort we reach a barracks where the captain's adjutant volunteers to take me to the captain.

We find the captain sitting in a broken armchair under a canopy spread across one of those inner patios that always make me wish to be a Spanish householder. He reads my letter, which tells him that I am everything that is most desirable and that I am to be shown anything that I may desire to see. "Yes," he says, "but first let us have dinner."

The captain is an excellent specimen of *l'homme moyen sensuel*; quite like a movie star. I do not know the stars in private life, but I imagine them to be more body than mind, healthy, slow-moving and inclined to enjoy an armchair. This man gives out an air of huge but casual enjoyment of his physical existence, the sort of enjoyment that I rise to only occasionally on a hot day while bathing in a warm sea. He has the kind of eyes that best-seller writers have broken many typewriters trying to describe; usually with the help of the epithet "hot." The kind of eyes that women, they say, find effective; insolent eyes. In sober truth, I think that his eyes look as if they have successfully staved off a slight cold only the day before yesterday or may possibly have to be treated with boric acid in a day or two. Very handsome eyes, in fact, attractively half-extinguished, like a room which looks better by fire-light.

Dinner was a long time coming, and the wait was embarrassing. I could not fail to see that the captain was very shy of me. He found it hard to make conversation. Moreover, from the top story, just beneath the canopy, now on one side, now on another of the inner square, popped girls' heads staring down on me and the captain. By the time we sat down at table I had lost my Castilian and, though nobody knew it, my English too. I suppose they were all daughters of the house in which the militia officers were billeted. I found myself in the unpleasant position of making a table of fifteen adults so shy by my mere presence that nobody talked.

We stared at our plates and ate beans. I thought it incongruous to be so shy in a city where they were killing one another.

Dinner over, we sat in the patio. My chair was so broken that I feared a landslip, but I did not like to call attention to it. The girls sat and stared, chiefly at the captain. Orderlies came in with papers to be signed. And still we sat, and would be sitting yet had I not broken the intolerable mass timidity by taking everybody's photograph. More by luck than cunning I took them standing, and the new position seemed to remind the captain that I wanted to see the town.

First, we climbed on the roof of the barracks. The captain and I were bare-headed, his hair, dark and straight, was combed back and shone with, I suppose, a subdued insolence. The other officer was wearing a forage cap which on emerging on the roof he carefully removed. Apparently snipers were more ready to leave bare heads alone.

"You must keep your head well down," said the captain, and we edged round a parapet into full view of the rebel citadel.

A constant, though irregular, crackle of rifle fire came from their direction across the faded vermilion roofs of the thickset city. Immediately in front of me the smoke I had seen in the morning still rose from the burning cottages. To the right towered the Cathedral spire beneath which, locked up and deserted, lay Juan de Mena's San Francisco and El Greco's Espolio. And ever as I dodged along behind the captain I kept thinking to myself that the Count of Orgaz was lying amid the flame-like hands beneath these very roofs over which men were shooting. Crawling catlike over the roof, the captain was in his element; we began to like one another, and so I turned my back on the Alcázar and took his photograph with a clothes-line across his mouth, a convent with a red cross flag as a background, and the crackle of rifles dimly in the distance.

Immediately beneath us as we clambered across the roof there lay a tangle of human tragedy, sordid and insignificant except to the two or three people concerned. We climbed down one flight to find ourselves in its midst. A long corridor with many cell-like rooms giving off from it. Near the door piles of old mattresses on which militiamen and some girls lay resting, with that unattractive appearance that no one can avoid who has been for several days sleeping at odd moments in his clothes. Pasted on the doorpost was a brief notice forbidding entrance; it was signed "By order of the Cheka." Here were the detention rooms of the militia secret police; the sordid reality so often written up in accounts of the "Terror." One expects horrible dungeons, torture chambers, ruthless mechanical efficiency meting out secret punishment; one finds a corridor with the paint scratched, doors with frosted glass tops, old mattresses, tiredness. The captain stood silent taking it all in. His impassive face certainly showed no blood lust, no anger, no purging energy even; he was content to take it all in with a sleepy intensity.

A door opened; a young militiaman armed with rifle and bayonet, his feet in rope-soled canvas shoes, strolled out with two young men who had asked to be taken to a lavatory. Two prisoners of the Cheka. The captain stared at them, not with hate or anger, but with his usual impassivity. One felt that he never had any particular emotion unless it was needed for a specific action. He had nothing to do with these prisoners, not then at least, and so he stared at them without feeling. They disappeared behind a door; the captain turned and looked at me with exactly the same expression. "Fascists," he said quietly. A sleepy girl buried her face in another lump of mattress.

As the men passed me slowly I saw more of them. Young men in the early twenties; they, too, had been several nights in their clothes. They had neither collars, nor ties, nor shoelaces; they were unshaven, heavy-eyed, grey. They strolled very slowly back along the corridor, dispirited, lethargic. Nobody ill-treated them, nor would they do so; they would simply be shot in due course; and when the militia made up their mind to shoot them, it would be, as much as for any other reason, to break the intolerable tension, the shyness of having to do with these specimens of another race of animal.

For a moment, as they passed, I saw one of them side by side with the captain. Considering them as two animals at the Zoo, the one in fine feather, the other mangy, I could not help thinking how easily their attractiveness could have been reversed. If the Moors could be brought to Toledo to slaughter half the town, then the captain would be unshaven, grey, heavy-eyed; and his prisoner, after a face massage and a visit to the tailor, would once more be a senorito, a leader of Toledo's smart set, with a racing car and a querida and as much physical beauty as the captain.

The noble qualities are only skin deep. In war time your propagandist waits until your enemy has had to sleep in his clothes and remain unshaven and then photographs him next to your well-groomed self, beauty and the beast. No more need to wonder on which side justice lies, for God is always on the side of the Beauty Parlour.

The captain turned his head slowly, and followed their retreating forms up the corridor, but he made no comment and betrayed no feelings.

What would I like to do next?

"I would like to get nearer the Alcázar."

"There are some barricades very near the Alcázar; perhaps you would like to go there."

We walked downstairs to the street; but before we left the barracks we went and stood in what had been the barracks chapel. Uncouth mattresses lay along the floor and a few slightly sick young militiamen sprawled on them. Near the door a confessional turned on its side had been improvised into a sort of box office, and an orderly was writing out passes. I looked at it and smiled. The captain looked at me looking, and smiled also, and then to my astonishment he made a comment:

"What sadness has been produced in that box!" he said. It was the first time he had volunteered an opinion on anything, and as he spoke he stared at the confessional in a way that made me suspicious. This man of action, apparently without feeling, certainly without desire to express feeling, was he not living a life of intense contemplativeness? He was like an artist at a picture gallery; he was approaching every experience that his eyes gave him with the humility of a mystic. He was an El Greco who could not paint; a primitive using action as a medium. El Greco would have brought out that look which I had just caught only by accident.

Young men came up to him and asked questions. These men who are described as sexually attractive always turn out to be worshipped by their own sex.

We walked uphill into what had once been the Archbishop's Street, but had become, early in the Republic, the Street of Carlos Marx. For some reason the Gil Robles régime forgot to change the name back again, and no one had ever tampered with Trinity Street; so there at one street corner Carlos Marx and the Trinity share a corner stone. Here is the meeting place. Below the name plate of Trinity Street you can read: "Stick no Bills"; below that they have stuck a recruiting poster, "Enlist in the Fifth Regiment"; next to it is something about the "Fascist Canaille"; and next that is a Spanish Red Cross notice. And in Carlos Marx Street, beneath the ancient Archbishop's Palace is a militia woman in full uniform of overalls, rifle in hand, scarlet scarf about her neck. "Are you sure you got me in your photo, comrade?" she says.

Carlos Marx Street has the Archbishop's Palace on one side and the Cathedral on the other. We stood beneath the walls of the latter and watched a line of women outside a soup kitchen lower down. Another officer joined us.

"An English journalist," the captain explained, and before I knew what was happening we had plunged into a rapid discussion of the Spanish temperament. The newcomer was explaining why Spain would never be communist. The Spanish temperament was anarchist and individualist. I would remember how in Don Quixote—how by making Sancho Panza say so and so, Cervantes was— Moreover, the whole Castilian history... Hermandados ... Regionalism ... Individualism ... the Spanish Ego. The captain nodded from time to time, watching the effect of this new barrage upon me. Presently I noticed how constantly rifle bullets seemed to be sailing somewhere overhead. It made me unable to concentrate on the Spanish character. The captain saw that too. He would never have noticed the rifle bullets but for the expression on my face.

"We are nearer the Alcázar," he said. "Do you see that rope?" I saw a rope stretched triangularly across the opposite side of the road. It had once been supported a few feet above the ground by a post knocked into the cobbled surface; but that had fallen down and no one had bothered to put it up again.

"Put your head the other side of the rope," said the captain, "and look up there, but draw your head back very quickly."

I did so. Towering above me a hundred and fifty yards or so away was the grey wall of the Alcázar wreathed in little gusts of smoke. The rope was a warning that that side of the road was within death's reach.

On the other side we had talked safely of Quixote; women had passed us screening their faces from the sun with paper fans. "Last week," said the Captain, "a little girl, nine years old, was playing here with a ball. It rolled beyond that rope and she followed it. A sniper got her through both cheeks.

We said good-bye to the Cervantist and turned the Cathedral corner.

We were now approaching the burning houses I had seen from a distance in the morning; but it was absolutely impossible to remember that behind them loomed the Alcázar at a very few yards distance unless one was constantly reminded of the fact. Life was so normal everywhere; a line of women bargaining about milk; the milkman and his donkey cart; the donkey half asleep, whisking his tail against his hereditary enemies, the flies; three little girls skipping; a boy of two sitting on the edge of the pavement, his head shaved close to cheat the insects, playing with a sardine tin and a broken spoon; an old woman on a balcony emptying heaven knows what liquid into the middle of the road; window-boxes of carnations. At the top of the road one saw a group of men clustered near an improvised shelter of logs straddling the narrow street.

"You must be careful now," said the Captain; "we are very close, and at some places the streets are under fire. Then we must hurry." The shelter was built across the road at its juncture with a narrow side lane, leading straight up to the Alcázar, from which hand grenades could be thrown. The end of the lane was packed with sandbags in which an occasional bullet could be heard embedding itself. In the picture you can see a man leaning on his rifle to the right; his rifle is stuck between the sandbags, and the enemy are forty yards from its other end. Between is no-man's-land, the restricted, concentrated no-man's-land of street warfare.

I climb up on the sacks and raise myself for a moment above them; immediately ahead are the burnt-out shells of cottages still smoking, and beyond them, through what were once their windows, I see again, but very near now, the besieged fortress.

The noise is irritating; a constant ricochet of bullets coming I knew not whence, going I knew not whither. I raised my arms fully above my head to discharge my camera right into no-man's-land; a cheerful militiaman hidden behind a window three yards above me, bent on adding to the confusion, began shooting bullets at the opposite wall nine feet away, and my hands trembled violently. A laugh broke out from the barricade below: "Ha! Ha! Look, there is an Englishman who is frightened." I turned round and explained that I had always been sensitive to noise, and to show them how brave I was took deliberate aim once more at no-man's-land. Some of my readers may have expected that I saw piles of bodies at every street corner; the truth is; in street warfare the more exposed sections become hopelessly congested with empty tin-cans.

Now we continue our journey to the next barricade a few yards up the street. We are going parallel to the whole length of the Alcázar; every lane to the left leads straight past the smoking houses to its foot.

To take the Plate captioned "Firing from Barricades", I stepped out in front of the barricade, looking back to the platform lower down the road. Above it you can see the street sign which tells the name of no-man's-land in my picture. Immediately in front of this barricade the road widens out and comes once more under the direct fire as you will see from the accompanying photo. Here the captain, out of focus, is looking at his men, while they look at the camera. To the left of the men in the distance is a side-street leading to the Alcázar, and across it is barbed wire; almost all this space is swept by rifle-bullets and at any moment a sortie may be made down it; but only to be caught in a cross fire from this barricade and the next and last.

In spite of his proximity to all this activity Jesus Palencia has kept his shop open at the corner of X. street. He is a grocer, and I expect that many of the cans thrown out into no-man's-land came from him. In "A Danger Zone" you see Jesus Palencia's shop from the other side. To take this photograph we had had to hurry. You will see the barricade which we have just left, in the distance; between it and us is a ten yard strip exposed to point blank fire.

"Now," said the captain, "I will cross first; then you must count ten and follow. If you come at once you may get the bullets meant for me." He ran; not very fast; his arm bent over his head, nicely exposing his heart, when you come to think of it; but who does not instinctively protect head rather than heart. In the very middle of his stride he paused and gazed up at the Alcázar, with the same deliberate, insolent stare, like a man at a show who has paid and expects to be amused, but has not been amused yet. As he turns round on the other side of the danger zone, three sharp cracks ring out, three rifle bullets embed themselves in the opposite wall. I have counted ten and follow, trying hard not to run fast enough to make the watchers laugh. Three more cracks and bullets follow me; and the captain stares silently at the wall opposite, where pock marks tell of a month of this sort of thing.

Now we have reached the most advanced barricade of all; beyond which it is quite impossible to go. If you follow the stone house that is the background to the picture called "The Last Barricade" you come to a gap at the left hand side; the mottled mass that fills the gap is the Alcázar. There is no posing about the picture; each rifle is aimed directly at the enemy's position. The men standing on the left are using the wall as a protection, those on the right are being a little careless. And in the centre you can see a figure with a whiter arm than the rest, and the ends of what looks like a pair of white gloves at its side. It is an interesting figure; not Spanish but German; not male but female. In the most advanced trench at

Toledo were three German anti-fascists, two men and this girl.

The arrival of an Englishman seemed to complete the international front, for though I had nothing more lethal than a camera, the very presence of another foreign sympathiser was almost like new stores of ammunition. We cheered the anti-fascist cause and damned the fascists so loudly, that the captain raised his voice. "Less noise," he said. "Why attract hand grenades?"; and as he said it we were treated to a more vigorous outburst of rifle firing accompanied by the impotent spatter of a machine gun. Three million rounds of rifle ammunition and nothing to do before dying but shoot them off.

But it is time to think of the men and women and children entrenched within the Alcázar. Who are they and why are they there? There are some hundreds of rebel guardias civiles, officers and cadets; besides these three are perhaps two hundred fascists properly so-called, rich local capitalists and implicated priests who fled to the Alcázar for refuge. There are a number of soldiers, many of them loyal and unwillingly caught up in a situation that is none of their making, and there are women and children, wives some of them of rebels, others of entrapped loyalists.

Horrible stories get out of the life within. A few soldiers, protesting loyalty, have escaped to the barricades; some have let themselves down by sheets and ropes into the river; some have committed suicide. You will find the same company in Teruel and in Cordoba, a group of rebels who miscalculated their strength, who hoped to gain the day by one sudden act of treachery and who are left to face nothing but punishment.

The officers, they say, are keeping their spirits up with drugs from the chemist's shop. Every day as more masonry is torn away, more people must cluster in the cellars. Nobody knows what they are eating. They are the last fragments of age-long despotisms starving to death.

If only someone could write their history; how as the days of futile agony pass on some have grown cruel and others religious; some have grown beards, and others have kept themselves as clean-shaven and dapper as if there was an alternative to lingering death; the stealthy hunting of women; the mothers watching their children; wondering if to-morrow there will still be a thin drop of nourishment to be squeezed from their starved breasts; the children still thinking of new games, playing fascists versus reds no doubt. Some souls are growing daily more noble beneath the strain, others are cracked and go squeaking, like bats, to hell.

Wives are finding themselves pregnant without any possibility of their coming to full term; some hardened minds without illusions seek whimsical ways of making the last hours of life tolerable; others persistently hope and expect General Franco to come with Moors to their help. One can imagine them clustering round the loud-speaker, listening to the drunken Queipo de Llano in Seville. Can his filthy jokes make them laugh? What does make them laugh? Do they argue and find good reasons for disbelieving all the government wireless station says? Probably they believe that General Mola has already marched down the Paseo del Prado, or at least they are persuaded that next Thursday, or even next Wednesday he will be there; and then, quite soon, a paella, maybe a rice with chicken in it followed by coffee and a liqueur.

Certainly they believe that every nun in Toledo has been raped; that Moscow gold paves the hostile streets around them; that the militiamen have robbed and slaughtered; that they themselves are crusaders. What on earth do they not in their feverish state confess to the priests? And some are promising themselves a life of purity if they ever get out, others a visit to the nearest brothel.

The captain hurries past the exposed corner: I follow him. We are on our way back to a good supper. Here is the Plaza de Zocodover! (see illustrations) We will go by the way of the Plaza de Zocodover, where there is a beer shop. When on July 18th, the rebels gathered their forces and the guardias de asalto were rushed from Madrid to oppose them, they took up their positions in the Plaza de Zocodover.

"Now proceed," says the best of guides, Richard Ford, "to the Zocodover, 'the square market,' a name which, to readers of Lazarillo de Tormes and Cervantes, recalls the haunts of rogues and of those proud and poor Don Whiskerandos who swaggered and

starved with their capas y espadas. *Suk* in Arabic, *Zoco* in Spanish, and *Soke* in English, signify a 'market place,' and a vicinity to
cathedrals; for while commerce and religion went hand in hand,
the shrine attracted multitudes and 'money-changers,' while the
sanctity protected the cash. This *plaza* is most Moorish, with its
irregular windows, balconies, blacksmiths, and picturesque peasantry, and in summer evenings is a fashionable promenade. It was
for years the site of national sports of fire and blood, of the auto-
da-fé and the bull-fight; it was planted in 1840."

Here is the Plaza de Zocodover to-day; not one stone lies upon
another; between the camera and the ruins all the ground is swept
by fire from the Alcázar lying to the right out of the picture; to
the left a huge barricade of sandbags is waiting to be occupied in
an emergency, for that way lies the one chance of a sortie from
the fortress and out of the city. Suppose the rebels made a desperate sally they would race for the Plaza and hurl themselves upon
that barricade, but as they did so they would be machine-gunned
by the cheerful souls whose photograph I take. Most of them are
guardias de asalto, trained men, for this is a vital position, and
mere bravery and enthusiasm are not enough. To the left is an
armoured car of an amateurish and doubtful design: it has been
hastily constructed by the men in the steel industries, and it would
not commend itself to a mechanized army expert. Just out of the
picture to the right is an enormous gramophone, a lethal weapon
to the man with a sensitive ear, filling the square with a distorted
blare and assuring us against our better judgment that the music
goes round and around and comes out here. Immediately behind
me as I snap my camera is a thick rope across the road to keep
back the general public who stand vaguely like a crowd which has
arrived too early, and is not sure whether the game has been put
off on account of the weather. Above our heads a constant smack
of rifle bullets followed by little pieces of cement and plaster dislodged and crumbling to the ground. In front of the barricade and
visible in the other picture is a café table lying on its side. One has
an irresistible impulse to go and put it on its legs and be shot in
doing so. One wonders what has happened to its marble top.

I try hard to visualise what the Plaza de Zocodover was like when last I sat in it, and all I can remember is my own irritation at the touts who wanted to show me round Toledo. When will the next tourist come to Spain? And from out of the sky suddenly, to everybody's intense surprise, there swoops an enormous airplane.

Is it ours or theirs? Has it come to bomb the Alcázar or to bomb the loyal city? It hovers above the fortress; it is Italian; everybody suddenly knows that. I confess that I have not the slightest idea as to how one tells an Italian airplane from one of any other nationality, but I, too, am suddenly certain that this is an Italian. It is trying to drop hams on the Alcázar. Why everybody in twenty seconds knew that it was hams, and not beef or bread or beer, I cannot say; but we all said that the Italian 'plane was dropping hams for the rebels. Hams of Montanches, no doubt, those juicy, succulent products of the oak forests of Estremadura; those hams which the Marquis had tried to buy for his plump little daughter. "The fat," says Ford, "when they are properly boiled, looks like melted topazes, and the flavour defies language, although we have dined on one this very day, in order to secure accuracy and inspiration. The flesh of pork, a test of orthodoxy, as being eschewed by Jew and Moslem, enters largely into the national metaphors and stew-pots. The Montanches hams are superb." And so we all knew that this Italian plane coming up from Badajoz and the western piggeries was dropping ham for the rebels.

A wave of fury swept through the whole visible world; rifles, machine guns, anything began to pepper the upper air. I saw a lad of fourteen race to his cottage and run out with a pistol six inches long, and try to cover the intruder; he could not fire for he had no ammunition. And then with a spatter of machine-gun fire spraying the town the 'plane disappeared as suddenly as it came and within forty-five seconds of its first arrival. Half a minute later everybody knew that two men had been killed as it swept low over the arms-factory. A blanket of talkative indignation covered the little crowds up and down Toledo. An Italian 'plane had come from Badajoz, dropped Montanches hams on the Alcázar, killed two people with machine-gun fire, and disappeared. We all knew that. And yet I do not see how anyone had been in a better position to know it than I, and I only knew it because everyone else knew it. By the time I had got half way to Madrid on the return journey the men at the barricade knew that a rebel plane had bombed Toledo and all they wanted from us was the details.

Meanwhile in the Alcázar the twenty-eighth night was falling and a meagre supper of garbanzos and mule flesh was being served out. The rebel aeroplane had brought a more valuable thing than probably mythical hams, for now once more hope could lift its aching head. 'They will certainly relieve us in a day or two. They are coming up from Badajoz. General Mola will enter Madrid by Sunday. We shall drink coffee in the city in a very few days. We shall go to the cinema and see Shirley Temple. The child will not die after all. The child will be born after all. I wonder if the brothel has been burned…"

Two or three days later I was walking down the Grand Via, in Madrid, when a muffled roar from a passing car stopped me. It was followed by the shaggy face of Alvarez Del Vayo. "You must get in this car and come with me."

"But I have an important engagement with Paco."

"This is more important. The Alcázar is about to surrender, and you will be the only foreign correspondent to know it."

Del Vayo was not then what he is now— Spain's Foreign Minister, but he was already the power behind the throne, and the ear, the voice, of Largo Caballero. He is one of those men whom you must forgive, whatever he does, a man without guile, a genial mystic. He wore brown instead of the usual blue overalls, and every day he would be so full of appointments as to be inevitably an hour or two late for all of them. Most afternoons he would drive out to the Sierra to do his bit of fighting, but every now and then he would be so late with his morning appointments that he would have to ring up Paco, to go and do the bit of fighting for him. And although Paco would probably be busy putting his paper to bed, he would have to go.[1]

---

1. Caballero's visits to the front line made him extremely popular.

At this moment Del Vayo was extremely excited, to the detriment of his English, which out of courtesy he always insisted on using. But I gathered that I was being whisked off to see Caballero and to take him at once with us to Toledo. At the U.G.T. offices I waited with the stoicism that is necessary when it is a matter of Del Vayo, and at last he shot out into the street and into the car and we were off to the Ministry of War. It seemed that two hours ago the rebels in the Alcázar had hung out a white flag.

But it came to nothing at all. As Del Vayo said when he emerged once more from the Ministry of War, it was all a little premature. A white flag had been held out from a hole in the wall and a request for a parley made, but when the War Office sent someone post haste from Madrid, he arrived to find that the white flag had disappeared and he was greeted by a rain of bullets instead. "So," said Del Vayo, "we must wait, I am sorry to have made you late for Paco." But as I was only an hour and a half late I was still able to get there half an hour before Paco, who had been delayed by something that had occurred during his bit of fighting on the Sierra. It is very odd to keep appointments with men who can always give you the perfectly good excuse that they have been made late by a bit of barbed wire, a machine gun or a trench mortar.

Yes, it had been premature all right. The intolerable length of the days during civil war makes everyone think that next week has come long before its time. Thirty, forty, fifty, sixty days were to pass, and still the agony of the Toledo Alcázar was to continue. The militia were to sit about in the streets and behind the barricades and the rebels in the Alcázar were to go on listening to the wireless and cheering, more feebly perhaps each time, the fifth, tenth, twentieth report that General Mola had entered Madrid, had captured Madrid's main water supply, had joined up with the southern forces and was about to relieve Toledo from Talavera de la Reina. And as they listened to the wireless day after day, they picked their teeth and dislodged fragments of the last mule; that last mule which had been reached, we had been told, early in August, and yet was still to be eaten, with fourteen other mules, in mid-September.

Not that no progress was being made on either side. By mid-September the rebel forces were really at Talavera and by mid-September the tunnel patiently mined by experts from Asturias had penetrated beneath the cottages until the drills were grinding and picking at the solid rock under the Alcázar's one remaining tower.

One morning the commander of the militia, bareheaded, his arms crossed over his chest, walked out into the centre of the Plaza de Zocodover, past that pathetic iron café table without a marble top and down the avenue of death to the gates of theà. At the gate the rebels blindfolded him and led him in. He had come to plead with them. Very soon they were going to blow the whole fortress into the air. In the name of humanity let them send out the women and children. They should be given safe conduct, and be fed and looked after.

"They shall die with us," the commanders of the rebels replied. The government officer returned and one minute later the stupid process of shooting off three million rounds of ammunition began again. The horror of civil war had reached its height. The Toledo forces faced necessity, the ghastly bravery of their enemies must reach its appointed end. Irun had fallen, San Sebastian had been abandoned; the rebels had brought columns of Moors almost within striking distance; more and more German and Italian aeroplanes were helping; man, woman and child must be blown into the air.

The tunnel was complete. Two tons of dynamite were in position.

On Friday, September 19th, the sixty-third day of the siege, the civilian population of Toledo was told to leave the town. They filed out of the city gate which we have seen a few pages back and from the previous dusk and through the night a constant stream of old and young dodged their way behind the row of cottages and the pile of sandbags across the main road until many of them were sitting on the hill from which I first looked across at the Alcázar.

Dawn broke. All eyes were fixed on the smoking, partly ruined, monster building, which had brooded over the brawling mobs of Toledo for so many centuries. Of the four towers in my photograph only one remained, the south-western one, and the four-square majesty of the structure was altogether gone. From this tower, although nobody in this waiting crowd could see them, two rebels, knowing what was coming, jumped to a quicker death than would otherwise have been their lot.

At a quarter-past six someone seventy yards from the Alcázar pulled a switch, and the distant crowds saw the last tower rise into the air and fall in fragments. While the horror of the sight was still only half grasped, there came the horror of sound, a roar of man-made thunder, and the horror of touch, the tremble of a man-made earthquake.

Within the city huge blocks of masonry scattered themselves in every direction, crushing roofs and falling shattered in the empty streets. There was a pause for a few seconds as the brown cloud of smoke steadied itself around the building, and then two hundred picked militiamen rushed upon the ruins.

For six hours they fought the survivors, hand grenades, rifles, machine guns took their toll, and at the end of six hours half their number had been killed and the rebels still held on. As night fell once more a few refugees crawled out of the ruins and reached the government lines; half crazed women were helped over the barricades; militiamen returned carrying children in their arms; the state of affairs in the dungeons can only be guessed. The end had not yet come.

In the Plaza de Zocodover the armoured car used as a barricade was cut in two by the explosion and half of it landed on the fire station nearby.

But even now the Alcázar had not fallen, and the Moors were coming up in sober truth from Talavera de la Reina. A few days more and news came that the city was captured.[1]

---

1. This was a turning point in the war. Victory in Toledo confirmed Franco as the leader of the Nationalists and militarily opened the road to Madrid.

Stop Press News.   *Thursday, Oct.* 1. Toledo

Mass Suicide: Anarchists Burned To Death.

General Varela said that yesterday about forty anarchists committed suicide en masse in a seminary when they were trapped after the capture of Toledo.

Shouting 'Viva la Muerte' meaning 'Long live Death' the anarchists drank large quantities of anisette (a liqueur resembling absinthe), and then set fire to the building, burning themselves to death.

General Varela also said that 100 Anarchists were burned to death in San Juan Hospital. The hospital was surrounded, but the Anarchists resisted capture, and the building was shelled and set on fire.

Loyalists Besieged.

According to News reaching St. Jean de Luz, the insurgents in Toledo have turned the tables on the men who besieged the Alcázar. Fifty Government troops are said to have taken refuge in the seminary there, and are desperately holding out against the insurgents. It is believed that there are a number of women and children with them.

To which I may add a few notes. The seminary which is said to have been set on fire by "anarchists" is the building from whose roof I photographed the Alcázar. The "anarchists" are doubtless the men you have seen in the barricades. It would be more sensible but less colourful to call them the troops defending the democratically elected government of Spain. My friend, the Captain, has either been killed, or set himself on fire, or is defending himself in the ruined Alcázar.

One October evening in London I sat showing my Toledo photographs to a World-War veteran. I described the barricades, the corners where one ran from the bullets, the natural site on which Toledo is built. He listened with growing surprise and pity.

202 Behind The Spanish Barricades

"That street corner," he said, "do they have to cross it often?"

"All day long."

"Then, my god, why don't they hang a sheet across the road; then they could walk across without any sniper being able to do a thing! We used to blanket miles of communication roads. Can't somebody tell them how to fight?"

Of course I would never have thought of that; and now I kicked myself for not having suggested to the Captain that a blanket would be a good idea. And yet, thinking of the Captain, I doubt whether the blanket would have been welcomed. There is that appalling element of stupid contempt of death, of being ashamed to take cover. Probably every militiaman insisted on crossing exposed places a few times a day to make life more interesting.

"And why didn't they mine the thing properly? And how the hell did they manage to lose Toledo in the end? Why, twenty good men with machine guns could hold up twenty thousand indefinitely. And surely they can buy barbed wire, or make it? A few yards of barbed wire and a machine gun, and nobody could take Toledo."

Yet Toledo was taken. Machine has triumphed over man. The men in my photographs were burned to death or shot against a wall.

An English newspaper of conservative complexion records that Toledo to-day is empty. "It is a mystery," it says, "where the population has gone." Well! well! Instead of welcoming their Moorish deliverers with open arms they seem to have shown them a clean pair of heels.

CHAPTER 8
WHAT IT MEANS TO US

Well, there it is! What does it all mean to the average Englishman.

First of all, how does the Englishman think that he reacts towards trouble abroad? He thinks that he wants the right man to win, and that he has a sympathy with the underdog. He thinks that he is a firm believer in democracy, and that anything that goes wrong in a democratic country goes wrong because democracy *has* "never had a real chance" there. He thinks that, as an Englishman, he is luckier than foreigners —because democracy has had a real chance here, and that this gives him a moral right to lead the rest of the world, and even occasionally to read it lectures. He is certain that, whatever goes wrong in other countries, "it can't happen here." He thinks that the moral superiority of his country gives him a right, or as he calls it a duty, to protect the *status quo*, for example the free all-red routes to India and elsewhere. Provided this "sacred trust" is not endangered, he wishes to interfere as little as possible. He believes, in fact, in minding his own business, in both ways. Finally, he thinks that when he reads, let us say, Mr. J. L. Garvin, he is reading the words of a man who believes as he does about fundamentals; and when he is governed, let us say, by Mr. Baldwin that his rulers are carrying out a policy based on these fundamentals.[1]

What does he think about Spain, apart from bull-fights, gipsies, sherry and port, which, in spite of the latter's name, he believes to be the leading Spanish wines?

When the monarchy came to an end, he reacted both ways at once. Thinking of his own king and his loyal sentiments, he was sorry for Alfonso and suspicious of his enemies; but he fully re-alised that the fall of the monarchy was due to absolutism, and that if the Spanish king had been like the British king it could never have happened out there any more than it could in England. In the same way, thinking of the village church and green, with the vicar keeping wicket on Saturday afternoon, he did not like republican legislature against the church; but remembering the Inquisition, Bloody Mary, and the attempted prayer book revision, he fully realised that something had to be done to stop priests interfering with politics.

When, in 1934, there was an armed revolt from the left, he asked how it was possible for a country to have democratic government if the defeated side started a revolution to regain power. If he heard of the vile repression afterwards, he thought that it was probably six of one and half a dozen of the other. His natural sympathies being with "law and order," he was inclined to agree with the professional propagandists of the red-terror school in 1934; but when, in 1936, there was an election and the Popular Front won, he was less impressed with these same gentlemen because his democratic sentiments led him to believe that victory at the polls should be accepted gracefully and the victors should be wished good luck to get on with the job. I think this is the point of view of the average non-political Englishman. It is when he finds that he has been deceived that he becomes political overnight.

Now what I have to say on the Spanish tragedy, as it affects us,

---

1. James Garvin (1868-1947), editor of the *Observer* (1908-1942), was an admirer of Mussolini. The paper came out immediately in sympathy with General Franco's uprising.

is spoken to this man. I am not speaking to communists or socialists or fascists, but to the majority of Englishmen and in doing so I believe that we are all together facing a tragic and decisive moment in our lives as Englishmen and human beings.

The incontrovertible primary fact is that on July 18th, 1936, a legal democratically-elected government was attacked by a small group of rebel military officers, aided by a few thousand "fascists" largely representing the absentee-landlord class, and helped by the church hierarchy who, as the clerical party, had so powerfully influenced politics in the *ancien régime*. These three classes saw their privileges attacked by a liberal government, prepared to overthrow it by any means in their power, and struck on that date.

If it were not that certain groups in England have denied this incontrovertible fact, it would be a waste of time to give the evidence which proves it true. Briefly, let us state why the Spanish government was a legal government.

It was elected in February in accordance with the Spanish constitution. It had very nearly half the votes cast, and vastly more than the Labour Governments in England. Those who say it was "illegal" because it had not an absolute majority of votes are saying that the Ramsay MacDonald government was illegal; and those who say that the fascists had a right to rebel, because the government had 60,000 less votes than the opposition in over 8,000,000 votes cast, are suggesting that if there is another minority government in England Sir Oswald Mosley will have a legal right to try and destroy it by force.

Moreover, this government legally elected in February, 1936, had, in accordance with the Spanish constitutional electoral law, a large majority of the delegates in the Cortes supporting it. Its majority was so large that the right-wing opposition decided to hide their impotence by boycotting it. They also boycotted the election to form an electoral house to decide on the new President, knowing that no popular support would come for any candidate except Azaña. It is worth adding that the February elections were controlled by the Gil Robles-Lerroux reactionary government, so that there can be no question of the liberals having won through rigging the ballot boxes. What was this Spanish legal government elected last February? It was a mildly liberal, middle-class government containing not one socialist, communist, or anarcho-syndicalist.

Why did it immediately antagonise the three parties, the military, the landlords, and the church hierarchy, so that—as ample evidence proves—they began promptly to perfect their plans for its overthrow?

It antagonised the military by continuing a policy based on the belief that, so long as Spain had a Pretorian Guard, it could not have a safe democratic government. It therefore reduced the opportunities and power of the officer class. There were over 800 Spanish generals in February, 1936. The Baldwin government would never tolerate 800 British generals. The Spanish liberal government was determined to destroy so dangerous a force. Moreover, knowing that the armed forces, both military and civil guard, were full of anti-republican and anti-democratic interests, the government of Spain proceeded to counter these and to strengthen democracy by establishing the republican Guardia de Asalto, made up of elements that could be trusted to be loyal to their republican oath. This policy antagonised the army officers and civil guard, who saw their position of dictators in Spain vanishing before a new and powerful democracy.

The legal democratic government of Spain antagonised the landlord class by carrying out agrarian reforms. These reforms were in no way extreme. The only expropriation was at the expense of members of the *ancien régime* who had been legally proved disloyal to the Republic. Land was provided for the starving peasantry by insisting that landlords rent their waste land at a reasonable rent. Everything was paid for. Cultivated land was not interfered with. The Spanish government simply said to the landlords, "We will not allow you freedom to continue keeping your lands uncultivated; we will force you to hire it to people who need to use it; but we will guarantee that you receive rent." Not a very revolutionary policy; but a sufficient attack on privilege to solidify opposition.

The Spanish government antagonised the clerical elements by curtailing their powers, especially by insisting on secular education. When we think how hard the British democracy has fought to prevent the Church of England, the Non-conformists, or the Catholics from using the educational system of England for mildly sectarian purposes, we should surely sympathise with the Spanish government in its effort to make education a reality. A thousand years and more of clerical instruction had left almost half Spain illiterate. The clericals had had ample opportunity, and wasted it. Moreover, everybody in Spain knew that the clerical party was using church property, church treasure, and church influence to destroy the Republic. In the body of this book we have shown why Spanish liberalism must be anti-clerical.

So on July 18th the legally-elected democratic government of Spain was attacked by a small minority of vested interests without popular support, but with the weapons of modern war.

It has been suggested that this statement is not true; that a very large proportion of the Spanish population supported and supports the rebels. Some propagandists have even trotted out the figures of the February election, suggesting that as 4,000,000 voted against the Popular Front government, the fascists have that much support. This is the same as saying that, if Sir Oswald Mosley took up arms against a British liberal government, he would have the support of the millions of conservatives who voted against that government.

Moreover, certain very important elements of the extreme right opposition in the February elections have been among the Government's supporters against the rebels. Thus the Basque Nationalist party is so strongly Catholic as to desire Basque independence, so that they may have a separate Concordat with the Vatican. Yet this party, the most powerful in the Basque provinces, has been fighting loyally for democracy against fascism—a fact that those who wish this to be considered a religious war wisely conceal.

Except for a certain proportion of the people of Navarre and neighbouring districts, the Rebels have no popular support. Then, if they are a miserable minority, how have they defeated a nation of 21,000,000?

They are winning a military victory because such victories are won not by men, but by machines. The original intention was to rebel in October, by which time plans to seize all the centres where armaments are kept or made would have been secured; but as we have shown elsewhere, an earlier start was advisable, so the legal government could not be deprived of all sources of arms, technical knowledge, and trained support.

In consequence the Rebels could not win as they had hoped in forty-eight hours, and had to play their trump card, namely the intervention of the Fascist International.

Now those are facts. Every one of them can be verified by simple attention to the known evidence. Yet on October 25th, 1936, Mr J. L. Garvin, in the London *Observer*, writes: "The Spanish drama is at its climax with the assured triumph of the national uprising over class-war anarchy and total disruption. The fall of Madrid will mean the shattering and humiliating defeat of Moscow as the open partner of Communist revolution in other countries."

Now with all the modern means of communication, telegraphs, telephones, wireless, after three months, it is possible for a respectable Englishman writing for respectable Englishmen to make a statement like that.

Consider for a moment. "The national uprising" is a minority rebellion of army officers and fascists, using Moorish mercenaries and foreign legionaries, equipped by Italy and Germany to destroy a whole people and its legal government. "Class-war anarchy" is an admittedly weak and young attempt at democracy in a country emerging from centuries of autocracy. Far from there being a "class-war" government *before the rebels forced it on the country*, there was not a single socialist or communist in the Spanish government on July 18th. That there is what Mr Garvin would call a class-war government to-day is due entirely to the Rebels who destroyed the democracy they were pledged to support.

"The fall of Madrid will mean the shattering and humiliating defeat of Moscow." In the same way, I suppose, if Sir Oswald Mosley, helped by Sikhs and Bantus, transported to England in Italian and German planes, succeeded in occupying London that would be a "shattering and humiliating defeat of Moscow."

Later in his article Mr Garvin goes on: "The Red *régime*, under Largo Caballero in Madrid, represents nothing but the desperate minority of Communists, Anarchists, and extremists of other stripes... The Government of Spain already is the Government of Burgos. The Red *régime* now in its last throes at Madrid has never had the shadow of a claim to the former title."

"The Red *régime*," with Largo Caballero at its head, is the legal descendant of the previous government. It came into being on the initiative of the previous prime minister, S. Giral. It was appointed in accordance with the Spanish constitution. It contains every element of the Spanish democracy, including, for the first time, the *Right Wing Catholic Basque National Party and one communist*. Even if Mr Garvin cannot distinguish between a socialist and a communist, he ought to be able to understand that anarchists are not and cannot be in this government, and if he regards this as hair-splitting, he should at least be able to distinguish between a communist and a catholic.

This "Red *régime*" counts among its supporters such prominent Catholic intellectuals as Ossorio y Gallardo and Menéndez Pidal, appointed by it to the Presidency of the Spanish Academy. Are these gentlemen paid by Moscow or are they misled by what Mr Garvin calls "sincere ignorance."

In case an impatient reader may feel that all this was written in one of Mr Garvin's off-moments, let me quote from the same paper's "Diplomatic Correspondent:

"General Franco so clearly has the best present title," he tells us, "to be the Government of Spain— will have to be recognized as such the moment he captures Madrid—that any further evidence of Russian assistance to the Reds will become in international law a matter of Russian aggression against Spain."

In short, now that it has been abundantly proved that Italy, Germany, and Portugal have been assisting the Rebels against the legal democratic government of Spain, and that Russia alone

among the anti-fascist countries is threatening to assist that government, the people who read and write the *Observer* believe that
international law is being broken, not by Italy, Germany, and Portugal, but by Russia.

Let us remember precisely what Russia threatens to do. It is not
a question of Russians fighting Franco. It is simply a question of
Russia allowing a legitimate government of a friendly power to
buy arms with good hard cash.

Under international law it is illegal for a foreign country to
supply rebels against a legal friendly government in any circumstances. Germany, Italy, and Portugal have broken international
law in this particular; for though the British Foreign Office claims
to have no evidence of this, such evidence has been put before the
public in a form that cannot be denied.

Under international law it is perfectly legal for a foreign country to supply arms to the legal government of a friendly power.
It is also legal, no doubt, to refuse to supply arms, as France and
England have done, but there is nothing to stop Russia selling if
she desires.

Yet in these circumstances it is probable that the majority, or at
least many millions, of Englishmen would back up the contentions
of Mr J. L. Garvin and the *Observer's* Diplomatic Correspondent.
It is equally certain that a very large number of Englishmen will
oppose with life and liberty the logical outcome of such a point of
view. And that brings us to the really vital thing revealed by the
Spanish tragedy. *We have come to the end of a period of National
Wars. There will never again be a united nation fighting against another united nation. War from now on will involve civil war.*

It does not matter what combination of powers is opposed to
another combination on paper; in every country those who think
like Mr Garvin will be on one side and those who think otherwise
on the other.

It is of value to compare the attitude of Englishmen to-day
to Spanish affairs with their attitude in 1808. When at its birth,
nineteenth-century civilization was overshadowed by the force of
military dictatorship, English conservatives were united with the

rest in determination to resist Napoleon. On May 2nd, 1808, the first blow was struck against Napoleon by the spontaneous rise of the Spanish people, and the English government, seeing that it would be better to defeat the tyrant on the arid deserts of Aragon rather than in the home counties of England, sent the Duke of Wellington and thousands of English soldiers, who are now some corner of a foreign field. As a result the nineteenth century was freed from despotism.

To-day a far more dangerous despotism overshadows Europe; Mr Garvin and his friends are hoping that it will succeed in engulfing Spain. Our government has interpreted expediency in a different way from their predecessors of the Peninsular War, and has by every action done its best to see it shall engulf Spain.

It is no use mincing matters—we English have a habit of fixing our attention on the delinquencies of foreign governments and letting our own be forgotten —the British Government has not been as generous as certain others in its aid to Spanish fascists, but it has been fully as parsimonious in its sympathy to the Spanish Government. Our consuls have not even troubled to disguise their sympathies with the illegal enemies of the legal government to which they have been accredited. In some cases they have even refused to help British subjects who have got into difficulties because they have been sympathetic to the lawful rulers of Spain. Our Home Office has refused admission as "undesirable aliens" to scores of Spanish citizens who could not remotely be considered "red." I know of cases of Spanish business men turned back at Croydon, although they had come to give orders to British firms, simply because they came from the part of Spain controlled by the Spanish legal government. Our Foreign Office has not even yet (October 25th, 1936) been able to find a particle of evidence that Portugal has helped the rebels, although such evidence is forthcoming in quantity.

The simple fact is that Europe is divided into two halves, the Fascist International and the Anti-fascist International, and our government has done all it can to give comfort to the first and to embarrass the second.

What is the Anti-fascist International? It is Russia, nine-tenths of France, one-half of England, and some smaller and more civilized countries, such as the Scandinavian. Our government, judged by its actions and inactions, belongs to the Fascist International, along with Mr Garvin and the average reader of the *Observer* and the rest of the conservative press, both dignified and gutter.

Thus divided we face a war. A war which began actively in Abyssinia; which became more clear and urgent in Spain; which may quite possibly have spread to France by the time this book can be published. In that war England will be divided almost exactly in two. It will not be a question of a tiny minority of pacifists as in the last war, but of a formidable opposition to whatever government happens to be in existence at the outbreak of war. Neither a pro-fascist nor an anti-fascist government can expect loyalty and unity again.

Nor will it be possible to pretend much longer, as Mr Garvin would like to pretend, that those who will oppose any attempt to bring England into the Fascist International will be communists. The assumption that the only opponents of fascism in this country want England to "follow the Moscow road," is too puerile to impress intelligent people. It is quite certain that the danger to our institutions *in the international field* comes from fascism and not from communism; and without Russian assistance in the international field, Germany, Italy and Japan are paramount in world affairs.

Meanwhile our British government has consistently followed a policy which involves the abandoning of all those policies hitherto regarded as "patriotic." And that is the second thing that has been made clear by its attitude to the Spanish Tragedy. *We have come to the end of a period when capitalism dressed in democratic fashions prided itself on being patriotic; we are coming to the period when capitalism in its fascist phase abandons even patriotism in the cause of profit.*

When General Franco, in the name of patriotism and Christianity, brought Moors to slaughter Spaniards, it was bad enough; but from an Englishman's point of view it was far worse when respectable English journalists began to call those Moors "the Nationalists," for it showed that here, too, we have men perfectly prepared to go to all lengths rather than see the economic evolution of England go in directions of which they do not approve. It may be a long time before Sikhs and Sepoys will police depressed areas—after all we shall begin by asking blackshirts to do the dirty work—but already the British government has embarked on a policy which no conservative before 1920 would have considered patriotic. For we have hastened the victory of Fascism in Spain and thereby already lost what was left of the Mediterranean route to India. We have done more; we have seated Fascism firmly astride the long sea-route also, for the Canaries, once Franco wins, will be under the domination of the Fascist International.

The coming of Fascism to Spain involves the following direct threats to British Imperial Sea routes:—

1.   Majorca is now virtually an Italian colony. Our Foreign Office must know that. There is incontrovertible evidence that Count Rossi rules the island; that there are several hundred Italian bombers on the island and fifteen thousand troops officered by Italians in the interests of the Rebels; there is uninterrupted landing of Italian war-supplies from Italian ships, and at the same time the island is almost completely cut off from the outside world. Does anyone really suppose that Italy will abandon Majorca? Is it not certain that she will remain, and thus establish a powerful base in the Eastern Mediterranean? The immediate value of this is that Barcelona, the most important port on the Mediterranean, and except for Marseilles the only non-fascist port, is threatened with destruction—may have been destroyed by the time this can be read in print. But beyond this, Majorca is a first-class prize for Fascism and a long step forward to turning the Mediterranean into a Fascist lake.

2.   Ceuta, opposite Gibraltar, in Fascist hands closes the Mediterranean. British Imperialist policy has always taken great pains to see that the opposite coast to Gibraltar should be held by a weak power. It was for this purpose that British imperialists participated in the breaking-up of Morocco; they feared the effect on the Mediterranean route of a French menace opposite Gibraltar, and they insisted on Spain being left

in charge, because Spain, they assumed, could be more easily managed. So vital was this policy considered that British Imperialists on more than one occasion risked a war to perpetuate it; for in those days they were not represented by a "Peace at Any Price" government. So important indeed was this policy that it finally had a very important part in the causation of the Great War.

A Fascist Spain will still certainly be a weak Spain, but its weakness will play into the hands of Italy and Germany and *against* traditional British policy.

3.   The Canary Isles are already halfway to being controlled by Germany. Luft-Hansa aeroplanes paved the way, and when on July 18th the Rebellion broke out, their wings, decorated with the Swastika, hovered over the villages of the islands, while their pilots dropped leaflets in favour of the Rebels. It will be interesting to see how South Africa reacts to a situation in which the Canary Islands have passed into the power of the Fascist International.

4.   Fernando Po, of no possible importance to General Franco's present plans, has staged a rebellion in his favour in the course of this month of October. The really interesting point to note about this is that Fernando Po is an island immediately off the particular piece of Africa that Germany hopes one day to have as a colony.

So much for the effect of a Fascist victory in Spain on the British Imperial Sea routes. Let us consider another aspect. Our only real ally is France. Of course in theory we are all members one of another and of the League of Nations, but any practical statesman knows that there has been substituted for that League two Internationals, one of Fascist powers, the other of potentially Anti-fascist powers. Our government is far more afraid of communism than of fascism; it refuses, therefore, to regard Russia as a potential ally; if it has any hope of saving democracy in England from fascism abroad, its one chance is a powerful France. Consider how France has been weakened by permitting the Fascist International to triumph in Spain.

France has lost control of the sea-routes between her African possessions and herself. In any war with Germany and Italy it will now be possible to prevent the landing in France of any colonial troops. Thus one of the essentials of German preparatory strategy has been accomplished. Instead of enjoying immunity on her southern frontier, France will now have to expect in any future war air attack from beyond the Pyrenees. In a few brief months fascism has created two new frontiers for France to defend, one towards Belgium, the other towards Spain. A democratic England's sole ally has been crippled.

There can be only two explanations of the complacency of the British Government in the face of such facts as these. Either it has no real policy but only a vacillating hope-for-the-best attitude, or it is very well satisfied with the way things are going. Most people at present seem to believe that the first is nearer the truth.

The Government itself claims that a weak policy has been forced on it because the Peace Ballot and Labour opposition to re-armament and recruiting has left it defenceless. Actually, if we adopt a realist attitude and admit that the natural alignment for any future war is England – France - Russia versus Germany -

Italy-Japan, the anti-fascist powers have a far greater armament superiority, especially in the air, than they are ever likely to have again. A Government determined to save democracy from fascism would call the bluff of the Fascist International now, before it is too late. By so doing it would not only threaten the growing danger before that danger was fully grown, but capture the very groups who refuse to help to strengthen a government for purposes which they believe to be suspect.

Mr Duff Cooper cannot get anyone to join his army, and blames the pacifists.[1] It would be possible to recruit five thousand men in a few weeks to go to the aid of democracy where democracy is at present in danger, between the Straits of Gibraltar and the Pyrenees. But the mere fact that the British Government has seen fit to thwart democracy in its struggle there has strengthened the feeling that it cannot be trusted to defend democracy anywhere, and that will increase the opposition to rearmament and recruiting.

---

1. Duff Cooper (1890-1954) was a Conservative politician and in 1936 was Secretary of State for War.

But the opinion is growing that there is nothing vacillating and weak about the British Government's policy at all; that it is consistent and well-planned. Abyssinia and then Spain seem to be ample evidence that we as a nation are being sold into fascist captivity. If that is the object of their policy the Government have done admirably from their own point of view. We need not suppose that Mr Baldwin wants democracy to go under in England, we can do him the credit of assuming that his real delight would be to escape into eighteenth-century England; but the betrayal not only of democracy but of imperialism is being forced upon him by the one overmastering necessity of his policy. That necessity is simply this: *that in no part of the world must a Popular Front government be allowed to succeed.* That is why the route to India is no longer to be defended; that is why the greatest crime against humanity that our generation has seen, the murder of the Spanish people, is regarded with more than complacency in official quarters.

As I have been writing this book, I have tried to describe those things which I have seen in Spain. I have not troubled to attempt propaganda because to me the truth is so clear that propaganda is not necessary. So I have described many of the sad and ugly things; I have not pretended that churches have not been burned; I have not obscured the fact that, owing to rebellion on the part of the natural defenders of the republic, left wing elements have become more powerful; I have tried to be faithful to those of my Spanish friends who have followed what I believe is the wrong road; I have not spared the many worded intellectuals who are still philosophising negatively while others act. There is never a war between angels and devils; especially when it is a matter of civil war, every other atrocity is likely to be added to the first and greatest atrocity, and is to be imputed to those who brought the civil war, the mother of all atrocities.

But behind the human scenes and memories out of which I have tried to build a three-dimensional picture, there has always been in my mind the one terrible fact. Month after month in these days we are seeing all over Europe the lights that shine in the faces of free men and women go out one by one. In many places they are not likely to be rekindled in our generation. When we realise that here, too, in England there are those who desire this new Dark Age to come, not only over there, but here also, the Spanish tragedy becomes a human tragedy, the battle they are fighting, not theirs alone but ours also. We turn in humility to the humble folk of Spain, republicans, socialists, communists, syndicalists, anarchists who are groping in horror with their bare hands to save the light from flickering out. We turn in anger to those in England who want the light to die, and we cry in words to which Spain has given a new meaning, No Pasarán; They Shall Not Pass This Way.

DONATION

PLAN INTERNATIONAL is one of the world's biggest child sponsorship charities and works in 60 countries worldwide. To donate to PLAN please send a cheque to Plan UK, 5/6 Underhill St, London NW1 7HS quoting reference RPBTSB.
Find out more at: www.plan-uk.org. 5% of the profits from the sale of this book go to PLAN INTERNATIONAL.

APPENDIX

John Langdon-Davies's fifteen-year-old son, Robin wrote this account of his trip to Spain with his father for the Mid Devon Times. The article appeared on 19 September 1936.

Impressions of a visit to Spain
Anarchists who got "somewhat annoyed"
By Robin Langdon-Davies

The writer of this article, Robin Langdon-Davies, was accompanied by his father, a London newspaper correspondent, on a visit to Catalonia last month, much of the journey being accomplished on the back of a motor cycle. The lad is now staying at Dartington.

It was with some uncertainty of mind that I crossed over the bridge from Bourg Madame in France to Puigcerda in Spain. Alarming but scandalously untrue reports had riddled the British reactionary Press. But, when I had finished formalities on the French side and had crossed the bridge to where two Militia-men were sitting in wicker chairs, any doubts I may have had were expelled from my mind and I realised that everything was quite safe; quiet, unshaven young men of about 25 sat in their ordinary work-shop overalls fondling their guns and reading the paper. One of them accompanied us to the Customs house some hundred yards further up the road. The first thing of interest that I saw was a house with a notice on it: "Requisitat per la Generalitat de Catalunya". In completing the numerous formalities for my father's motor cycle and in getting various permits from the local committee of Anti-Fascist Militia, I saw much that was interesting and new. Outside the Parish Church were three little boys playing about with the smouldering remains of a bonfire which had once been the church furniture. All the cars had the trade union letters, U.G.T, C.N.T, and F.A.I. on their dusty bodywork. In the town all the cafes were open as usual, and were full of people, mostly Militia-men.

A few bad elements

From the moment of my arrival, I could see that although the place was under the strict martial law of the Anti-Fascist Militia, life was quite normal, for the civilian population of Catalonia. In every town and village in Catalonia there is a barricade at each road approach to protect the people from a few bad elements among the Anarchists which, during the first hectic days of the revolution threatened the peace of the civilian population. Every vehicle is stopped by the patrol of Militia at these barricades, and the occupant must show a permit from one of the committees before he is allowed to pass.

Everybody is doing what he or she can to help a democratically elected Government beat off an attack of ruthless military Fascists, who, with the help of German and Italian aeroplanes and pilots, and with their military base in Portugal, are threatening Spain with the most unspeakable terror. In the small mountain village where I stayed for some time, everyone was giving poultry and other farm produce to their comrades at the front. In Barcelona every day, thousands of young men and girls are enlisting and marching off to the front. In the streets are many Militia-men and girls taking perhaps their last stroll down the beautiful boulevards. All the way down the Ramblas are stalls selling books, ties, handkerchiefs, and badges to get money for the Militia. Militia-girls are busy collecting money from passers-by who give willingly.

Somewhat annoyed

An aspect of the revolution which must give rise to much consternation among the British public is the destruction of the churches in some parts of the Government territory. Having been in Catalonia, where the church destruction has been most severe, I now understand the motives which burned the churches. For centuries since the Inquisition, the Roman Catholic Church had ruled the Spanish people and had extracted from it so much wealth that, before the Revolution, the church was the biggest landowner in Spain. Thus, when the priests fired on the workers with machine guns from the roofs of churches, some of the Anarchists got somewhat annoyed and tried to get some revenge by burning a few churches. Now, however, the Government of Catalonia has stopped all ruthless destruction, and has saved the majority of articles of artistic value. The churches are now merely being dismantled and put to very good uses as garages, markets, and hospitals. The English reactionary Press has caused many of its readers to think that in Spain there is a war between the "Reds" and religion. This is, of course, quite untrue. The workers, many of whom are devout Catholics, are seeking their revenge on a rich and corrupt church organisation which had tyrannised over them for centuries, and had used their sacred buildings as Fascist fortresses.

Robin Langdon-Davies
Mid Devon Times, 19 September 1936

REPORTAGE PRESS

REPORTAGE PRESS is a new publishing house specialising in books on foreign affairs or set in foreign countries; non-fiction, fiction, essays, travel books, or just books written from a stranger's viewpoint. Good books like this are now hard to come by – largely because British publishers have become frightened of publishing books that will not guarantee massive sales.

The DESPATCHES series brings back into print some of the best reportage and travellers' tales from the past.

At REPORTAGE PRESS we are not averse to taking risks in order to bring to our readers the books they want to read. Visit our website: www.reportagepress.com. 5% of the profits from our books go to charity.

You can buy further copies of *Behind The Spanish Barricades* directly from the website, where you can find out more about our authors and upcoming titles.

To The End Of Hell
One woman's escape from the Khmer Rouge
Denise Affonço

In one of the most powerful memoirs of persecution, Denise Affonço recounts how her comfortable life was torn apart when the Khmer Rouge seized power in Cambodia in April 1975. A French citizen she was offered the choice of fleeing the country with her children or staying by her husband's side. Chinese and a convinced communist, he believed that the Khmer Rouge would bring an end to five years of civil war. Affonço chose to stay at his side.
The family was, then, like millions of their fellow citizens deported to a living hell in the countryside where they endured hard labour, famine, sickness and death.
Part of the profits from *To The End of Hell* go to the *Documentation Center of Cambodia*.

Hardback £15.99

UNDER THE SUN
Justin Kerr-Smiley

A gripping tale of love, loss and the tragedy of war.
It is the final weeks of the World War Two and Japanese forces
are in retreat. Young Spitfire pilot, Edward Strickland is based in
the South Pacific. His task is to search and destroy any remnants
of the once mighty Imperial Army.
During a dawn patrol he is forced to ditch his aircraft near a remote
island. Close to death he is hauled up onto the deck of a Japanese
ship by the commander of a small Japanese company who have
remained hidden on the island throughout the war. Although, the
Japanese commander treats the young pilot with appalling brutal-
ity Strickland refuses to be broken. The battle of wills that follows
brings the men the men together as 'brothers in arms'.
But there is little space for mutual understanding and friendship
in war. A storm is gathering, which will sever the two men's relationship for ever.
Part of the profits from *Under the Sun* go to *The Japan Society*.

Hardback £16.99

Copies of the above are available at: www.reportagepress.com
or at any good bookshop.